The **BEST** Dream Book Ever

Eric

Happy

Dreaming in 2018

Love

J

Selected Books by Kevin J. Todeschi

Non-Fiction:

Dreams, Images and Symbols
Edgar Cayce's ESP
Edgar Cayce on the Akashic Records
Edgar Cayce on Soul Growth
Edgar Cayce on Reincarnation and Family Karma
Edgar Cayce on Soul Mates
Edgar Cayce's Twelve Lessons in Personal Spirituality
God in Real Life

Co-authored:

Edgar Cayce on Auras & Colors (with Carol Ann Liaros)

Fiction:

A Persian Tale
The Reincarnation of Clara
The Rest of the Noah Story

The BEST Dream Book Ever

Accessing Your Personal Intuition and Guidance

Kevin J. Todeschi

Yazdan Publishing • Virginia Beach • Virginia

Published by:

Yazdan Publishing
P.O. Box 4604
Virginia Beach, VA 23454

ISBN 13: 978-0-9845672-7-0

Cover art: "The Book of Life"
by Anne Richards Brewster (1870-1952)

Cover design by Richard Boyle

Text and design layout by Cathy Merchand

To Kurt, Heidi and Kellie
and the dreams of youth we shared

And to Margrethe, whose encouragement
moved the book forward

Contents

Introduction

Most individuals remain totally unaware of the fact that they possess a personal source of insight and guidance that is timely, helpful, and extremely accurate. Having had the opportunity to work with dreams for decades, I often ask people to consider what they might do in their own lives if they lived with one of the wisest counselors, advisors or psychics of all time. Would they check in occasionally for advice, counsel or personal encouragement, especially during times of great confusion or stress? Obviously, the answer is yes. However, these same individuals generally remain totally unaware of the fact that they possess a wealth of intuition and personal guidance within their own subconscious minds. Actually, no one knows an individual and his or her life better than that person's subconscious. At this level, each and every one of us is much more in touch with ourselves, our relationships, our surroundings, and even our personal futures than we could possibly be aware. With this in mind, ignoring the deeper substance of a meaningful dream is like deciding not to open a letter from a trusted and close personal friend. Why would individuals not want to hear from someone who loves them unconditionally, knows them intimately, and only wants what is best for them? What may be even more surprising to some is that it's truly possible to ask for a dream on a very specific question and then have a dream that contains the answer!

In our contemporary world, most of us were not brought up to pay attention to our dreams and so for much of our life we simply ignore them. The earliest dreams I remember are from around the age of seven. I still recall two with relative ease even now. Both dreams had a profound effect upon my waking mind and my thoughts during the course of the many days that followed. One of those dreams was a nightmare; the other was a pleasant adventure. The nightmare caused me a great deal of fear and apprehension. The adventure gave me much joy and an excitement that nearly rivaled a child's anticipation of Christmas morning. The nightmare made me afraid to go to sleep, as I worried that a similar experience might trouble my dreams. The adventure filled me with anticipation when it was time to go to bed, as I was hoping to pick up the story once more—something I actually managed to do on several occasions.

These two dreams have stayed with me through the years. If I could speak to myself as a seven-year-old from my present vantage point, I could provide an explanation that would probably set my mind at ease with one and totally ruin a childhood fantasy with the other. If I had told my parents about either experience, I know that they would have listened but ultimately reassured me that dreams were "only my imagination." After working with dreams for more than thirty years and speaking throughout five continents about the topic, I know that children all over the world have heard this very same phrase. What is not stated, perhaps because it is not generally accepted or known, is that although dreams are pulled together from within the recesses of the subconscious mind—a place we too easily relegate to "only the imagination"—these imaginative wanderings have meaning. By suggesting that the imagination is unimportant in terms of dreams, we are unfortunately negating a wealth of insight, direction and personal counsel and guidance that is easily accessible by every individual.

Having taught dream interpretation workshops to thousands of people, I know that a frequently asked question is "Do all dreams really have a meaning?" I have come to believe that the answer is a resounding, "Yes!" To be sure, sometimes that meaning is not very important but every dream has a meaning nonetheless. For example, let's say that a student stays up late at night watching television, speaking with friends or studying and then has the urge for a midnight snack, devouring a pizza just before bed. After falling asleep that individual dreams about a horrendous war, a military conflict, or the explosion of an atomic bomb. The dreamer might wonder whether the dream is a prophetic vision of things to come but in all likelihood it is simply suggesting that the individual's digestion is "at war."

Another misperception about dreams is that it takes an expert to somehow decipher their meaning. However, the truth of the matter is that each individual is ultimately the best interpreter of her or his own dreams. Why? Because each of us is aware of the events occurring in our lives, as well as the feelings we hold and the personal relationships we are experiencing with other individuals. These are some of the various topics that are readily explored in dreams. Although someone who has had experience with dream interpretation can often facilitate the discovery of a possible meaning, it is generally up to the dreamer alone to decide what truly applies and what does not.

In my own life, other than remembering an occasional dream, I really was not actively involved in dreamwork until I became interested in the work of Edgar Cayce (1877-1945). Called the "father of holistic medicine," "the Sleeping Prophet," and "the greatest psychic of the twentieth century," for forty-three years of his adult life, Cayce was able to enter into a self-induced sleep state and provide psychic information, called "readings," to virtually any question imaginable. In addition to subjects such as health, philosophy, spirituality and psychic ability, much of the Cayce material deals with dreams and dream interpretation. That information first opened up the world of dreams to me and provided a foundation and an understanding that has stood firm for decades.

Edgar Cayce emphasized the importance of working with dreams, stating as early as 1923 that attempting to understand what he called the subconscious, the psychic, and the soul forces of each individual should be "the great study for the human family." The rationale from Cayce's perspective was that through the study of the subconscious and psychic part of ourselves we would come to an understanding of the nature of the soul, our connection to one another and our relationship with the Creator.

Almost nine hundred of the more than 14,000 Cayce readings on file at Cayce's Association for Research and Enlightenment (www.edgarcayce.org) deal with the subject of dreams and dream interpretation. Generally, when Edgar Cayce was asked to discuss the meaning of a dream, his wife would simply hold a copy of the dream in her hand and ask that the dream be interpreted—without the dream itself ever being read! Even more amazing is the fact that on numerous occasions when Cayce was provided with an individual's request for interpretation, he would remind the dreamer of forgotten portions of his or her own dream!

In terms of the dream material, one of Cayce's most involved enthusiasts was a wealthy, young Jewish stock broker named Morton Blumenthal who received more than 500 dream interpretation readings for himself and members of his immediate family! Extremely interested in the nature of the soul and each individual's relationship to God, one of Morton's dreams explored this very topic in a humorous vein:

Morton dreamed that he was in his apartment in New York City. Suddenly the doorbell rang and his maid went to answer the door. She announced the presence of a "distinguished visitor" and Morton jumped to his feet in exhilaration with the sudden knowledge that God Himself had come to call. Morton ran up to God and embraced Him with a hug. God's appearance was very business-like. He was clean-shaven and clean-cut, wore an expensive suit and a derby hat. He also seemed strong and intelligent, just the sort of man with whom Morton would like to do business.

Because God was visiting, Morton decided to give Him a tour around the apartment. Things went well enough until Morton realized they were approaching the living room and that he had mistakenly left his liquor cabinet half-open. Understanding that God was omniscient, Morton decided to reveal everything rather than trying to hide his liquor supply. He flung the cabinet wide open and pointed out the bottles by stating, "In case of sickness." God's reply was matter of fact: "You are very well prepared!"

Later, when asked for an interpretation, Cayce stated that much of Morton's dream indicated that each and every individual can have a personal relationship with the Divine. This interpretation becomes obvious when we consider that God comes to meet us in the form that we might best recognize Him, that he comes not as some supreme deity but as someone we might relate to, and that the Creator is extremely accepting of us in spite of our imperfections.

The Cayce information suggests that dreams essentially analyze, compare and contrast the events, thoughts, and issues of each day. This process enables us to see things from a more objective perspective. For example, it is very common for individuals who are tense, worried, or unsettled about something in their lives to go to sleep and, after a night of dreaming, awake feeling refreshed and ready to deal with life's events anew. It is this unconscious process of correlating and contrasting the events of the day in our dreams that can provide a psychological support and even "healing," enabling us to deal with life's confusions. Dreams can have physical, psychological and even spiritual significance. In addition to understanding the nature of the soul and our relationship with God, the benefits of their exploration include such practical issues as problem-solving, understanding relationship and work issues, intuitive insights into all area of life, a deeply personal look into self discovery, and a very practical tool for personal guidance. So the reasons for exploring dreams are numerous. Conversely, when talking to individuals about their dreams, they may offer several excuses for not exploring their own dreams: (1) "Dreams don't mean anything"; (2) "I don't dream"; and, (3) "I don't know how to interpret them."

Contrary to the first response, I have personally witnessed countless individuals become puzzled and even amazed by what their dreams revealed about them. Whether it was a personal secret that had not been told to another individual, an issue with which the individual has been struggling, or an event that was occurring in life, oftentimes dreamers have been completely surprised by what their dreams revealed about them. One of my favorite instances occurred during an Exploritas (ElderHostel) program where I had been asked to work with a group of conference attendees one night on the subject of dream interpretation.

During this particular event, I was standing in front of an audience of approximately fifty individuals and had just given some background information on dreams and how they worked. I then asked for any volunteers from the audience to share any dreams that they would like to have discussed and analyzed. After a moment's hesitation one gentleman of about sixty-five raised his hand. He began by stating, "I have a dream, but it doesn't mean anything." I simply nodded and asked him to relate the dream to the group. The dream seemed to cause his wife, who was sitting next to him, some measure of embarrassment.

In the dream, he found himself on the second floor of a two-story house. He was in the master bedroom in his pajamas. His wife was lying in the bed completely naked, waiting for him. Before getting into bed with his wife, he related that he had suddenly remembered something, although he couldn't consciously remember what that something had been. As a result, in the dream he left his wife and the bedroom and proceeded downstairs to the first floor. He seemed to "putter around" doing something for awhile before suddenly remembering that his wife was upstairs naked in bed and this was his (as he put it) "chance for romance." The thought caused him to retrace his footsteps, but he was surprised and "very frustrated" to find that the stairway to the second floor had suddenly disappeared, and he couldn't get back to his wife. That was the end of the dream.

One of the mistaken assumptions regarding the subject of dream interpretation is that each dream should have only one interpretation. This is wrong for a variety of reasons. One is that two individuals might have a similar dream but the actual interpretation for each could be very different. Why? Because each individual may have her or his own feelings or beliefs about the images or events being portrayed in the dream and each may have completely contrasting experiences in waking life. Another reason is that dreams often have multiple meanings, corresponding to the various aspects of the individual as well as her or his physical, mental and spiritual self. Keeping these factors in mind, I attempted to analyze the man's dream by diplomatically suggesting that sometimes a dream like this might indicate that there was some kind of a sexual issue or problem. Obviously a dream of this nature—a husband not being able to have sex with his wife—could be interpreted in this manner.

After my suggested "possibility," the dreamer emphatically rejected any such idea, insisting, to his wife's red-faced embarrassment, that there had "never been a problem and never would be a problem." When the audience had stopped laughing, I then offered a second interpretation: "Do you have the habit of starting projects that you never really follow through on, which is causing a great deal of frustration to members of your household?" The dreamer looked at me in complete confusion but his wife enthusiastically nodded her head in total agreement. She then volunteered the fact, "Even now he has the beginnings of a deck out back that he has been working on for six months and still hasn't gotten around to finishing." I thought the not-following-through interpretation was likely because in this instance the house could represent his current situation, the wife that he doesn't make love to something that he doesn't follow-through on, and his own emotion of being frustrated a likely feeling being experienced within his own household.

The second reason individuals give for not exploring the topic of dream interpretation is the claim that "I don't dream." Scientific studies have proven otherwise. In a 1953 article in the journal *Science*, Eugene Aserinsky and Nathaniel Kleitman of the University of Chicago, discussed for the first time their findings that REM (rapid eye movement) sleep indicated dream periods. Their discovery led to countless additional scientific investigations of the topic. As it turns out, dreams are not necessarily limited to REM sleep but rapid eye movements can be a major determinant in indicating the possibility that a dream is taking place. It is now believed that most individuals dream a number of times each night, for a total of ninety minutes or more on average.

The issue is not so much a lack of dreams, as it is an issue of individuals not bothering to reflect upon their dreams when awakening, let alone attempting to record them. Because dreams are the substance of the subconscious mind, they are extremely fragile, illusive and easily dissolved by the intrusion of waking consciousness and the left brain. Often, students have told me how they have awakened from sleep, aware of the presence of a dream but that as soon as they attempted to put all the pieces together and "remember the whole story," the dream disappeared. A better approach is simply to begin writing down whatever is on the verge of consciousness immediately upon awakening. Even if the dreamer only remembers a feeling, a color, or a specific character or place, it should be written down. With this approach, individuals will often find that more pieces fall into place as they are writing and dream recall becomes not so much a goal of remembering but a process of re-experiencing the dream on paper.

The third reason individuals give to explain their hesitation in undertaking an examination of their own dreams is "I don't know how to interpret." But interpretation can be straightforward with just a little practice. Working with dreams is a process. Individuals need to keep in mind the fact that they already know the possible meaning of many more symbols then they may consciously be aware. It is not even necessary to memorize the meanings of hundreds of symbols. These meanings can be discovered in a variety of ways—by using a good dream dictionary, an unabridged dictionary, one's own logic, or even asking friends to help brainstorm possibilities. What is more meaningful is becoming comfortable with the dream interpretation process.

Many dream symbols are actually quite easy to interpret. For example, most people know that bad luck can be symbolized by a black cat, walking under a ladder, or breaking a mirror. Conversely, good luck might be indicated by such things as a rainbow, a four-leaf clover or finding a genie's lamp. Places also lend themselves to interpretative meaning: a library suggests knowledge, a post office suggests communication or a message, and a place of worship suggests spirituality. Most individuals could easily decipher each of these symbols.

In addition to their usual meanings, many words also have a variety of metaphorical or symbolic meanings. A fish might suggest something's fishy; a book could symbolize playing by the book; and, a forest might show that an individual is so caught up in details that she or he can't see the forest for the trees. Metaphors often present themselves in a variety of ways in dreams. Dream interpretation is something that virtually anyone can accomplish. In fact, dreaming might be considered "a right-brained process" whereas their interpretation is perhaps best undertaken with logic and "a left-brain approach."

One dream student who told me that she did not know how to interpret her dreams related the following example: She dreamt that she saw her brother in her backyard. He was standing next to a compost pile with a rake in hand, as though he had been gathering some of the material together. To the dreamer's surprise, a telephone sat on top of the pile of compost. When I asked the dreamer if she was having problems communicating with her brother, she looked at me in compete astonishment and inquired, "How did you know?" I explained to her that one possibility suggested by the imagery was simply that her communication (telephone) with her brother (who appeared in the dream) was rotting (compost pile), and it appeared that he had been trying to work (rake) on the situation, whereas she had not. After my explanation, the dreamer could clearly see how I had arrived at the interpretation from the images provided in her dream.

If I could speak to myself as a seven-year-old and explain why I had dreamed that a hideous monster had come to fetch me, I would say that it was simply in response to my having taken something that did not belong to me from a neighborhood child. The guilt had begun to devour me. Even though I was not aware of the dream's meaning, shortly thereafter I returned the rubber-band gun I had taken, and the dream never occurred again. My other childhood dream of being with a girlfriend that I did not really have (who somehow made my life complete) turned out to be partially prophetic. More than twenty years later I met and married a woman very much like the one portrayed in the dream. The dream had come in response to my loneliness at the time. It was also a subconscious prompting to incorporate the various aspects of my being, and learning to like myself so that I could truly like and have relationships with others. Although I have learned a great about dreams from working with other people, perhaps more importantly I have learned a great deal about myself and how to show others how they can do the same.

This book is written in the hope that it might make some small contribution to a day somewhere off in the future when each and every individual is encouraged to work with dreams as a normal part of everyday life, when no child is ever again told that a dream is "only your imagination," and where many more people might come to understand that they have always possessed a source of helpful intuition and personal guidance within themselves—they just didn't know where to look.

1

Finding Insight in Symbolism

As long as there have been human beings, there have been dreams. Whether our ancient ancestors regarded dreams as messages from the gods, omens or simply extensions of daily life is subject to much conjecture. What is known is that the evidence of our fascination with dreams dates back to the first written word.

One of the earliest indications of dream interpretation comes from Egypt in the form of the Chester Beatty papyrus. Perhaps one of the oldest "dream dictionaries" in existence, this document is approximately 4,000 years old and contains a number of dream symbols and their possible corresponding meaning. For example, to the early Egyptians, dreaming about seeing one's bed on fire could represent the rape of one's wife, whereas dreaming that you were looking at a snake might signify abundance. Although not necessarily maintaining the same meaning today, both of these are examples of cultural symbols, which will be discussed later.

For eons, many cultures believed that God literally spoke to His human children through their dreams. With this in mind, no wonder the Bible contains approximately seventy-five references to dreams throughout the Old and New Testaments, including the Creator's announcement that "If there be a prophet among you, I the Lord will make myself know unto him in a vision, and will speak unto him in a dream" (Numbers 12:6). In early Judaism, symbols such as the rainbow, the rite of circumcision, and recognizing the Sabbath were signs that signified the mystical relationship between God and humankind. The rabbinical contributions to the Talmud also contain hundreds of references to dreams and the logical connections between symbolism and consciousness. As one example, according to the Talmud, salt symbolizes the Torah because just as the world cannot exist without salt, it cannot exist without the Torah. This would also be an example of a cultural symbol.

The Greeks also placed much significance on the ability of dreams to relate important information to the dreamer. During the Greco-Roman period, dream incubation was a common practice in which individuals were able to obtain divine guidance from the gods. At the temple dedicated to the god Asclepius, the Greek god of healing, patients attempted to have a dream that would provide them with information enabling them to recover from whatever ailment was troubling them. Temple priests were on hand to assist dreamers in interpreting whatever guidance came their way.

It is also from the Greeks that we get the word "symbolon," which means an insignia or a means of identification. In simplest terms, a symbol is a visible representation of an object or an idea. A word or an image is symbolic when it implies something more than its obvious and immediate meaning. Symbols provide mirror images of feelings, situations, fears, experiences, needs, potentials, and desires.

The interpretative meaning assigned to symbols is not some random definition that has to be memorized; instead, there is generally a logical connection that can be discovered by the dreamer. In other words, a symbol does not mean something simply because that meaning may be listed in a dream dictionary, invariably there is a rational explanation. For this reason, dreamers often experience an "aha!"

when a possible meaning for their dream is discussed—generally the meaning becomes apparent and is not simply a matter of conjecture. Certainly this was the experience of a thirty-year-old Navy wife who related the following dream[1]:

Dream of thirty-year-old woman:
I dreamed that my husband, Bill, and I were on a little bitty island (like in the cartoons) in the middle of the ocean. The dolphins were swimming by and the water was beautiful just like the island of Guam from which we recently moved. I was watching the dolphins when suddenly Bill jumped in the water.

Before I could do anything I saw a killer whale. I was afraid to get in the water and I couldn't see Bill. I was scared because I thought I had lost him. Then this huge killer whale jumped out of the water onto the little island. Its head had a huge hole in it as if it had eroded from toxic waste or something. I started to cry. I wanted to help it but I was afraid to get close.

The whale knew what I was feeling and started flapping these things inside its head and I understood perfectly what it was saying to me. It was as if we could read each other's minds because no words were spoken. It was telling me that its sore didn't hurt and not to worry because the missing skin would grow back. It then told me that if I wanted to go find my husband I could ride on its back.

The whale stated that although we (the whale and I) had a hard time communicating, we would be able to understand one another and everything would be okay. The whale had a big smile and a beautiful laugh that made me smile as well. I remember feeling guilty for being human and allowing bad things to happen to these beautiful animals but I felt so good when the whale seemed to forgive me.

---

[1]Each of the dreams used within this volume is real, although the names have been changed to maintain confidentiality.

Looking at the major symbols, the little island could be indicative of the dreamer's present situation or experience. It might also indicate some type of personal or emotional isolation. Dolphins can be a symbol of new thought or higher intelligence. Because of their enormity and the fact that they have very thick layers of internal fat or blubber, a whale can be symbolic of someone holding in personal emotions. Because this is a killer whale, it may be suggesting that the act of holding in these emotions is creating volatile outbursts.

Although the dreamer expressed total confusion regarding the possible meaning of her dream, a few insights can lay the groundwork for clearer understanding. To begin, the whale seems to symbolize the dreamer's husband. The rationale is two-fold: the whale does not appear until after the husband's disappearance and in the dream she also expresses that she is having a hard time communicating with this creature, even though there is deep affection between them. The fact that the whale has a "toxic waste" sore on its head may suggest that the husband has been constantly worried or concerned about something, which is basically eating away at his thoughts.

Since the island can be symbolic of their life together, the husband appears content with the tiny world in which they live (the cartoon island); however, she is looking for broader horizons. Upon questioning, the woman admitted that she and her husband were arguing about their life situation—her wanting more meaning in life and him not understanding why.

According to the dreamer, she and her husband had just moved to the states from an overseas military assignment. In the process of moving, she had decided to give up her career in administration and pursue "something more meaningful." Her interests turned to holistic health and spirituality (hence the images of the dolphins). She returned to school to get a job as a health care practitioner. From her husband's perspective, this change in his wife had been the cause of much concern: "My husband is a man of few words but I knew all my talk of holistic healing was driving him a little crazy. He wanted me to have a paycheck every two weeks and continue to be 'normal.'" The husband's "craziness" and mental concern is obviously reflected in the toxic waste sore that appears on the killer whale's head.

The dreamer confessed her fear that she had begun to worry that her beliefs and her desires for the future were so different than his that she and her husband would begin to grow apart. She was relieved to see that the dream suggested otherwise. In the dream although it had been difficult to communicate with the whale it ended with the knowledge that they "would be able to understand one another and everything would be okay."

Oftentimes, individuals pursuing the topic of dream interpretation often ask questions like: "Why do dreams have to be interpreted anyway?" or "Wouldn't it be easier if the unconscious mind just told me what it wanted me to know in plain English?" This is an extremely common inquiry for individuals looking into the meaning of their dreams, and perhaps the best answer in this regard is that the language of the brain is symbols; it is not English, nor is it any other spoken language. For this reason, individuals can often help one another with dream interpretation even when they might not be able to communicate in the same verbal language. Although our ability to communicate verbally may be limited, each of us shares the language of symbols because it is connected to the nature of our own consciousness. For contributing to this very understanding, we owe a debt of gratitude to two pioneers in the field of psychology, Sigmund Freud and Carl Jung.

The founder of psychoanalysis, Sigmund Freud (1858-1939) was a pioneer in the exploring the unconscious and dreams. Although many now regard Freud's work on dreams as somewhat narrow in perspective, he is often credited with generating a modern-day interest in dreamwork. To be sure, Freud was not the first scientist to explore the topic of dreams, but his publication of *The Interpretation of Dreams* (1900) laid the groundwork for a great deal of dream analysis that followed.

Essentially, Freud worked with the assumption that dreams are not a matter of chance but are instead associated with conscious thoughts and problems. In his approach, dreams are the unconscious mind's expression of deeply rooted experiences and even traumas. This idea was based in part on earlier studies that recognized how some neurotic psychological symptoms are symbolically meaningful. For example, physicians had previously discovered such problems as psychological asthma, whereby one had the feeling of being stifled or being unable to breathe, or eating disorders in which the individual felt as though she or he could not eat, swallow or accept something.

Freud's original technique became known as "free association." In this process, individuals would discuss their dream images and thoughts over and over again until they got to the unconscious core regarding what the dream was really about. The dream itself was the manifest content whereas the unconscious prompting that had created the dream to begin with was known as the latent content. In this regard, the nature of the conscious mind is like the tip of an iceberg—it is only a small portion of what exists just below the surface.

Later, Carl Gustav Jung (1875-1961), a student of Freud's, abandoned this approach. Jung felt that dreams were much more than simply tools to get to the core root of an unconscious problem. He suggested that there was actually much to learn from the form and content of a dream and that the symbols themselves had meaning. He also suggested that there was a level to the unconscious that Freud had overlooked, and this level he called the collective unconscious. This collective unconscious was also the level from which universal symbols or "archetypes" originated. According to the story, Jung's theory of archetypes first originated because of an experience he had with a patient in an asylum. One day the patient was looking out the window and commented on the fact that the sun was wagging something that looked like a tail, creating the wind in the process. Apparently Jung thought nothing of the unusual comment until years later when he came across the translation of an Egyptian papyrus that told the myth of how the wind was created by the activity of a tail-like protrusion coming from the sun. Since the patient could have had no knowledge of the Egyptian account, Jung theorized that there must be some type of symbol that was universal in nature and connected individuals across time and cultures. Later work would confirm that his theory seemed to have a great deal of historical and other verification.

Jung's approach to the nature of consciousness closely parallels that of Edgar Cayce's, although the two men apparently had no knowledge of one another. Cayce's approach came as a result of a dream he had in 1932, while giving a reading to another individual. In the dream, he saw himself as a tiny dot that began to be elevated as if in a whirlwind. As the dot rose, the rings of the whirlwind became larger and larger, each one encompassing a greater span of space than the one preceding it. There were also spaces between each ring that the sleeping Cayce recognized as the various levels of consciousness development. Cayce also uses the terms conscious, subconscious and superconscious to describe the various levels of the mind.

Regardless of which model we use, subconscious (or unconscious) images often contain mini-stories of events, thoughts, feelings, and experiences that mean much more than simply the image itself. These symbols and images can arise from each level of human consciousness. Essentially there are only three different types of symbols. There are *archetypes* that have meaning for individuals across time and cultures, there are symbols which are *cultural* in nature and appropriate for a given nation, culture, or group of individuals with something in common (e.g. a career, a workplace, a lifestyle, a family, etc.), and there are those which are *personal* and specific to an individual.

Personal symbols have the most significant meaning to each individual regardless of what anyone else might think about that same symbol. As an example, many individuals have very emotional feelings about their pets. To a pet lover, the image of her or his dog in a dream could be literally associated with the dog or it could be symbolic of the love that the individual feels toward her or his pet. Someone else who is allergic to dogs might think of dogs as representative of allergies, an irritation, or even the possibility of health problems. If a person had a fearful encounter with a dog at some point in her or his life, than a dog could be associated with something else about which that person is afraid. Someone without a dog and no particular feelings one way or another might be culturally predisposed to associate dogs with friendship or faithfulness because of the well-known saying that "a dog is man's best friend." The underlying meaning of a specific symbol is oftentimes closely associated with whatever the dreamer equates to that particular image.

Other examples of pets in dreams and their corresponding possible meanings include the following:

Dream of twenty-something-year-old woman:
I dreamed that I was standing in my kitchen petting and holding my kitten. Suddenly, to my surprise, cowboys and Indians started fighting and chasing one another through the living room on horseback. I held on to my kitten and wondered what to do.

Looking at the major symbolism, a kitten can call to mind comfort, security or playfulness. Cowboys and Indians could certainly be an image of conflict. So, in this instance, the dream may be suggesting that the woman's comfort and security is being threatened by some kind of a conflict (cowboys and Indians), occurring perhaps within her own home or work environment (living room). This conflict is causing her enough concern that she is wondering what to do about the situation.

The dreamer revealed that she was having problems fighting with a new roommate. This conflict was ruining her home life to the point that she often dreaded going back to her apartment after work. The woman decided that the dream was confirming her feelings that she needed to get a new roommate.

Dream of middle-aged woman:
I am holding a large dog in my arms. One of my hands is clamped over the dog's mouth. I am holding onto the dog, squeezing its mouth shut because I am afraid to let go of the mouth for fear that the dog will bite me.

One possibility suggested by the dream is that the woman is holding on to some kind of anger or aggression (angry dog). She is clutching the dog's mouth shut either because she's afraid of being "bitten" (hurt by something) or because she worried about words that might be spoken ("biting words"). Another possibility suggested by the symbolism is that the woman may be fearful of something being spoken (either toward her from another or by her toward someone else) that is angry, aggressive and ultimately hurtful, and is therefore clamping down on the spoken work (e.g. clutching the mouth shut).

When asked about her personal experience with dogs (e.g. "Do you have a dog?"), the woman confessed that she was terrified of dogs because in the past one had bitten her.

The woman also admitted that she had a "problem with anger" and that she often found herself "biting her tongue" for fear of expressing something that she might regret later. Obviously, the dream portrays the woman's need of finding a better way to express her feelings.

Generally, a personal symbol represents whatever the dreamer most closely associates with that symbol. For example, different places are generally symbolic of whatever an individual may associate with that place (e.g. a church = spirituality; a library = learning or knowledge; a post office = communication or a message; the cleaners = that which needs to be cleaned or tasks that need to be taken care of, and so forth). In the same manner, rooms in a house can be symbolic of whatever is associated with that particular room (e.g. the master bedroom = relationships or sexuality; kitchen = home and family or diet; bathroom = that which needs to be eliminated). Either an automobile or a house can sometimes represent a person's physical body since both are obviously extensions of one's self.

In a dream in which the house represents the individual, the roof could indicate thoughts or ideas, the attic the subconscious or the higher self, the basement the unconscious or repressed emotions, etc. In the same way, when an automobile represents a person's body, the headlights can correspond to sight, the tires to one's foundation or feet, the exhaust to eliminations, the engine to the heart, and the electrical system to one's nervous system. By looking at the thematic content of a dream an individual can generally deduce whether a house or a car actually represents a physical body or if it is instead symbolic of one's life or current situation (house) or one's present experience and direction (car).

In the case of a middle-aged man, his dream of a car suggested that he was losing control of his life.

Dream of middle-aged man:
I am driving my car very fast and going down a winding mountain road. The car keeps going faster and faster. I try to

apply the brakes but they do not work. I panic when I realize that my brakes are out of control. I try my best to keep the car on the road but I'm losing control. The dream comes to an end when I slam right into a tree.

In addition to the possibility that the dream is literal, suggesting that the dreamer needs to have his brakes checked, the imagery also suggests that the man's life is out of control. Although he is doing his best to keep everything on track, he has got to learn to slow down and "apply the brakes" to his life. When it was suggested that the dreamer had too many things going on in his life and that he wouldn't be able to keep up the pace much longer, he wholeheartedly agreed and decided to begin looking into ways to "slow down."

A sixty-something-year-old woman's dream of her house suggested that the very foundation of her life had been pulled out from underneath her.

Dream of sixty-something-year-old woman:
I came home and was shocked to find that my very expensive carpets were being torn out of my house. They were just being ripped up by the carpet people. It appeared as though they were being haphazardly replaced with something cheap that looked much less valuable. I was horrified.

The imagery could indicate that there is something occurring in the dreamer's life (at home or possibly at work) in which she feels like the foundation is being "ripped up" from underneath her. It also appears as though she has no control over the situation and is fearful that she is going to end up with something "much less valuable." After describing her dream, the woman began to cry and stated that her husband of thirty-some years had totally surprised her with his request for a divorce. She was devastated and understandably concerned for her future. Echoing the process of dreams contrasting and correlating the events in one's waking life, the dream was simply reflecting back her conscious feelings and worries.

In the case of a nineteen-year-old student, the condition of his yard indicated that there was a great deal occurring in his life and that in spite of his organization skills he did not yet have everything totally under control.

> *Dream of nineteen-year-old student:*
> I was back home in my backyard. I walked around the corner and I was stunned to find weeds at least ten feet high in the yard. I was shocked because I had spent so much time and effort to keep the yard clean. I kept saying, "No! This can't be happening!"

In terms of the symbols, a backyard can be associated with one's present situation or experience (it might also indicate that which in the past or something hidden from public view). The existence of weeds can obviously correspond with something that needs to be attended to.

The dreamer went on to provide his own interpretation. He stated that the dream had occurred after the first day of his anatomy and physiology class. During class he had discovered that they were going to be required to go through twenty pages of "very difficult text" before the next class and that there would be a thirty-point quiz on Friday. He admitted that the class was turning out to be much more work than he had first anticipated. The dream also suggests that the dreamer was exactly where he needed to be (his own back yard) and that the task before him was exactly what he needed to be doing.

Other common symbols in dreams include dreaming about other people. When other individuals appear in our dreams it is important to keep in mind that they usually represent something the dreamer associates with that individual or some aspect of the relationship with that individual. Generally we do not dream *for* other people. If an individual dreamed about the President of the United States, for example, he or she would probably not contact the White House and express to the President, "I had a dream for you," and yet this exact sentence is often stated to friends if they appear in a dream. Unless we are very much concerned about another individual we do not dream for them and even if we do (an approach that will be discussed in chapters seven and eight), the dream still has a personal meaning for the dreamer. Other people in our dreams generally represent traits, talents, faults, activities or experiences we most associate with that individual. Two examples follow:

> *Dream of forty-something-year-old woman:*
> I am walking with my brother (who is dead!) arm and arm through a field and a forest. We seem very close and happy, even though I begin to wonder in the dream, "Isn't he dead?" Suddenly, I see my brother's wife and she is dressed like the Virginia Lottery's Lady Luck [an advertising symbol for the Virginia lottery]. She waves her hand at us and I start to feel very good about what is going on.

Obviously, it is much easier to help someone interpret his or her dream if it is possible to dialogue with that individual about some of the imagery being portrayed, as each person is most intimately aware of her or his own connection to symbols and personal life experiences. In the case of the above dream, whatever the dreamer associates with her brother and seems to be involved in personally (the dream shows her arm in arm with her brother) may turn out very lucky, even prosperous.

The dreamer stated that four years ago her brother had been on the verge of much prosperity in his personal business when he had suddenly and unexpectedly died. After his death, she had taken over her brother's business. She added that her brother and his wife had been very close and gotten along well.

From the dream, it appears that the dreamer herself is on the verge of much prosperity with the business that is now hers. The "brother's wife" in the dream might also be symbolic of the company business (e.g. the "other woman" with whom the brother had had a relationship). Overall, the dream suggests that the business is about to become very lucky and the hopes, dreams, and expectations that the dreamer had shared with her brother regarding the company's future are all about to manifest. Much prosperity is about to come into the dreamer's life (Lady Luck).

People in our dreams can also be indicative of whatever positive or negative traits or qualities we associate with them. Such was the case in a thirty-something-year old woman's dream of her grandmother.

Dream of thirty-something-year-old woman:
I dreamt that I was given a birdcage by my grandmother. Although it was a good size cage, it was much smaller than the bird I seemed to own. The bird was about three feet tall. I wondered what I was supposed to do.

For a variety of reasons a bird can often symbolize a message or a messenger. Those reasons include the fact that a rooster crows to signify the dawn of a new day, the singing of birds is associated with the arrival of spring, a vulture can be a messenger of death, and in scripture Noah sent forth two birds to bring back evidence of whether or not the waters of the Flood had abated. Since a cage can be a symbol of confinement, the message to the dreamer seems to be that she has outgrown something that she associates with her grandmother.

Instead of hearing about a grandmother's love or nurturing, the woman proceeded to describe how the thing she most associated with her grandmother was criticism. All of the dreamer's life, her grandmother had been highly critical of her and everything about her: her appearance, her friends, her decisions, her direction in life, and her choices; the list went on and on. She volunteered the fact that this criticism had rubbed off on her so that she had struggled for a long time with being very critical of herself. The dreamer felt like she had finally overcome some of her own self-criticism, a fact that was being portrayed in the dream by the cage (imprisoned by criticism) being too small. In other words, the woman had outgrown her grandmother's and her own perception of herself.

Although another individual was not present in the dream, an additional dream that seemed to explore a dreamer's self perception occurred in the case of a fifty-something-year-old woman.

Dream of fifty-something-year-old woman:
I had a little box of crayons. Someone (I never saw another

person in this dream) took the box of crayons away and I was handed a large shoebox full of crayons of every color imaginable. It was larger than the biggest Crayola box that exists and there were many more colors than I had ever seen. I heard a voice tell me that I could sharpen any one of these crayons as sharp as I wanted to.

Perhaps the dream is suggesting that the dreamer has many more creative talents (crayons) than she believes about herself. The woman stated that she had recently bought a top of the line sewing machine with all of the "bells and whistles." She also admitted to feeling guilty about the cost of the machine: "Since I don't sew very well, I felt like sewing was something I could never do well enough to justify the expenditure." The woman herself perceived that the dream was telling her that "I have been given many, many talents and I can become as skilled in any of these areas as I desire." She decided the dream was telling her to discard her self-doubts and just "charge ahead" with her creativity and her sewing.

In addition to personal symbols, a second category is cultural symbols: symbols which have meaning to large segments of a society, a people, a race, a religion, or group, or even a nation. For example, the symbol of a country's flag often represents patriotism (or nationalism) to citizens of that country. A crucifix is a symbol of faith to many Christians; for many Jews the symbol might be a menorah or a mezuzah and for those of the Islamic faith, Mecca or even a prayer rug could represent the same thing. Students of the scriptures may associate a rainbow with a promise or a covenant, whereas others might associate a rainbow with luck or prosperity. In the United States, Friday the 13th, a black cat or walking under a ladder can all be considered bad luck. In Egypt, a beetle (or scarab) is symbolic of abundance and good luck. In Ecuador, dreaming of a funeral is thought to be symbolic of an impending marriage. However, in the United States the same dream would usually indicate the end of something. In Japan, dreaming about Mount Fuji, the highest mountain in the country, suggests to the dreamer that something magnificent is about to transpire in her or his life.

Countries often have icons that can represent what other people and nations most associate with that country. For example, the Statue of Liberty can represent liberty, independence and freedom—qualities that a number of individuals throughout the world may associate with the United States. Many people in the world associate France with being the country of good food and wine, romance and passion, and a great place to visit. For this reason, if an individual dreamt about the Eiffel Tower, the dream could be associated with a romance, with a relationship or even with travel. In the case of the Eiffel Tower, because its shape is phallic in nature, the tower could also represent some type of a male relationship or energy. For the same reason, the Washington Monument can represent the same thing. Anything that appears in the shape of a phallus (e.g. a banana, a tall building, a gun, or a hammer) can be symbolic of a man or male energy. Conversely anything that is more receptive and womb-like (e.g. a cave, a box, a basket or a tunnel) can be symbolic of a woman or female energy.

Dreams that are commonplace and frequently experienced by individuals within a society can be considered cultural in nature. Examples include such typical dreams as the dream of falling, which is generally symbolic of not feeling in control of some situation or experience.[2] It can also indicate a loss of personal power and will. Conversely, the dream of flying can symbolize having everything in control, experiencing great euphoria or an elevated experience of some kind. Other common dreams include appearing naked in public (feeling vulnerable or exposed), or having one's teeth fall out (having things come out of one's mouth that shouldn't, e.g. gossip). The dream of finding one's self back at school and suddenly realizing there is a test you didn't know about or being in the hallway and completely forgetting one's locker combination both suggest the possibility of not

---

[2]An often-repeated "old wives tale" is that if an individual dreams she or he is falling and then hits the ground in the dream that person would die and that is why the individual wakes up. The truth of the matter is that we often have normal physiological responses while dreaming. Many people have been around a sleeping dog or cat dreaming of running and then watched as the animal's paws move in response. In waking life, a long fall would cause an individual's heart to beat faster with an adrenaline rush, therefore the same thing occurs in the sleep state and the adrenaline and the heartbeat simply cause the individual to awaken from slumber.

feeling prepared for something that is presently occurring in life. Cultural symbols exist because throughout the world, groups and masses of individuals have often given meaning to specific images and symbols based upon their history and experience, and that meaning has been passed down to people sharing a similar culture and background.

Symbols, stories and images that are universal are called archetypes, the third type of symbol. In addition to having meaning to masses of people, archetypes can also be defined as encapsulated symbols or prototypes of human behavior and experience. For example, the archetype of the hero is portrayed in such stories as *Superman, Hercules,* and *Xena: Warrior Princess.* The archetype of a tragic star-crossed love affair is told in tales like *The Tragedy of Romeo and Juliet, West Side Story, Torch Song Trilogy,* and even the relationship between Leonardo DiCaprio and Kate Winslet in the *Titanic* movie. For every possible human condition there is an archetype.

Mythic tales and legends also illustrate archetypes regardless of whether or not the basis for the story has any historical validity. Examples include the Creation Myth, which is at the root of all civilizations and societies, as well as the Flood Myth, which is told in a variety of ways in more than two hundred different cultures. Examining the Great Flood Myth more closely, most often the story describes the account of a family that survives a deluge of enormous proportions. Prior to the disaster, the family generally pulls together everything that is part of their world (such as the animals in the story of Noah described in Genesis) and finds refuge in a craft or a ship in which they can ride out the storm. Oftentimes, the family has no control over their journey for the ship is inundated from above and below and they are forced to simply ride out the storm. At the end of the Flood, the craft generally finds higher and stable ground and the occupants can disembark and begin their lives anew. Everything that was a part of their old world is now a part of their new (e.g. the animals get off the ark). The difference is that now all of the ship's occupants find themselves upon higher ground.

Regardless of whether or not the story of a Great Flood has any basis in fact, because it is so widespread the tale has an archetypal meaning at a subconscious level. Simply stated, that meaning is one of transformation and change because the ship's occupants underwent a journey over which they had no control and yet somehow ended up in a better place because of their experience. As an archetype the Great Flood Myth symbolizes the pattern of being overwhelmed by personal transformation and change and yet somehow becoming a better person because of it.

What is fascinating about this particular archetype is that the story of Noah seems to be experiencing a tremendous rise in popularity. The market has been flooded with numerous children's toys, night lights, magnets, collector's plates, ornaments, figurines and even programs about Noah's Ark. The reason is not because for some inexplicable reason this man and his family suddenly fascinate society. Instead, it is because so many individuals apparently feel in the midst of personal transformation and change themselves that the archetype has resurfaced. People feel motivated to put a Noah magnet on their fridge because subconsciously it resonates to something they are experiencing within themselves.

Another popular mythic archetype is the legend of the soul's journey. Simply stated, the story is that the soul was with God in the beginning, went off on a journey of self-discovery, and will eventually return to the same place it started only with an expanded level of awareness. The soul's journey archetype is reported in such diverse materials as Dorothy's experience in *The Wizard of Oz*, Christian's journey in *Pilgrim's Progress*, Pinocchio's challenges in *The Adventures of Pinocchio*, Bilbo's adventures in *The* Hobbit, and *The Parable of the Prodigal Son* in the book of Luke (Luke 15:11-24). To be sure, no one ever reads *The Wizard of Oz* and exclaims, "That's the best story of the soul's journey I've ever read!" but it is a classic because so many individuals relate to the tale due to its archetypal significance. Whenever a story, a legend, a myth or a movie can encapsulate an archetype of human behavior, it has the potential to resonate to an enormous audience.

In addition to stories, myths and legends, symbols can also have archetypal significance. For example, the symbol of an old person (or a grandmother or a grandfather) can be an archetype of wisdom and experience because the longer a person has lived, hopefully the wiser she or he has become. Even if individuals are not consciously aware of it, there are many archetypes of which they already have personal understanding. Another common symbol is a lion or a great cat. Just as the lion is considered "the king of the jungle," it can be associated with personal power or vitality. A very common symbol in dreams is a great body of water. Water is oftentimes the symbol for spirit or emotion. The rationale is simply due to the fact that water is the source of all life on the earth but ultimately spirit is the source of all life. As human beings, much of life is experienced through our personal emotions. For that reason, water can be the archetype for spirit or emotion.

In regards to symbols, the most important consideration to keep in mind is an individual's own feelings, thoughts and experiences about that symbol. Symbols are profoundly and deeply personal. If, for example, an individual dreams of drowning in water it would be senseless to attempt to impose the archetype for spirit or emotion on that individual's dream if she or he had literally had a near-drowning experience. In another instance, a dream about the Vatican for a Catholic could be symbolic of spirituality or religion but to a Cardinal employed in the Holy See it probably represents work.

The interpretation of symbols is primarily dependent upon whatever the individual associates with that image or his or her personal experience with it. When these associations differ from the thoughts and feelings of others, personal feelings of the dreamer generally take precedence. Sometimes a dream dictionary or another person can be helpful in discerning the possible meaning of symbols, but ultimately it is left for the dreamer alone to decide. Therefore, regardless of whether or not a symbol is archetypal, cultural, or personal, ultimately each individual will be the best interpreter of his or her dream images because only that person is fully familiar with his or her current situation, activities, background, relationships, experiences and thought processes.

Chapter 1 Sample Dreams
See Appendix One for possible interpretations

Dream of fifty-year-old woman:

(Background information: Woman has been extremely busy; her shelties have actually been dead several years.)

I dreamed that I was inside my house and all of a sudden I remembered that I hadn't watered or fed my shelties in quite some time. For some reason, I had put them in a shed out back of the house and never went back to check on them. Suddenly, I was in a panic and tried to go and check on them but a neighbor showed up and kept interfering with me trying to go see my dogs. Finally, when the neighbor left I was able to go out to the shed. I was horrified to find that the dogs were gone!

Dream of forty-something-year-old woman:

(Background information: Woman works in an office where there is a lot of backstabbing that really bothers her.)

I was speaking to the office receptionist about the fact that I was being promoted. I had decided that from now on there would be a new dress code that everyone would be wearing. I had on a smart-looking business-type pantsuit to show her what I was talking about.

Dream of middle-aged man:

(Background information: Man does not get along with his mother.)

I dreamed that I was speaking to my mother and as I was speaking my two front teeth kept falling out. I'd push them back in but they kept falling out. The funny thing was, I don't think my mother noticed. It made me feel uncomfortable to be around her.

2

Finding Insight in the Theme

Most often a story, a fable, a movie, a play or a book has an essential point or an idea that is trying to be related to the audience. Although individuals might express that idea in a variety of ways, essentially they will simply be articulating their personal perspectives on a central theme that the author is trying to portray. Whenever a story's theme can encapsulate a pattern of human experience or behavior that piece has the potential of resonating to the greatest number of people.

At some point in their educational process, individuals generally learn about the importance of a theme in one or more of their English classes. Countless students have discussed works such as *The Bridge of San Luis Rey* (Wilder) as exploring how love can be the bridge between the living and the dead. In *Lord of the Flies* (Golding), we are confronted with the horrifying thought that in spite of the dictates and morals imposed by society, left unchecked human nature may not ultimately change from its base animal instincts. In *Animal Farm* (Orwell), we are presented with the idea that even when we express our firm belief that "all men are created equal," too often some of us cannot help but feel more equal than others. The *Harry Potter* (Rowling) series presents the universal theme of coming of age in the face of tremendous adversity. A theme is essentially the foundation upon which a story begins to take shape.

When skillfully crafted, a story's theme enables an audience to recognize some truth about the human condition or something about themselves. The works of William Shakespeare, for example, have survived and remained popular for hundreds of years because the themes explored by his plays continue to have modern-day significance. Examples include *A Midsummer Night's Dream*, which suggests in part that in matters of love it is often difficult to discern the difference between an outer truth and one's inner fantasy. *The Tragedy of King Lear* explores how for many of us our individual suffering is most often brought about by our own choices and ignorance. *The Tragedy of Romeo and Juliet* presents the theme of star-crossed lovers who suffer misfortune and catastrophe because of the differing ideologies of their families. This same theme was expressed in the modern-day version of the tale, *West Side Story*, as well as in the love story of Bella and Edward in the *Twilight* series. It has also been experienced personally by anyone who has fallen in love and has faced family or peer conflict or antagonism because the individual's loved one was deemed "unsuitable" because of such factors as creed, race, sex, or station in life.

Although themes can sometimes be challenging to discover, most often given a little thought they can be straightforward and easily detected. Countless children can describe how *Star Wars* explores the struggle between good and evil. Later, in *The Empire Strikes Back* we discover how one of the most challenging aspects of this conflict is the struggle between an individual and the dark side or shadow side of him or herself. In plays, movies, books, and fairy tales, the theme is the central idea being expressed as the story unfolds. The same is true when it comes to dreams.

One of the most straightforward approaches to deciphering the meaning of a dream is to first establish a possible theme for the story being portrayed. When it comes to dreams, a theme can generally be described in terms of "what is happening to whom" and should be stated in no more than one or two sentences. Examples of themes might be such statements as "Someone is being threatened," "Something is uplifting someone," "Someone is able to overcome adversity," "Something appears to be easily discoverable," "Someone is running from someone else who appears fierce," and so forth.

Rather than being a waste of time or not worth the effort, discovering a theme can actually save a great deal of time for the simple reason that each symbol has a wealth of possible meanings but not all are appropriate for every dream. By establishing a theme the dreamer can discard those meanings that are not specifically important to the central theme of her or his dream. The following examples show how finding the theme can be extremely useful in unlocking the imagery contained with a dream:

> *Dream of twenty-something-year-old man:*
> I was alone in a sailboat in the ocean. I seemed to be looking out over the horizon when suddenly a large storm started heading directly for my boat. The sky got very dark, the winds started blowing and enormous waves began striking the boat, threatening to turn it over. The boat got tossed around again and again and I began to panic because the waves were so big. I was afraid of what came next because I was convinced I was going to die.

The water and the waves seemed to be the predominant threat in the dream. As stated previously, water can symbolize spirit or emotion. In addition, water can have metaphorical connotations such as "making one's mouth water" (having desire for) or "being in hot water" (being in trouble). Water can also be symbolic of eliminations ("to make water"). However, the theme in this dream seems to indicate that "Someone is on a turbulent journey" or "Someone is being overwhelmed by something." With this in mind, the most obvious meaning suggested by the dream is not about eliminations, or spirit, or desire but the fact that there seems to be something going on in the dreamer's life that is overwhelming him emotionally.

Upon questioning, the young man stated that he was having a great deal of emotional turmoil regarding his life's direction. He wanted to become more involved in theater and the arts; however, his father (who was apparently very much "the head of the family") had already decided on a business career path for his son. For a long time the young man had known he needed to stand up and speak to his father but he had not been brave enough to do so. The dream was reflecting the dreamer's emotional struggle regarding his own life's journey and his conflict with his father. The conflict was obviously coming to a head and before long the son was going to have to brave the storm and express his own desires for the future. In a metaphorical sense, the dreamer's conflict (and worrying about how he could deal with that conflict) was "killing" him.

Oftentimes individuals can get so caught up in the minute details or the complicated storyline being portrayed by their dreams that they want to decipher every element of the story and then try to come to terms with the meaning. This can become a monumental undertaking and frequently a waste of time. Over time, trying to go through every image or symbol one at a time and assign meaning to that symbol might help a dreamer memorize a bunch of symbols but it is not very effective in overall interpretation. The more an individual focuses upon the details the harder it can be to separate from the dream itself and see the storyline with any objectivity. Discovering the overall theme of a dream can bypass unnecessary details and enable the dreamer to get to the basis of what is being communicated by the images. The following dream provides a straightforward example:

Dream of forty-something-year-old woman:
I dreamed that my husband and I were walking and came upon the house of Donald Trump. Everything was gorgeous! Since the doors were opened, I suggested that we walk inside and tour the mansion. Everything about the home was beautiful and exquisite, until we came into the master bedroom. I was shocked to find the room a wreck—everything was out of place, towels on the floor, sheets thrown around, etc. Sud-

denly, I noticed two dogs fighting in the middle of the room, and all at once one of the dogs squatted and defecated in the bedroom. I didn't know what to think.

Rather than trying to decide what each symbol means first and then putting them all back together, the theme approach suggests that the first step is to discover the central storyline. One possibility suggested by the dream might be expressed in one sentence, as follows: "Something does not appear as good on the inside as it does on the outside." Certainly we can see how this is a possible theme since the beauty and splendor of the house is not maintained within the confines of the bedroom walls. Another way of stating essentially the same thing might be, "Something is worse than it first appears." Obviously, there are many ways in which a theme can be stated. Once a central theme is discovered, the next step is to interpret the primary images in the context of that storyline. Since the master bedroom is involved it suggests that the woman's marriage (or sex life or both) is in trouble.

In real life the two occupants of the bedroom are obviously the husband and wife who are symbolized by the dogs in the dream. The two dogs are fighting and at least one of them continually drops "crap" in the middle of the relationship. In real life, the woman and her husband had been married for nearly twenty years. The couple was highly successful and appeared to have everything that money could buy. To the outside world it appeared that they had it made, however, in real life the two hardly spoke to one another. Oftentimes, they did not even sleep in the same bedroom. Their marriage relationship was in chaos. The appearance of the bedroom in the dream accurately portrays the upheaval within the couple's relationship. The theme "Something does not appear as good on the inside as it does on the outside" or "Something is worse than it first appears" clearly relates to their marriage. The dream is presenting the chaos of the relationship that the couple has apparently been ignoring and obviously needs to address one way or another.

Discovering a theme proved extremely helpful in the case of a young woman who suffered from depression. She had dropped out of college, was dissatisfied with her life and did not really feel like wanting to do much of anything. She had tried some counseling but stated it had not been helpful. She was just very unhappy and truly did not know why.

After describing her situation, the young woman was told that her subconscious mind might give her insights into what was really going on in her life. She was encouraged to "incubate a dream" on the problem. That night she was to write out the question, "Why am I depressed?" She was to read the question a couple of times before she went to bed. When she awoke the next morning, she was to write down her dreams. If she did not remember a dream, she needed to repeat the process until she had a dream that she could bring back for discussion. The woman agreed to try. A dream followed a couple of days later:

> *Dream of twenty-year-old woman:*
> A friend of mine from elementary school (I don't even know her anymore) walked into the room with an enormous fish bowl that was almost bigger than she was. There wasn't much water in the bowl; it was about two-thirds empty. The water that was there was very dirty and I noticed that the goldfish in the bottom of the bowl appeared very sick. My friend said, "I've been taking care of this for too long, and now it's your turn!"

Rather than immediately trying to interpret the symbolism, a better approach is to decide what the story is all about. The theme in the young woman's dream seems to be that "Something is being neglected." This theme seems likely because the bowl is not full, the water is dirty and is in need of being changed, and the fish have not been cared for properly and are sick. We also have the friend's statement that "I've been taking care of this for too long, and now it's your turn," again suggesting that the dreamer is neglecting something in her life. The dreamer had attempted to incubate a dream on the question, "Why am I depressed?" If we can discover what she has been neglecting, we might get to the root cause of her depression.

Oftentimes, a dream will replicate the meaning of the dream in a variety of symbols. With this in mind, since both water and fish can represent spirit, the thing that is being neglected might have something to do with her own spiritual life. However, there is a reason that the young woman's subconscious mind chose this particular friend to appear in the dream. When asked what this person was like, the response was that this girl was very nice, very pretty, fun to be around and so forth. However, to the more specific question, "What was different about this friend than all the other friends you had at the time?" Without a moment's hesitation, the dreamer replied, "She was the most religious friend I ever had." Again, the subconscious mind tries to express the same meaning through a variety of symbols.

When asked about her own religious and philosophical beliefs, the young woman stated that she did not know what she believed. She had not been raised with any particular religion in her family and she did not really know what she believed about God or spirituality. She was not certain if she was an atheist or an agnostic. She just did not know. Unanswered questions like "Why am I here?" and "What is the purpose of life?" may need to be answered to her satisfaction. One possibility suggested by the dream is that part of her desperately wants to know what life is all about. That was the root cause of her depression.

Demonstrating how dreams can have different meanings depending upon the experience of the dreamer, if the young woman had instead described her friend as "the best cook I ever knew," the dream might be suggesting that her depression came as a result of a problem with diet, health or her physical body. In this case, both the friend as a cook and the fish as a food could have been symbolic of food and the dirty water might have indicated problems with her physical eliminations. The process of getting to the central meaning of a dream often entails dialoguing with the dreamer about what specific symbols and people mean to her or him.

Obviously, when attempting to find insights in a dream through working with the theme, there are a variety of ways to state that theme. Anyway the theme is stated simply allows the individual to build her or his interpretation upon the foundation of the central storyline. Possibilities suggested by the following dream include

"Something appears to be stolen and is not," "Something valuable has been replaced with something cheap," "Someone is mistaken about his perception," and so forth.

> *Dream of forty-something-year-old man:*
> I dreamed that I was looking at my Rolex. Suddenly, I realized that it was a fake, and that it had been replaced by a cheap copy. I ran to a police officer to tell him that someone had stolen my watch. However, the police officer told me that I was wrong and that my watch was still there. I looked at my wrist and saw that he was right.

Regardless of how the theme is stated, to the dreamer it appears as though something valuable has been taken from him. However, an authority figure points out that his perception is incorrect.

In real life, the man was a well-to-do business professional who owned a Rolex watch. He spent many hours at work in order to maintain the success of a business he had helped to create. Immediately after stating his dream, the dreamer volunteered the information that a number of years previously he had been robbed of another Rolex watch and had been extremely upset. He had purchased the first Rolex as a symbol of his success in business. The man wondered if his replacement Rolex was about to be lost or stolen as well.

Oftentimes, the subconscious mind uses previous experiences in life as mini-stories or events in order to bring to the dreamer's awareness that something thematically similar is about to occur. This does not mean that another Rolex is about to be stolen (although it could), a more likely interpretation is that the man is once again on the verge of losing something that is valuable to him.

In the dream, the Rolex could certainly symbolize material success but it can also represent "valuable or quality time." If the Rolex symbolized valuable time and it has been replaced by a cheap copy, then it might indicate that the dreamer has substituted what is really valuable with something less valuable. Whatever that something is, although the dreamer believes it had been stolen from him the man's higher self (police officer) states that he still possesses it. In fact, his time is still integrally connected to his free will (wrist). The wrist can be a symbol of free will because when we choose something at the store, for example, it is the hand, wrist and arm that reaches out to obtain whatever we have chosen with our free will.

In today's society it is not uncommon for a business professional to feel like she or he has to neglect family time (quality time) because of the need to focus on work time (cheap copy). Upon reflection, the man stated he had a wife and children and that more and more frequently his wife was becoming upset because of the long hours spent at the office. He was afraid that the two of them were growing apart. With this in mind, the dreamer's fear of losing the Rolex was a reflection of his fear that he might be losing his family. The dream also seemed to be suggesting that he was blaming his work for the fact that he spent so little time with his family but his own higher self pointed out that the decision continued to be his own. The dream's imagery suggests that he still possesses the ability to decide whether or not he will give more valuable time to his family or continue to replace it with his focus on work. After a moment, the dreamer admitted that he probably did have more control over his time and his schedule than he had first believed, and he was adamant that he really did not want to lose his family.

As illustrated by the businessman's dream, the more that is known about an individual and his or her background, the easier it can be to interpret a dream. For that reason, each dreamer is potentially the best interpreter of his or her own dreams.

The following is similar in nature to a common dream experienced by many dreamers, but ultimately it took the dreamer to express how the dream related to her own life.

Dream of fifty-something-year-old woman:
I was going through a building looking for a restroom because I had to go to the bathroom. Every time I came to a restroom, however, the stall or the seat was really dirty (filthy), and I didn't want to go in, in spite of my need to use the bathroom. For that reason, I kept looking for another bathroom, but every time I found one it appeared just as dirty.

Certainly, many people have had a dream about the need to go to the bathroom and have been unable to find a toilet in their dream or have been unable to relieve themselves once a bathroom was found. Oftentimes these same individuals have literally awakened and discovered that they *really* needed to use a bathroom. In these instances, this type of a dream illustrates how the body's physiological responses can become the substance of dream imagery. It also demonstrates how our conditioning about where it is appropriate to go the bathroom carries over into the dream. Since it is only appropriate to use a *real* bathroom, most often in a dream a real bathroom cannot be found or the dreamer cannot go once a bathroom is found for the reason that it is not real. In the example of the fifty-something-year-old woman, she expressed that although she had dreamt bathroom dreams before and found that she had to use one upon awakening, on this occasion that was not the case. She wondered what this particular dream was all about.

The dream is suggestive of the theme that "Someone is trying to eliminate something but has not been able to do so." In other words, the dream may be suggesting that the dreamer has something in her life that she wants to eliminate or get rid of but has not been able to figure out how to do it. The dirty restrooms might also indicate the woman's own sense that whatever she is trying to get rid of is not appropriate and was perhaps even dirty or shameful. With these possibilities in mind, the dreamer suggested that the dream was probably about her relationship with a daughter.

Apparently the daughter was in her early twenties and had graduated from college. Although the young woman had lived away at school for a time, after graduation and because she had yet to find the job she really wanted (her mother stated she had been offered several and had turned them down), she had moved back home. Since the girl's return, the mother had experienced one frustration after another. The girl was lazy and refused to do anything around the house. She did not do any laundry nor did she offer to cook any meals. She stayed out until all hours. She often went places and did not say where she was going or when she would be returning. She was rude and belligerent to her parents. The list went on and on.

The woman expressed her frustration but also insisted that she wanted to be supportive of her daughter. She felt that her child was going through a challenging "What's next?" period in life. Many times the woman had wanted to say something to her daughter about her behavior or her selfishness, but she had not really been able to do so. The mother added, "I have a problem with conflict...it just doesn't seem spiritual to me."

Obviously, the dreamer had been holding onto all of her frustration and anger in regards to her daughter instead of finding a way to eliminate (e.g. communicate) how she was feeling. As a mother, she felt that any kind of confrontation would be inappropriate, even "dirty" or "filthy." The dream was pointing out that all of her suppressed feelings had become toxic waste products that needed to be released. After a moment's contemplation, the woman indicated she still felt some trepidation regarding expressing her thoughts and feelings but she also agreed that she had to find a way to confront her daughter, helping them both in the process.

In another example utilizing the theme for interpretation, a woman expressed her sadness and anxiety over the fact that her life was "spinning out of control." She was very depressed about a short-term relationship that had come to an end. Previously divorced, she admitted that she originally had high hopes and expectations about this new relationship, believing the two of them made a great couple and would eventually marry. Her dream reflected this overall storyline:

Dream of fifty-something-year-old woman:
I am attending a high school play that seems to be some kind of a musical. It is a really good show and I am enjoying myself. Unfortunately, after the play some of the actors in the production are on a train, including the lead singer and one of the most prominent couples in the musical. There is a horrible train wreck. The train smashes into a car that was spinning out of control. To my horror, the lead singer and the couple are killed in the collision.

Themes applicable to the above include such statements as "Something is in the midst of disaster," "Someone is acting a part that does not turn out positively," and "Something that first appears beautiful, musical, or harmonious leads to disaster." The fact that the dream begins in a high school suggests that the entire episode has been a learning experience for the dreamer. Obviously the musical that is "a really good show" is the harmonious relationship that the couple started out with in which the woman was enjoying herself. The train symbolizes the direction in which this new relationship was ultimately headed. Since this is the woman's dream, the lead singer is a symbol of herself and the prominent couple is associated with their relationship. The train wreck is connected to the car spinning out of control—in other words, the woman is totally confused, heartbroken and devastated by the abrupt end of the relationship. With the death of the relationship, part of the dreamer feels as though she has died as well.

As will be discussed later, many dreams do provide a suggested course of action. It is also possible to incubate a solution on a specific question or problem. However, this particular dream does not provide resolution in regards to the woman's situation. It simply illustrates what she had been experiencing. Because dreams contrast and correlate the activities of one's life in order to make sense of them, the subconscious mind often explores the thematic content of a situation in order to understand, clarify, resolve, enhance or come to terms with that situation or experience.

In a final dream detailing the use of theme interpretation, a teenage girl was given an objective look at a situation in her life that she already knew about but had yet to share with any family member.

Dream of teenage girl:

I am standing on the sidewalk next to my boyfriend. Suddenly an old woman driving a car pulls up next to us, throws open the passenger door and grabs me into the car. She drives off quickly, leaving my boyfriend behind. I look through the back window and notice that he is running after the car. When I turn back around I see the cutest little bear cub up ahead of us but when I look again it suddenly turns into a ferocious gigantic bear.

Possible story lines for this dream might be phrased as "Someone is leaving someone else behind," "Someone is trying to be forcibly taken from something," or "Something that appeared cute and cuddly is actually quite dangerous." Each of these statements turned out to be applicable to the girl's relationship with her boyfriend.

For about one year the girl had been going out with a young man that her family did not approve of. The girl's parents had frequently mentioned their disapproval and had repeatedly tried to get her to date other boys. The girl admitted that although she had immediately been drawn to him because "he was so cute," she continued to stay with him more out of habit than desire. She had not told any of her family members but her boyfriend had also begun to display a very "explosive temper" and she expressed some concern that he might end up hurting her.

Obviously, the old woman in the dream represents the girl's higher self or some authority figure in the family. The fact that the old woman is driving the car suggests that this individual is trying to change the girl's direction. Leaving the boyfriend behind indicates that the relationship is probably going to come to an end. It also suggests that the girl may have been thinking of ending the relationship herself because she looks out the window at him as the car is driving away. It does not take much thought to understand that the cute little bear cub that becomes a ferocious beast is representative of the girl's personal experience with her boyfriend's temper. In the end, the young woman's dream became the final impetus she needed to end the relationship.

One of the best approaches to working with dreams is to find the essential theme that is being portrayed by the storyline. That theme might be stated in a variety of ways but it will ultimately be expressed in no more than one or two sentences. This approach enables the interpreter to simplify complex storylines and bypass a variety of meanings for individual symbols that may not be appropriate for the dream. When discerning that "Something is happening to someone" it is important to remember that the something is generally an activity or a situation with which the dreamer is involved and that someone is most often the dreamer.

Chapter 2 Sample Dreams
See Appendix One for possible interpretations

Dream of eighteen-year-old woman:

(Background information: This is a reoccurring dream. The woman stated, "I do occasionally chew gum but only regular size pieces." She has been trying to make changes in her life.)

In the dream I am chewing a really big piece of gum. When I'm ready to take out the gum, it will not come out. In my attempt to remove the gum, it becomes stringy and sticks to my teeth. The gum never comes out!

Dream of forty-something-year-old woman:

(Background information: Woman's husband has asked for divorce.)

I was working in a hospital. A man's wife was dying of lung disease. He and his son came to me and asked me to steal some meds for her. They kept telling me how she was suffering. I told them that I of all people understood but I could not steal drugs or bring in herbs that would interfere with her treatment. I also said there was a lot of security and I just couldn't do that. I reached over and got my stuff to leave and I was crying saying that I couldn't help them. I woke up crying.

Dream of fifty-something-year-old woman:

(Background information: Woman expresses concern about her friend.)

I dreamed about going into a big house with one of my female friends. To our horror, in walking through the house there were all of these disembodied heads that we had to walk around just to get through to where we were going.

3

Finding Insight in Emotional Content

Although individuals might have similar experiences in life, each person's feelings about those experiences can be very different. As just one example, two people can be coworkers in a similar job at the same company and possess conflicting opinions about that workplace. Two individuals might be acquainted with the very same person and one may consider the person a friend and the other may feel antagonistic toward her or him. Individuals often have very different emotional experiences in regards to their work, their families, their acquaintances, their surroundings, their relationships, even their life in general.

Conversely, in spite of our individual differences, there are also emotional experiences that we have in common as a human family. Most of us can relate to the sadness of losing a loved one, the thrill of an amusement park, the apprehension of starting a new job, the anticipation of the holidays, the joy of spending time with someone we love, and so forth. These same emotional feelings can be evoked in such things as a good movie or a good book. We understand the emotional content when someone tells us that something was a comedy, an adventure, a mystery, a thriller, a drama, a tear-jerker, a horror, etc. Whenever a personal experience or something we take part in as a spectator touches our emotions and elicits some response from deep within us it becomes truly memorable.

When it comes to dreams, working with the emotional content can be as important as understanding symbolism or discovering a theme. On occasion, it can also be the easiest approach to working with a dream because everyone can answer questions such as "Does it feel like a positive dream? a frustrating dream? a frightening dream? or, an inspiring dream? Just what does it feel like?" The most important thing to remember in regards to interpreting a dream based on the emotional content is that whatever emotion is being aroused within the dream generally corresponds to a situation or experience in the dreamer's waking life that evokes a similar feeling or emotion.

With this in mind, if an individual experiences a frightening dream, the dreamer could be asked, "What is happening in your life right now that is causing fear or apprehension?" A dream in which the individual is being chased might elicit the query, "Are you trying to run away or avoid something?" An uplifting dream might prompt the question, "What is the one thing about which you are most excited, most looking forward to, or are most joyful?" As the following dreams will demonstrate, if the individual can deduce what activity in life is reflective of the same emotion being portrayed in the dream, discovering what the dream is all about can be fairly straightforward.

Dream of thirty-four-year-old man:
In the dream I am at some kind of a barbecue with a bunch of people from work. At first everything is fine. Some people are carrying plates, others have a drink in hand. Everyone is standing around and talking and having a good time. All at once I look down and notice that I am totally naked! I am horrified and feel very insecure, afraid that someone is going to notice. No one seems to notice before the dream ends.

However, I wake up still feeling very insecure.

Since the outstanding emotion being portrayed deals with the dreamer's feeling of insecurity, we might get to the basis of the dream by asking the dreamer, "What is going on in your life that makes you feel a little insecure?" However, because all of the other characters portrayed in the dream are co-workers, a logical assumption is that this dream could be about work and the dreamer might be insecure about something related to his job. Because work is obviously an aspect of life in general, it is also possible that this dream relates to something else in life causing the dreamer insecurity, but in this case the dreamer acknowledged that his feelings had to do with work. He discussed his job as follows:

He was a stockbroker with a number of years' experience and had just started working for a new brokerage firm. He liked his job and got along well with his coworkers. He admitted, however, that the new firm "did things a little differently than I am used to." He added that he was sometimes worried about making a mistake and he wondered if his coworkers had started to think that he wasn't catching on fast enough.

In terms of the dream, it's important to note that although the dreamer had been naked in the dream, feeling unprepared, insecure and perhaps even vulnerable in the midst of his new coworkers, no one else noticed that he was naked. This suggests that the dreamer's insecurities are his own and not necessarily shared by anyone else in the company.

A similar dream came to a twenty-something year old woman who had just started school.

Dream of twenty-something-year-old woman:
I was standing in the middle of class with the rest of the class and we were all saying the Pledge of Allegiance to the American flag. Everyone else had clothes on except for me. Some people had their shirts off but I had everything off except my underwear. I felt very uncomfortable but there was nothing I could do about it.

The emotion is one of feeling uneasy and the imagery suggests that the young woman is uncomfortable because she is not feeling as prepared as the rest of her classmates (she is not dressed whereas most of them are). The other students reciting the Pledge of Allegiance could correspond to their acceptance of the curriculum or it might be suggestive of their common desires, hopes, and beliefs about the school. It is also indicative of a shared commitment, as is the flag. The dream suggests that she is afraid that she is not going to be able to do as well as the other students, or that the school is more challenging than the dreamer initially believed. However, because she has already enrolled and taken the pledge to commit to the curriculum, at some level she is aware that she is going to have to face her insecurities and do as best as she can because she does not appear to have any other choice.

Since dreams reflect our personal feelings and perceptions, it's often necessary to dialogue with the dreamer about what is occurring in her or his life. Without the possibility of dialogue, sometimes a dream can only be interpreted in basic generalities. For example, the following dream of a thirty-something-year-old man suggested that panic and fear were somehow occurring in his life. Probable themes included "Someone is isolated and afraid," "Someone is in a dangerous situation," and "Someone is falling into a great divide." However, the imagery lent itself to so many possible interpretations that choosing the right one would have been extremely difficult without some sort of interaction with the dreamer.

Dream of thirty-something-year-old man:
I am standing on a cliff—it looks like the edge of the Grand Canyon. Suddenly, I slip and began sliding over the edge. I begin to panic, calling out for help. No help comes, and I continue to slide. As I began falling over the edge, I awaken very much upset.

The dream suggests that the dreamer feels like he is in the midst of some kind of a situation in which he feels totally alone and losing control. Upon questioning, the man responded gravely, "My wife is divorcing me."

Obviously the dream is indicating that the man felt as if his life was falling apart and he did not have control over the situation. To be sure, the dreamer may need to find someone to talk to about his feelings: a counselor, a minister, or even a friend, as he is alone in the situation, causing him to feel panic-stricken. In this instance, the Grand Canyon turns out to be a perfect symbol for the enormous divide that has occurred in the couple's marriage.

In another situation dealing with divorce, a forty-something-year-old woman's husband had asked for a divorce. The emotion evoked by a dream she experienced was one of much sadness. The imagery seemed to deal with the end of her marriage.

Dream of forty-something-year-old woman:
I came home after vacation and found a blue cat very dehydrated. It had thrown up and had the runs on the corner of the living room rug. As I put it into a box to take it to the vet, I asked why didn't someone take care of this. My husband said, "I cleaned." And my daughters said, "We didn't know, we weren't here." I was not sure the cat could be saved. The cat had big sad eyes like the pictures of the moppet kids that were popular in the 60/70s. I was very sad.

Without knowing the woman's personal situation, the meaning of the dream could have been interpreted by asking the dreamer what was going on in her life that was making her very sad. For the purpose of dialogue, additional questions suggested by the imagery include: "How do you feel about cats?" The dreamer loves cats. "What was going on in you life in the 60/70s that is now making you very sad?" This is when the dreamer's relationship with her husband began. "Do you really have daughters?" The couple had two girls. "Is there something going on in your life that they don't really know all about?" The girls did not know all the details of what was occurring in the couple's relationship. And so forth.

Although it is not really necessary to interpret all the other details once the meaning becomes clear, additional interpretive insights include the fact that the woman has been away on "vacation." This may suggest that she has been oblivious to her problems or is in a place (state of mind) where she really doesn't want to deal with them.

Since the dreamer loves cats, the cat may be symbolic of love and since the cat is dehydrated, it suggests that in spite of the fact she doesn't want a divorce the marriage has not really been feeding her emotionally. In all likelihood, this emotional neglect has caused the woman to do things that her husband refuses to deal with (the cat being sick on the carpet). His perception may be that he has more important things to attend to or he thinks he has already done his part to clean up the problems in their marriage. The cat is blue either because the situation is making the dreamer very depressed ("blue") or because only her interest in spirituality is keeping her going in this situation or because of both reasons. The daughters may be grown and not really a part of the home environment, not always around, and not really aware of the extent of their mother's unhappiness and that is why they state, "We didn't know, we weren't here." The woman looks for someone to help her with the problem but it doesn't seem salvageable. The whole situation is making the dreamer feel as sad-eyed and vulnerable as the moppet pictures of the 1960s and 70s.

In another case involving a sixty-something-year-old woman, it would probably require dialogue and a number of questions before the substance of the dream can be determined:

Dream of sixty-something-year-old woman:
There was an old man who was a cannibal. He was running around eating legs off of people. I was very much afraid and didn't want him to get me so I ran to hide in the forest. He saw me and seemed to get very close, but I don't think he ever got to me.

In this example, fear and anxiety are the predominant emotions in the dream. Obvious questions include such things as: "Is there something you're trying to run away from?" and "Is there someone or something that you're anxiously trying to avoid?" Afterwards, the next step is to begin working with the predominant symbolism. The "bad guy" in the dream is a cannibal who is chasing the dreamer. This lends itself to a question such as "Is someone (probably a strong male energy) causing you anxiety by trying to interfere with your belief system or direction?" since both can be associated with the symbol of legs.

Hiding in the forest can be associated with trying to avoid a situation, since a forest is a place where one might become easily lost. A forest can also deal with growth and prosperity, neither of which seem appropriate to this particular dream, or it can correspond with the metaphor of "not being able to see the forest for the trees"—getting caught up in details. Only the image of trying to avoid the situation appears relevant.

When dialoguing with a dreamer, oftentimes it is necessary to re-phrase something that has already been stated, attempting to verbalize it in a way that finally strikes a cord. In this instance, that restatement became: "It seems like the dream is suggesting you are trying to avoid something that is causing your direction or personal foundation to be threatened." That statement ultimately led to under-standing what the dream was all about.

In real life, the woman had recently signed a contract to buy an old farmhouse located out in the country. After legally agreeing to pur-chase the property, a follow-up inspection had revealed that the building's foundation was rotten and would need to be completely replaced. Because the costs of replacing the foundation were enor-mous, the woman desperately wanted to get out of the contract but had not signed the agreement with a conditional waiver pending an inspection. The whole experience was "eating her up" with worry just as replacing the foundation would have eaten her up financially—both suggestive of the cannibal. Thankfully, the woman did not have to follow through on the contract. Just as was suggested by the dream, "He saw me and seemed to get very close, but I don't think he ever got to me," she was able to get out of the purchase agreement because the seller had not revealed his knowledge of the property's condition to her.

Since dreams contrast and correlate experiences occurring in the dreamer's waking life, very often insecurities, fears, anxieties, hopes and expectations all become the substance of dream imagery. Because each of these conditions has corresponding emotions, the emotion portrayed in the dream can become the pathway for enabling the dreamer to take an objective look at some situation in her or his life.

The following dream of a young woman seemed to highlight some new activity occurring in her life as well as her own insecurities regarding that activity:

> *Dream of twenty-something-year-old woman:*
> I was pregnant and now was the time to deliver. I had no contractions or pain. The doctor checked me and left (guess he thought I wasn't ready) but birth had already started. I could not push it out no matter how hard I tried. I was not in a hospital but outside on a chair. Later, after it was born, I was embarrassed because I had asked for two days off to deliver and the baby was a black and white cat. I loved it and we had a special bond but it was still a cat. I was ashamed that I missed work for a cat.

When the dream occurred, the young woman was two months away from graduation. She had returned to school in order to receive training as a massage therapist. She realized that the "birth" was probably related to graduation or her new career. She thought that the cat was black and white because some part of her was still wondering whether or not her decision to return to school for massage training had been "right or wrong." In addition to the dreamer's insights, the fact that the time is "now" to deliver suggests that the young woman feels like the time has come to decide what her life is going to give birth to—in other words, what is she going to do after graduation? In the dream she is having a difficult time with delivery, indicating that she is having a hard time giving birth to her goals for the future. Her feelings of embarrassment corresponded to her own insecurities regarding whether or not her choice of careers was as good (or as potentially successful) as other members of her family.

In real life, the woman loved going to school just as she loved the cat in the dream. School had also given her a number of new ideas (new births) that she really wanted to incorporate into her life. In addition to reflecting the dreamer's thought about her personal future, the dream was also giving her an objective look at herself. In the end, the dreamer realized that her career path was something she loved and the dream was encouraging her to begin looking at those issues related to her own sense of self-esteem.

Although appearing complicated at first, the dream of a sixty-year-old woman could have been deduced through the emotional content, through the theme, or through symbolism.

> *Dream of sixty-something-year-old woman:*
> I dreamt that I was standing in my kitchen feeling very much depressed. Suddenly, I started sobbing and crying until it got to the point where I had to blow my nose. I took a Kleenex, blew my nose and noticed that a "N-shaped" nail came out of my nostril. When I looked at it in the Kleenex, I became even sadder. I awoke from the dream feeling very despondent.

The emotion is one of great sadness. Possible themes suggested by the images include, "Something is making someone very sad," "Something is where it doesn't belong," and "Something is causing pain and suffering." The major symbols include the kitchen (suggestive of home and family, or diet), the sadness (associated with whatever is making the woman unhappy), and the woman's nose. Oftentimes the nose can be symbolic of one's self. It can correspond to the sense of smell, and it is also associated with a number of metaphorical meanings, including: "Getting your nose into someone's business," "Being led by the nose," and "Being nosey." The "N" probably corresponds with whatever the dreamer associates with the letter "N." A nail can indicate that something is being held together but it can also be a symbol associated with crucifixion—the woman came from a strong Catholic background. The Kleenex is symbolic of sadness or with trying to give comfort to one's suffering. After discussing some of the symbolism and asking the dreamer, "Is anything making you despondent?" and "Do you know anyone whose name begins with a 'N'?" the woman volunteered the following:

The dreamer was extremely upset about Nancy, her twenty-year-old daughter (home and family). Apparently the young woman had a serious addiction to cocaine (associated with the nose). That addiction had led to an ongoing need for money to help pay for her habit. In desperation Nancy had sometimes turned to prostitution in order to finance her habit. Understandably, the dreamer was very despondent about the whole situation. She had managed to have her daughter taken in by a halfway house on numerous occasions for rehabilitation but invariably Nancy escaped and returned to the cocaine and the streets. According to the dreamer, as a mother the whole situation was "killing" her and she didn't know what to do about it.

Looking back at the dream, obviously the woman is despondent and upset about Nancy's situation. The nail is probably associated with the fact that the mother is crucifying herself by trying to take responsibility for an adult daughter or, more bluntly, for putting her nose where it does not belong. In reality, Nancy cannot be helped until Nancy wants help. Although still depressed about her daughter's situation, after discussing this fact the mother actually felt relieved that she was not ultimately responsible for whether or Nancy decided to help herself. The woman no longer needed to take responsibility for the situation. She could only offer love, assistance and support for her daughter. It was up to Nancy to decide when she was ready to accept it.

The final dream is somewhat long and complicated. The dream belonged to a forty-something-year-old woman who had experienced a number of emotions during the course of her dream, including nervousness, anxiety and fear. However, the feeling the dreamer most recalled upon awakening was of "heart wrenching pain." In real life, the dreamer had two sisters, Aggie and Carol, and she was extremely worried about what was occurring in Carol's life at the time of her dream, as well as what she was supposed to do about it in order to help Carol.

Dream of forty-something-year-old woman:
I dreamed that I was walking on a large piece of property. My sisters Aggie and Carol were there. I walked over to Aggie and she told me that she had been bitten by a snake on her back.

I could see that there were bite marks on her back, but she told me that the snake's teeth had not fully sunk into her. Aggie said she had been bitten over six hours previously and she appeared not to be effected.

As I turned toward Carol she was talking about another snake that was on the fence next to the property. At first it appeared as a harmless garden snake, but as she moved closer to it I became very nervous. I couldn't warn her in time. The snake lunged out and bit her on the forehead twice. She turned to me, not fully realizing the seriousness of the situation. The bite areas were beginning to swell.

I looked at the snake and it appeared to be wearing a cowboy hat. I was aware that I needed to remain calm and not panic. I asked Carol what doctor she would call if this had happened to her son. She mentioned her pediatrician's name. I looked at her wounds on her forehead again. I couldn't tourniquet the surrounding area or place direct pressure on it as it was a critical area to her head. I gazed at her with love, very saddened to see the wounds, knowing the danger and not sure that it would turn out okay.

I hoped that as Aggie had been okay, Carol would be as well. But I knew that the fangs on Carol's bite had penetrated more deeply. I looked at her and seeing her expression—that of a young girl, innocently unaware of the harm. It was heart wrenching. I awoke from the pain as in a nightmare.

In this case, working with the emotional content of the dream would suggest that the dreamer is deeply troubled about something related to her sisters (probably Carol) or something associated with herself in relationship to one of her sisters. Taking it a paragraph at a time, the interpretation and the actual situation starts to take form.

A piece of property is suggestive of a current situation or experience in the dreamer's life. The fact that it is large indicates that it may be a big issue. Being with her sisters can indicate that the dream is about her relationship with them or that it is about something she associates with her sisters. In the dream, Aggie has been bitten on the back by a snake. A snake can be associated with temptation or with energy, but as a phallic symbol it is often associated with male energy. Being bitten on the back indicates that this "bite" has perhaps affected the dreamer's (or Aggie's) support (backbone), or it is something that happened in the past. The fact that the fangs did not sink in deeply can suggest that the situation may not have been that problematic. Aggie's statement that she had been bitten six hours previously led to a dialogue with the dreamer regarding the number six and how it related to Aggie. The dreamer stated that Aggie had been divorced six years earlier, leading us to believe that the snakebite had been the divorce and that Aggie had survived the situation rather well.

In real life the dreamer was not married and Carol was having serious problems with her own husband. Since we eventually learn in the dream that something that once happened to Aggie is now happening to Carol, the possibility of Carol considering a divorce starts to seem feasible. One of the possible themes in this dream is also "Something that happened before is happening again."

In the second paragraph we find Carol discussing the fact that a snake is "on the fence." Being on the fence is a metaphor for being undecided, so one possibility is that Carol, her husband, or both, may be undecided about getting a divorce. Another possibility is that there is a need to keep something out of one's personal space or seek protection from the snake. The imagery suggests that the snake becomes more aggressive as soon as Carol gets closer to the decision or to her own need for protection.

The whole relationship between Carol and her husband causes the dreamer to be very nervous and she can't do enough to warn her sister. The snake biting Carol on the head twice might indicate that twice before Carol has given serious thought to the possibility of divorce. The dreamer is also worried that Carol is not fully aware of the seriousness of the situation or of her sister's concern for her. The imagery of the forehead swelling may represent the idea that Carol has been thinking (again and again) about her situation with the snake and what she's supposed to be doing about it.

In case we did not already know it, the snake is wearing a cowboy hat in the third paragraph to let us know that it symbolizes a man.

The hat may also give some indication of the snake's personality. Both Carol and the dreamer need to remain calm in the situation and figure how to best deal with it. In Carol's case she needs to decide what to do regarding her husband, and in the dreamer's case she needs to decide how she can best serve as a support system for Carol. From the mention of the son and the pediatrician, we get a possible reason as to why Carol has not followed through on her desire for a divorce—there are children involved.

The repeated allusions to danger may suggest some kind of physical or emotional harm. The critical nature of the injury probably corresponds to the fact that the marriage may be beyond repair. The dreamer not being able to apply help to the sister's wound is representative of the fact that Carol alone needs to decide what is best and how she is going to follow through. The dreamer cannot take responsibility or serve as a decision-maker in this situation. She can only stand ready as a support system. Still, the dreamer is very concerned about whether or not her sister is going to be okay.

The last paragraph simply reflects the dreamer's hope that just as Aggie had survived her divorce, Carol will be able to do the same thing. The dreamer is very worried for her sister and feels badly that there is not really anything she can do about it by taking on the situation for herself. The whole issue is causing the dreamer an emotional nightmare. In the end, the dreamer accepted the fact that she couldn't live her sister's life for her and promised to support Carol in whatever happened, providing any assistance within her power.

Working with dream interpretation by using the emotional content of the dream imagery is easiest when the dreamer can relate his or her feelings in the dream to similar feelings and emotions that are being prompted by a real life situation, experience or person. Interacting with the dreamer with such questions as "How did the dream feel?" or "How do you feel about that person?" or "What are you feelings about dogs, or automobiles or forests?" or whatever symbol is most prominent, often leads to solving the dream. Most often a dream is an encapsulated story detailing some situation in the dreamer's life—the emotional content can serve as the key to peering inside and seeing what that story is really about.

Chapter 3 Sample Dreams
See Appendix One for possible interpretations

Dream of thirty-something-year old woman:

[Background information: Dreamer complained of relationship with her aggressive mother, a woman prone to critical comments.]

I was going home and being followed by a Velociraptor dinosaur. I had reached home and the Velociraptor had followed me inside. I raced up the stairs and went into one of the rooms and shut and locked the door. Although the door was shut I knew the dinosaur would be breaking through the door at any moment. Afraid, I climbed out of the window and crawled out onto the roof of the porch that was below the window. I was kind of hanging below the roof so it wouldn't see me. It finally went away but I knew it would be back.

Next, my family was packing our belongings: the pets, the food, and the things that we needed quickly so we could leave and be safe from the dinosaur. The dream ended with my being able to watch the car, all packed up and loaded, with all of us inside, driving away.

Dream of teenage boy:

[Background information: Middle-aged man recalls reoccurring dream that he often had growing up.]

The dream is that I am at home in my parent's home where I grew up. All at once I look out the window and am frightened to see that a number of tornadoes are heading right for the property. Although afraid, I suddenly remember that this is something I have been through many times before. The thought comes to me that just as I have survived previously, I'll probably be able to survive this most recent storm. The last thing I remember is being afraid and simply hoping that I will be okay.

Chapter 3 Sample Dreams
See Appendix One for possible interpretations

Dream of forty-something-year-old woman:
(Background information: Woman lives out of state from the rest of her family. Elderly parents are still alive.)

I was driving back to Iowa (where we use to visit my grandparents) with my Dad. We were going back to honor my great, great grandfather. We finally drove into a dinky town in Iowa and drove up to a large house that looked almost like an office building or a courthouse. A crowd of people, Blacks and Whites, scattered about the lawn just staring. For some reason the scene seemed eerie.

I went into the house and was confronted by an angry lady who seemed to resemble me. She was irate and screamed at me for failing to visit my dying great great grandfather. She said that I could not see him anymore and then she proceeded to abruptly escort me out of the house.

After a little reflection, I was determined to see him anyway because I had come a long way for that very purpose. I went back in the house and insisted on seeing him. Finally, the angry woman relented and led me back into the bedroom.

My great great grandfather was so old and aged and frail that I could hardly believe his condition. He was curled up in a fetal position and was as tiny as an infant. As I stood there looking at him in sadness, he opened his eyes as if to speak.

Suddenly, my alarm clock went off and I was awakened. I found myself desperately sad from the feeling of the dream and from my desire to know what he would have said to me.

4

That Which is Metaphor and That Which is Literal

Even if you are experienced in the art of dream interpretation it is possible to make mistakes when trying to decipher the meaning of a dream. Frequently, those mistakes include such things as imposing your interpretation upon the dreamer, relying upon the association of one's own personal symbolism and assigning it greater relevance than the dreamer's, or giving a metaphorical dream a literal interpretation.

Imposing your interpretation upon the dreamer occurs whenever the interpreter insists upon the dream's meaning regardless of what the dreamer states in response to that interpretation or to the questions that occur during the course of dialogue. Even when an interpreter is one hundred percent convinced of a dream's meaning, that meaning should never be forced upon the dreamer. In the first place, there is always the possibility that the interpreter is wrong in spite of his or her conviction. Secondly, a forced interpretation is not likely to be accepted by the dreamer or even reconsidered later on.

On one occasion, a dreamer's wife related her husband's dream. Another individual had already interpreted the dream and insisted that because of the imagery in the dream the wife needed to obtain a medical check-up. However, the dreamer's wife felt that the dream had to have a different meaning, as she was in good physical shape. The husband's dream follows:

> *Dream of sixty-something-year-old man:*
> The dream is reoccurring with some change in detail but the essential story remains the same. My wife is driving her new car. Suddenly, out of nowhere, another car broadsides her and she ends up in very serious condition in the hospital. In another version, my wife cannot get the car started because there seems to be something wrong with the engine. A third version has my wife driving down a very steep hill when the brakes go out and it appears as if she is headed over an embankment.

If the dream is literal, it indicates that there is either a problem with the car and the brakes need to be checked or that "Someone needs to watch her or his driving," or both. However, since the car was new and both husband and wife had a very good driving record, a metaphorical interpretation seems more likely. It was this same conclusion that led another individual to interpret the fact that the husband needed to encourage his wife to watch her health, watch her stress, watch her diet, and have a physical check up "as soon as possible."

We can certainly see this possibility. In the dream the car is hit broadside, suggesting that something is going to come out of nowhere, interfering with the direction of the vehicle (life path or physical body). Not being able to start the engine could be associated with having low energy, having an emotional (feelings) or nervous disorder (electrical system of the car is impinged), or with having some kind of a heart condition (engine). Driving down a hill without the brakes (going too fast in life or having too much stress) can be indicative of danger unless the driver manages to slow down. All these images led the interpreter to insist that the dreamer have his wife get physical attention before something serious happened. To the husband's credit, he repeatedly tried to relate to the interpreter that his wife was in very good shape and took excellent care of herself but apparently the interpreter was adamant, "Your wife needs to see a doctor!"

From the wife's perspective, she also believed that she was in excellent health and maintained a good diet. She exercised regularly by walking, handled any stress with meditation, taking a walk, or escaping into a romance novel. In addition, she had already been for her annual physical, including a mammogram, six months previously. Nonetheless, her husband's insistent nagging was prompting her to go ahead and make an appointment for another check-up, but she was worried that the dream might have another meaning that was being overlooked.

Although she still worked full-time, she described her husband as being retired and lacking any interests or focus rather than "tooling around the house and waiting" for her to get home. She tried to serve nutritious meals when she was home but while she was at work her husband always went out for fast food and "loved it when Burger King offered their Whopper specials." As a result, since his retirement he had put on twenty pounds. She said that her husband's only exercise besides mowing the lawn was "finger exercise on the TV's remote." She added that in spite of his retirement, he was still pretty stressed and handled that stress "by yelling a lot."

With the above in mind, it seems likely that the dream is actually about the husband's need to see a doctor, as the symbol of his wife in the dream could represent the dreamer's relationship and his own hopes for the future. This interpretation suggests that the something unexpected is going to broadside the dreamer's intended direction, that he needs to slow down (e.g. cut back on his stress and out-of-control habits), and that he needs to have a check-up immediately. The wife agreed with the assessment and planned to get her husband to the doctor immediately.

On another occasion at a large dream seminar, a woman related her dream and during the process of dialogue repeatedly rejected each and every possible interpretation suggested by the imagery:

Dream of forty-something-year-old woman:
I am standing on the ground looking up at an office skyscraper.
The building is surrounded by a fence that makes it impossible
for me to enter. I notice that the building is very modern and
intriguing and I want to go inside, but I don't know how.

In the dream the woman is unable to enter the office building
(work), which might indicate her unhappiness with her job and her
desire to do something else. The dreamer rejected that possibility. If
the skyscraper instead represents a phallic symbol, it could indicate
that there is some kind of a relationship issue with a male; in other
words, the imagery might be associated with someone who has put
up an emotional wall, keeping the dreamer out. Again, the dreamer
discounted the possibility that it had anything to do with relationship
issues. She repeatedly told the audience that she loved her job and
that her husband was very caring. The final very broad suggestion
was that the dream might be indicative of someone who wanted
something in life but that there appeared to be something that stood
in the way of attaining it.

Interestingly enough, during a break one of the woman's best
friends quietly volunteered the fact that although the dreamer liked
her job, she was an artist and was extremely frustrated that she had
never been able to move into the career full-time. In addition, on their
way to the program, the friend stated that the dreamer had expressed
some concern about the fact that there was definitely an issue bothering her husband but for whatever reason he was refusing to speak
about it.

As it turned out, obviously the dream could have been dealing with
both work and relationship issues but for whatever reason the
dreamer did not understand how the imagery in the dream and the
suggestions related to that imagery applied to anything occurring in
her personal life.

Another mistake often made by individuals who erroneously interpret a dream is to give personal associations related to symbolism
greater relevance than the dreamer's own feelings and thoughts about
that same symbolism. This occurred in the case of a thirty-something-

year-old man whose friend had helped him with a dream:

> *Dream of thirty-something-year-old man:*
> I dreamed that I was under water. The water was great and I
> was really enjoying myself as I swam through various schools
> of fish and looked at the beauty of the coral reef. Although I
> didn't have on an oxygen tank or a mask, I didn't seem to have
> any problem breathing or seeing in front of me. I woke up
> really refreshed and energized because of the experience.

In general, a dream of this nature might be associated with an individual undergoing some kind of a very positive emotional or spiritual experience (water), since water can be a symbol for either. The dreamer also appears to be enjoying himself and very appreciative of his surroundings. The dreamer's friend suggested that something was occurring in the dreamer's life that was related to an uplifting spiritual or emotional experience. As far as the dreamer was concerned neither of these possibilities seemed appropriate at the time of his dream.

The dreamer discussed the interpretation that had been suggested by his friend and how it did not seem quite right. He went on to say, "You know, I use to love swimming! Although I don't do it much any more, I was on the swim team in school and won a number of trophies. My father used to joke that I was more at home in the water than on land." In this instance, the dreamer personally associated water with his experience and success as a swimmer. When the dreamer was asked to describe what was occurring in his life in the present, he said that he had been offered a new job and was wondering whether or not he she take it: "It seems attractive but I just don't know."

Since the dream had occurred right after the job offer, one possibility being portrayed by the imagery is that he would love the job and feel very much at home in his work surroundings, just as he felt at home in the water. The attractiveness of the underwater surroundings could also be associated with the attractiveness of the job he had been offered. The various fish might be related to the groups of people he would meet in the new company or the various learning experiences (schools of fish) he would have and enjoy. The fact that he did not have oxygen or a mask could indicate that although his waking self did not feel totally prepared for the line of work being offered him, he would have no trouble with the new position. In other words, he would not be a fish out of water.

Perhaps one of the most frequent mistakes made in dream interpretation is attempting to give a metaphorical dream a literal interpretation. Long-time students of dreamwork frequently make this mistake. Individuals working with their own dreams repeatedly make it as well. One example occurred during a lecture program given by a prominent psychic. Several hundred people were in attendance, listening to some of the predictions that the psychic had foreseen for the immediate future. One of those predictions detailed a serious earthquake for the mid-Western part of the country:

Dream of prominent psychic:
I am sitting at my computer surfing the internet. Suddenly, a map of the country appears before me and I see a tremendous earthquake destroy a portion of the mid-West, near where my wife and I once lived. The destruction was devastating and I began to feel very sad and helpless because of all the people that had been killed or affected by the catastrophe.

Afterwards, members of the audience began raising their hands asking for more specifics out of concern for members of their families who lived in the mid-West. However, it seemed much more likely that the dream was metaphorical in nature, suggesting that the psychic and his wife were on the verge of getting divorced.

This interpretation is likely because he is sitting at his computer seeing the country where he and his wife had once lived. This can be associated with seeing the past associated with the dreamer and his wife. The fact that he was sitting before his keyboard suggested that he still maintained some element of control in the situation. However, he simply watched as the place where "my wife and I once lived" was destroyed by an earthquake. In the end, he had some regret and sad-

ness after becoming aware of all the other people affected by his marriage break-up (children? family members?). Rather than being literal
and about the outside, it is just as likely that the dream is metaphorical and about the dreamer's own personal world. As it turned out,
within twelve months of the lecture, the psychic apparently pursued
another relationship (surfing the net?) and he and his wife ended up
getting divorced.

Perhaps because of many people's fascination with earth changes
and potential global catastrophes, earthquake dreams are commonly
misinterpreted. Another example occurred in the case of a middle-
aged woman who had an earthquake dream. She felt that the dream
was encouraging her to move to another locale where she and her
family would be safe from earthquakes:

Dream of middle-aged woman:
There is an earthquake and my house is destroyed. I remember running through what is left of the house, looking for my
children and hoping that everyone is still okay. I am in a panic
and very upset by the devastation around me.

The dreamer was convinced that her dream was literal and that she
and her husband needed to move their family somewhere that would
not be prone to earthquakes. Although the woman listened to a discussion of the nature of metaphorical dreams versus literal dreams
and was encouraged to look at the dream from a metaphorical perspective, which would indicate that there might be something
unstable related to her or her family, she was not interested in
contemplating anything but a literal interpretation. However, approximately six months later the same woman returned and admitted
that the metaphorical interpretation had been correct: "Out of the blue
my husband asked for a divorce!" Her subconscious mind had known
about the instability of her home and family even before she did.

Whenever individuals have an earthquake dream, a war dream, a
nuclear explosion dream, or any kind of global catastrophe dream,
they may be so focused on the fear and a literal interpretation of what
they saw that is can be very difficult to encourage them to broaden

their perception. When this is the case, one approach is to ask them something like: "Do you think your subconscious mind is most concerned about you personally, or about events on the other side of the country/world?" To most individuals, the answer is obvious.

Sometimes the literal and the metaphorical interpretation of a dream are both very similar. For example, seeing yourself eat a salad in a dream might indicate the need for the specific nutrients that could be found in a salad (literal) or it might simply be suggestive of the need to change your personal diet (metaphorical). Dreams of pregnancy or a new birth can be suggestive of a literal pregnancy or they might simply be metaphors for a new beginning. Conversely, dreams of death can sometimes be associate with dying (literal) but most often they are simply indicative of change or a metaphor for the end of something. When both the literal and the metaphorical interpretation of a dream seem to deal with the dreamer, either might be correct. Each of the next two dreams dealing with diet illustrates this point:

> *Dream of a twenty-something-year-old woman:*
> I am sitting at a dinner table with all kinds of meat. There is turkey, hamburger, hot dogs, roast beef, chicken, fish, meatloaf, and a variety of other meals with meat. Suddenly, I start eating off of all the plates in front of me. I begin stuffing myself on all the different kinds of meat, chewing one mouthful after another without even stopping for a moment.

Although a young woman, the dreamer who related this dream did not look well. She was extremely thin and possessed a graying complexion. She also had dark circles under her eyes and did not appear either healthy or energetic. Considering the appearance of the dreamer and then looking at the imagery contained in the dream, one logical question might be: "Are you a vegetarian?"

The dreamer quickly admitted that she was and wanted to know how that was indicated by the dream. The literal possibility suggested by the dream was that the woman was not getting enough protein in her diet. Although the dream is not necessarily telling her to eat meat, it is definitely suggesting that she needs more protein in her diet. On the other hand, a metaphorical interpretation might be suggesting that she was perhaps gorging herself on too many choices that she was taking into her life (eating) and needed to take time to savor her experiences or her options rather than simply tying to attend to them all at once. In this case, however, the dreamer agreed that she might need to include more protein-rich, non-animal foods in her diet.

Another case concerning a diet dream also turned out to more metaphorical than literal:

> *Dream of a twenty-something-year-old man:*
> I am in the kitchen standing next to the refrigerator. I open the door and the only thing in there is an enormous container (bigger than a gallon) of milk. I reach in and take the container and pour myself a glass of milk. I think I was in the midst of drinking it when the dream ended.

The most obvious interpretation of the milk dream could indicate that the dreamer needs more milk or calcium in his diet. In this case, however, the individual stated that his diet included plenty of milk products and that he often had yogurt for breakfast. Another literal possibility might have been that the dreamer was eating too many milk products—after all that was the only item in the fridge. However, the dreamer appeared healthy and commented that his diet was fine.

A metaphorical interpretation could suggest that the dreamer may be having problems with his mother, or with a motherly relationship in his life. This is indicated by the imagery because the refrigerator could be a symbol for something that is cool or chilly. The symbol of milk can be associated with one's mother because of our infancy and early feeding habits. When asked if he and his mother had a "chilly" relationship, the dreamer admitted that he and his mother had been having difficulties and as a result had not spoken in several months. Because the imagery shows him drinking milk from the fridge, it suggests that he may need to make the first move in healing their relationship. The dreamer seemed to resonate to the idea and agreed that he needed to do something to resolve the problem.

Perhaps the most frightening dream that can be misinterpreted is one that seems to indicate someone's death. As stated previously, most often dreams of death deal with some kind of change or transition. Nonetheless, a long-time student of dreams had the following dream and wondered whether or not "a warning dream of this nature" would make it okay to call a co-worker and caution that individual about his driving.

> *Dream of a fifty-something-year-old man:*
> I dreamt that Alex—one of the company's spokespeople and representatives—was driving to work and was hit by another car right out front of the corporate headquarters. I got to the accident just in time to see the ambulance arrive. I was very sad because I knew Alex had been killed (or was dying) and I started to cry. Afterwards I woke up and wondered whether or not I should tell Alex to watch his driving.

It is important to keep in mind that most often dreams are about one's self. We do not generally dream for other people unless we are emotionally connected to them, seriously concerned about them, or have been asked to dream about them and even then the dream usually has a personal component in addition to any information concerning that other individual. With this in mind, rather than a literal dream about Alex, it is much more likely that the dream is metaphorical and relevant to the dreamer.

Since the dreamer has already described Alex as a company spokesperson and representative, in all likelihood Alex represents the dreamer's work. Since Alex's (work's) journey comes to an abrupt end right out front of the company headquarters, it could be suggesting that the dreamer's personal journey related to the company is about to come to an end. That ending may cause the dreamer some degree of sadness, as the dreamer starts to cry in the dream.

When the dreamer was asked: "Are you thinking of leaving the company?" the dreamer was stunned because that is exactly what he had been thinking and although he had decided it was the right decision, he still had a number of regrets. All of the information was being drawn from his subconscious and portrayed in the dream's storyline. In real life, the dreamer left his position a short time after having had the dream.

In a final example, a young woman expressed her hopes that one of her dreams indicated the fact that she would be getting together with a male associate—someone who was already married.

> *Dream of a twenty-something-year-old woman:*
> I am in a grocery store buying things for my wedding. I am excited because I am going to be marrying Ross. While looking at something in the store, I notice that Ross is speaking with a beautiful female cashier and I start to get very jealous. She is prettier than I am and I wonder if Ross might decide to be with her. Finally, I remember he is marrying me and I decide I don't have anything to worry about.

Oftentimes, being in a store can pertain to making choices and decisions. It appears that the dreamer may have a decision to make. Literally, that decision could be related to her getting together with Ross; metaphorically, that decision might be associated with whatever the dreamer associates with Ross.

When the woman was asked to describe what she thought of Ross, she replied that she had a crush on him but that he was already married. She went on to describe Ross as being heavily involved with computers and the data processing department of the company where they both worked. For that reason, Ross could symbolize another relationship (like Ross) or Ross could be symbolic of the computer field. The dreamer was asked, "Are you thinking of getting another job in the computer field?"

Surprised, the dreamer stated that she had recently heard of an opening at another company in the computer department and she had wondered about pursuing the position. Her hesitancy seemed to be that she did not feel totally qualified for the position. However, the beautiful woman cashier in the dream could be mirroring her own self-esteem issues and she could also represent the new job—something with which Ross had some degree of familiarity. The dreamer needed to set her insecurities aside and pursue the computer job. It is also possible that the dream is suggesting she will find a "marriage" (a relationship) at the new place of employment.

Essentially, there are two kinds of dreams, literal and metaphorical. A literal dream deals with some aspect of exactly what is being portrayed in the imagery. Conversely, a metaphorical dream generally symbolizes something else that is associated with the symbolism. It is sometimes possible for a dream to be both literal and metaphorical at the same time. Regardless of the kind of dream, most often the subconscious mind of the dreamer is concerned with the individual having the dream and not with some person or event totally disconnected from the dreamer. With this in mind, most dreams should be looked at from the perspective of how the imagery can be applied to the dreamer and what relevance the dream might have to the dreamer's own life.

Chapter 4 Sample Dreams
See Appendix One for possible interpretations

Dream of forty-something-year-old woman:
(Background information: Female Accountant expresses dislike for male co-worker, "Bob.")

I dreamed that I came to the office, and where my desk had once been, there was now a bed. Although I didn't seem surprised about it in the dream, Bob was waiting for me in bed. I smiled at him, took off my clothes and crawled in next to him and we started to kiss. I woke up feeling very confused and alarmed as to why I had done such a thing.

Dream of forty-something-year-old woman:
(Background information: Woman's daughter, with whom she is "very close," is about to attend college out of state.)

I was in the house and got a phone call that Amanda had been killed. The police were calling to tell me about her death. When I heard the news I screamed and dropped the phone. I ran through the house calling out to my husband, needing him to help me. I was horrified and sick to my stomach.

Dream of thirty-something-year-old woman:
(Background information: Husband is frustrated with business partner about finances; wife is frustrated with husband about marriage. This is the wife's dream.)

I dreamed that I was standing in the dining room next to my husband, looking at my husband's business partner. I said to the partner that I didn't want anything to do with him because of how he had treated my husband. I no longer wanted to eat with him or be in the same room with him.

5

Finding Insight in Life's Events

Dreams generally concern themselves with the activities, events, concerns, relationships, and thoughts transpiring in the dreamer's life. Just as individuals often communicate with their friends regarding what is happening to them personally, somehow coming to terms with current events in the process, the subconscious mind provides an examination of the very same information. With this in mind, ultimately the purpose of dialoguing with an individual when trying to help with an interpretation of her or his dream is simply to discover what is occurring in that person's waking life. Essentially, dreams contrast and correlate the events of the day, often providing the dreamer with an objective look at the very things with which he or she is presently concerned, sometimes even giving the dreamer additional insights and information.

The story of Elias Howe and his invention of the sewing machine presents a historical example of how dreams often explore the very same issues that confront an individual in waking life, while providing additional insights into that situation. Howe had been trying to automate the sewing process. As everyone knows, when sewing by hand the thread is threaded through the thick end of the needle. After many failed attempts, Howe finally created a machine in which the thread was threaded through the middle of the shank. Still, his invention was not a success. One night he had a dream. In one version of the story, he dreamt that he was going to be executed by some native guards (perhaps suggesting the pressure he felt in waking life) because he had not been able to finish the machine. Rather than being terrified by what was about to transpire, Howe instead became fascinated by the spears that each one of the guards was holding. In the dream, all of the spears had a hole in the center of the blade near the end of the point. Upon awakening, Howe created a needle, in which the hole was located at the end of the tip just as he had seen in his dream. The needle worked and finally Howe's machine was a success.

In a straightforward contemporary example that does not really need additional interpretation, a sixty-something-year-old woman also had a dream providing her with the needed insight regarding a creative project upon which she had been working:

> *Dream of sixty-something-year-old woman:*
> In waking life I had been crocheting a very difficult pattern and could not figure it out for weeks. One night I had a dream that explained the pattern in great detail and I saw myself crocheting the pattern step by step. The next morning I quickly went to my project and put to work the instructions I had received in the dream—they worked perfectly!

Because individuals do not always know how or sometimes do not wish to resolve the issues that are confronting them, dreams can encapsulate one's waking experiences into metaphor and symbol, enabling the issue to be dealt with more objectively. In this manner the situation can sometimes be explored by the mind in a non-threatening approach. The dream of a fifteen-year-old boy is a case in point:

Dream of fifteen-year-old boy:
I dreamt that I was barefooted out in the backyard. Although I must have walked out there, my feet were stuck in the grass and I couldn't move. I stood there totally stuck and unable to move in any direction. That was it.

The dream had been related by the boy's mother in the hopes that it might provide some indication as to what was occurring in her son's life. According to the woman, her son had lost interest in school and in sports and spent most of his time not wanting to do anything or complaining of feeling tired. The woman felt that the boy's lethargy had been the cause of his disinterest in life and she hoped the dream held a clue as to why he had become so "stuck."

Some of the imagery suggested by the dream is that the boy has made himself vulnerable (barefooted) because of something he had been doing. That something had caused him to become stuck (or even lethargic). The yard can be a symbol for one's current situation but the fact that this is the backyard could indicate that this something in the past (not likely for a fifteen year old) or something that is hidden from public view. The imagery of being "stuck in the grass" became immediately clear when the question was asked, "Does your son smoke marijuana?"

The woman lowered her eyes and nodded, "He says he only does it on occasion and it's not a problem." However, the dream seemed to be suggesting otherwise. Apparently the boy had become "stuck" (attached/addicted) because he had so firmly attached his life and his direction to smoking pot, immobilizing him in the process. Regardless of how infrequent he told his mother he was still doing it, the dream was portraying a very serious problem. Since the imagery had come from her son, it might prompt him to deal with the issue more so than if the advice had come from someone else.

Dreams can provide individuals with a variety of insights into every area of life about which they are concerned: relationships, work, health, desires, hopes, fears, and the future—every issue that confronts the dreamer in waking life. The dream of a forty-something-year-old woman seemed to provide precognitive information about a situation occurring at her workplace. In real life, many employees were dissatisfied with the way management was responding to their concerns. Therefore a number of her co-workers were attempting to bring a union into the company to help address their problems. One night the woman had a dream:

> *Dream of forty-something-year-old woman:*
> In my dream, I saw a battle between the North and the South. The South won.

In reality, the main corporate headquarters of the woman's company was located in the south and her particular branch was located in the northeast. As the conflict between the employees and the management continued, headquarters decided to close down the branch rather than accept a union and put the rest of their branches at "risk" of being unionized. In a very real sense, the south had won the conflict. As an aside, it is also interesting to note that during the Civil War the north had also been associated with the "union," as well.

In the case of a twenty-five-year-old student, a dream suggested that part of the current situation in her life was some unresolved relationship that her boyfriend was still wrapped up in:

> *Dream of twenty-five-year-old woman:*
> My dream was that my boyfriend and I were talking to each other. He said to me, "This doesn't mean we are getting engaged." The next scene we are on a waterbed making out. It seemed like he didn't want to have sex because he was worried about something to do with the condoms. The scene changed to me walking into the same room but he was wrapped up in a sheet waiting for someone else. I walked out and slammed the door. The scene changed back to us on the waterbed talking and I was going to tell him I was two months pregnant but my alarm went off and woke me up.

The dream begins with the dreamer and her boyfriend talking, suggesting that this dream might be about their communication dynamic.

The fact that her boyfriend tells her that he is setting boundaries on the relationship can indicate that he has essentially taken control (or is trying to take control) of how far the relationship proceeds. The waterbed might correspond to the relationship (bed) between the two being extremely emotional (water). Him not wanting to have sex because of a problem with the condoms might symbolize some kind of a sexual issue but it is more likely that he does not want to "merge" with her in a relationship because of his own fears about being emotionally vulnerable, or about his fears of a long-term commitment. A penis can be associated with male sexuality and vulnerability, and a condom insulates the user from the outside world.

The dreamer seeing her boyfriend wrapped up in the sheets can suggest that he is essentially wrapped up in the sexual aspect of their relationship (bed sheets). During the process of dialogue, the dreamer admitted that her boyfriend was separated but not yet divorced from his wife. Her slamming the door and leaving because he is waiting for someone else obviously suggests that the old relationship is still the cause of some kind of contention between the two. The imagery of being two months pregnant and wanting to talk about it has a number of possible associations. In real life, the couple had been dating for two years and the dreamer often wondered where the relationship was headed. Another possibility was that within two months from the time of the dream, the dreamer would have "birthed" her decision about the relationship. Finally, there is always the chance that the dream was precognitive and that the dreamer need to watch herself and be careful with birth control or else within two months she could find herself pregnant.

A second dream detailing a young woman's current relationship is seen in the following example:

Dream of twenty-two-year-old woman:
I was with my best friend and we were at my grandfather's house. We were about to eat dinner and had plates piled high with food. She went outside to look for a place where we could sit down and eat our meal. When I got outside she had run over to a neighbor's house to talk. She was showing them her

wedding ring. I walked over to the swing to sit down but there were two dead opossums on it. Instead, I walked over to the glider but saw a snake skin lying on it. I was going to move it until I realized that there was a snake next to it. I backed away and got behind the swing where I sat my plate of food to deter the snake away from me. He came after me anyway and wrapped around my legs so I couldn't stand. I fell to the ground and woke up.

In questioning the dreamer, she associated her grandfather's house with the ideal place for a loving home and family. Her friend in the dream was a newlywed and the dreamer expressed her own desire to get married and raise a family. She admitted to "playing around" in a relationship for the last four-and-a-half years but felt that neither she nor her boyfriend was truly committed to the relationship long-term. Certainly the symbols of the swing and the slide could represent their mutual amusement with one another and "playing around." Her looking for a place to sit or to put down her place are both suggestive of her desire to find out where and with whom she really belongs. With this in mind, the opossums might literally represent she and her boyfriend who were simply "hanging out" in the relationship, aware of its ultimate death but for some reason unwilling, unable, or too lethargic to do anything about it.

The presence of the snake throughout suggests that one difficulty the dreamer may be facing in breaking off the relationship is due to the sexual chemistry between the two. She thinks about setting aside the snake skin (the on again off again sexual relationship) only to find that the snake is still very much alive and is ultimately what prevents her from standing on her own two feet and leaving the relationship. The dreamer admitted that she often pretended to herself that her boyfriend would eventually become her future husband when she knew without a doubt that he would not. She felt that the dream was indicating her determination to finally make a change.

Another dream simply reflecting the dreamer's current situation occurred in the life of a middle-aged woman. A successful business professional, she had always considered herself to be very straightforward, practical and "down-to-earth." Recently, a friend had given her some metaphysical and spiritual books that were causing the woman to question some of her long-held assumptions about life. After having read a couple of the books, the woman had a dream that seemed important to her:

Dream of middle-aged woman:
I dreamed that I saw seven beautiful butterflies fluttering around my briefcase (where I usually keep some documents). I noticed that my briefcase was a different color than in real life. In the dream it was black and white stripes.

Numbers can have a symbolic meaning in dreams and seven is often associated with issues related to spirituality. Because a caterpillar enters a cocoon and then emerges as a beautiful new creature, a butterfly often symbolizes personal transformation. The dream seemed to be about some kind of a personal spiritual transformation that was occurring in the woman's life.

The briefcase probably represents the dreamer's work but it is also how she has seen herself up to this point—in all likelihood she has defined her individuality in terms of her job. Since the briefcase is where the dreamer often keeps documents or things she is reading or referring to, the imagery might also suggest that what she has been reading is causing her to become transformed. It is for this reason that the butterflies are flying around it. The briefcase is the color of black and white stripes, which is suggestive of the woman's own down-to-earth approach of everything being right or wrong, yes or no, straightforward and not complicated, etc. The symbol of the butterflies flying around her briefcase is probably indicative of the fact that her old approach to life is in the process of undergoing some radical change. However, it could also be possible that the dreamer is attempting to apply her old right or wrong philosophy to the information she has been reading.

Because dreams can provide additional insights into a situation, oftentimes they can enable the dreamer to have greater objectivity about a situation, to make a decision, or to even see the result of possible choices he or she could make. The dream of a forty-something-year-old man who had just graduated from massage school proved extremely helpful in this regard. Although he had graduated and was excited about building up his own massage business, he was also extremely low on money. This shortage of funds had prompted him to look for office work. Finally he found a job that he thought he could do but suddenly indecision had set in. He was unsure about whether or not he should accept the job because he realized it might take up too much of his time, causing him to neglect the massage business that he was trying to develop; however, he really needed the income. As he went to bed that night, he asked for guidance about what he was supposed to do. That night he had a dream:

Dream of forty-something-year-old man:
I am in my living room with my wife and looking out the front window. I notice a little girl out front of our house standing on the lawn. Suddenly, an office supply van drives around the corner and stops abruptly in front of the house. Two men jump out of the man, abduct the little girl and swiftly drive away. To my horror I realize that she is being kidnapped. I wake up in a panic.

Upon awakening the man knew that the dream had given him an answer to his query and he decided not to apply for the job but to instead build up his massage practice. He came to that conclusion because he felt that the dream was showing himself in his present situation (living room) with wife (family and need for income), trying to make a decision about something related to his future (looking out the front window). He felt that little girl on the front lawn was a symbol of his massage business that had not yet reached maturity—it was still a child. The office supply van stopping in front of the house was suggestive of the nine-to-five job he was contemplating. As a result of the dream, the man decided that if he took the job, his massage business (the little girl) would be taken from him.

Sometimes by presenting a dreamer's current situation in story-form, a dream can provide encouragement even if it is only to continue what the dreamer has already been doing. In one instance, a forty-three-year-old woman was feeling overwhelmed by her job. A webmaster for a large corporation, her assistant had suddenly left the company, leaving the woman with more work than she thought could be accomplished by one individual. As hard as she worked it seemed impossible for her alone to maintain and update the company's enormous web site. Extremely frustrated and defeated, one night she had a dream:

> *Dream of forty-three-year-old woman:*
> I was to perform a musical show with my big boss. I was playing the piano (something I do) and he was to sing. For various, totally ridiculous reasons we could not seem to get our performance started. One time I couldn't find the right page in the music book. Another try and the music had turned to text. Another try and the music was for guitar, not piano. Another time I had sat down on the piano stool and it was so low to the ground, I couldn't reach the keys. Another time my boss started singing without me.
>
> No matter what we tried, we couldn't get it together to start the performance. Finally we just looked at each other and started giggling and laughing about the situation. There were several people in the audience waiting for us to start. My boss's wife was there, too. She got so disgusted with us that she got up and walked out. We never did get the show going but we had a lot of fun laughing about the situation. At the end of the dream a little girl about six or seven-years-old walked up to me. I immediately recognized her as my boss's daughter (who he does not really have). She asked me, "Why did you have to change the passwords again?" which is something I do monthly at my job. That was the end of the dream.

After having the dream, the woman said, "I don't remember my dreams very often but this one helped me cope with the work situation very well. When I awoke, I knew the dream was telling me to lighten up at my job. My boss represented my job. The performance we were trying to do represented my job performance. The fact that we couldn't get anything accomplished represented my current situation."

Additional insights include the fact that the boss's wife could symbolize the company. The fact that the wife leaves suggests that the dreamer has become so frustrated with the situation that she has entertained thoughts about quitting her job. The boss's daughter might be indicative of the dreamer's length of time with the company, and her wondering why things had to change (assistant leaving) when things had been going so well. The dreamer added, "The dream was telling me to laugh and go with the flow because I could only do what I could do and there wasn't any point getting upset about it."

A precognitive aspect may have been included in the dream's imagery as well. According to the woman, at the time of the dream her boss's wife was expecting the couple's fourth child. The couple already had three boys. Because of the dream, the dreamer felt that the fourth child would be a daughter: "I remember her as having short, brown curly hair." Later, after the boss's child was born (a baby girl), the woman shared her dream. The boss was surprised and replied, "That's funny, my daughter does have brown, curly hair!"

Just as in other instances, dreams exploring an individual's current experiences can be easiest to work with by simplifying the imagery down to its essential storyline and theme. This approach can also enable the dreamer to become detached and more objective about the imagery being presented. This was certainly the case for a twenty-something-year-old woman. Recently married, she was fearful that a dream was telling her and her husband not to have any children. The dream had bothered her a great deal because family had always been very important in her life:

> *Dream of twenty-something-year-old woman:*
> I dreamed that my husband and I had a baby. We got the baby all dressed up to go to a party, even though the baby didn't want to go and cried about it the whole time. On the way in the car, the baby was crying and throwing a little tantrum. When we finally got to the party, the baby just sat in the corner

> sulking and then started to cry and throw a tantrum again. It
> was very clear that the baby wanted to leave. Very frustrated
> and not knowing what else to do, finally my husband and I took
> the baby home.

The dreamer was afraid that the dream was trying to show her that having children would not be a good idea for the couple. Because the couple was recently married, it appeared much more likely that the baby was a symbol of their marriage and some kind of frustration that the woman was experiencing as a newlywed. One possible theme suggested by the story is simply "Someone is being a baby." The dreamer had mentioned her appreciation of home and family and since going to a gathering of some kind had facilitated the baby's tantrum, the dreamer was asked: "How does your husband feel about going to family gatherings?"

Her response was immediate, "He hates them!" The dreamer went on to elaborate that she had always enjoyed visiting her family for picnics, on special occasions and on the holidays. However, her husband had made it very clear that he did not like going to visit her family. "I have to force him to go," she added.

When it was pointed out that it was the woman's husband that appeared to be acting "like a baby," the dreamer nodded as the dream suddenly made sense to her. It had nothing to do with whether or not they should have children but instead it was about her husband's childish tantrums and sulking that often occurred whenever she wanted him to do something that he did not want to do. It seemed very clear that she needed to discuss the importance of family with him and he needed to "grow up" in the situation.

In another case, a nineteen-year-old girl was contemplating dating on old boyfriend—someone who had once broken her heart. In addition to the break-up, her hesitancy about going out with him was because she was already involved with someone else. What was interesting about this example was that during the dialogue process, the young woman admitted that she did not think either of the young men had treated her very nicely. This fact also became obvious in the dream imagery:

Dream of nineteen-year-old girl:
I was walking down the street and suddenly two men jumped
out and robbed me at gunpoint. They took my wallet, which
in the dream I called my "lucky hope" wallet.

Obviously, the young woman is having something valuable taken
from her. The two men robbing her at gunpoint could symbolize the
two young men with whom she has been involved in a relationship.
The symbol of the gun could suggest that both males had been aggressive, controlling or even sexually domineering; a gun is also a
phallic symbol. Whatever she perceives as being valuable, which from
the process of dialogue turned out to be a long-term relationship and
eventual marriage, was taken away from her in spite of her hopes to
the contrary. In all likelihood, the young woman's dream was advis-
ing her not to date either male, as they were simply taking from her.
Neither was the long-term relationship she hoped to find.

A very practical dream came just as a thirty-seven-year-old man
and his wife were in the process of building a new home. The house
was to be a custom-built home located on a three-acre lot in the countryside, near other custom-built homes also with acreage. After the
final plans for the house had been approved, the man decided to lo-
cate the house one-hundred-and-seventy-five feet back from the main
road. Those instructions were given to the surveyors by phone and
the location of the house was to be plotted out on the lot later that
day—24 hours before the concrete foundation was to be poured. That
night the man had a dream:

Dream of thirty-seven-year-old man:
I was walking through our house, which had been fully built.
Everything was beautiful, just as my wife and I had imagined.
When I came into the kitchen, however, I heard a noise that
sounded like chewing that seemed to be coming from the
back of the house. I walked to the back door and was horrified
to find that the house was so close to the rear property line
that the neighbor's horse was able to put it's head over the
fence and eat off of our deck! The noise I had heard was the

sound of the horse chewing hay.

Upon waking the next morning, the dreamer drove out to his property and measured where the house had been staked out to the back of the property line. Although the dream had exaggerated the problem, the surveyors had mistakenly staked out the foundation fifty feet further from the street then they were supposed to—putting it much closer to the backyard neighbor than had been intended. As a result, the dreamer called the surveyors and had them re-stake the house, moving it more than fifty feet forward.

Although we don't generally dream *for* other people, frequently dreams can deal with people with which the dreamer is involved and about whom she or he is concerned. One possibility suggested by the dream of an elderly woman was just that. She began by stating that she had experienced the following dream about two years previously but its imagery still remained fresh in her mind:

Dream of eighty-something-year-old woman:
I was standing on top of a mountain overlooking everything down below. At the very foot of the mountain was an enormous lake. I looked down at my foot and noticed a beautiful pink rock was sitting on the ground just beneath me. I reached down and picked up the rock and placed it in my pocket because I wanted to keep it. To my horror, the rock fell through my pocket and started rolling down the hill toward the lake. I was totally devastated about losing the rock and I felt as though it was going to be gone forever. However, at the edge of the lake, just before falling into the water, the rock came to a stop.

To begin with, standing at the top of a mountain and looking down below could represent looking back at one's life journey. After eighty-some years, perhaps in the dreamer's mind her life had essentially reached it's end. However, in the process of reflecting back on a successful life (standing on top of the mountain), there seemed to be something still demanding the dreamer's attention. Since the color pink can be associated with love, the process of dialogue included the following: "It suggests that something you love (beautiful pink rock) is going to feel like it is going away or you're losing it. It is something you are very emotional about (water). However, even though it is going to appear like you are losing it, it won't really be taken from you."

The woman nodded and stated that a couple of months after having the dream, her sixty-one-year-old son's health problem had been diagnosed as terminal cancer. However, more than two years later her son was still alive and was undergoing periodic treatments. The family still hoped that his cancer would go into remission but doctors had yet to change their prognosis from being terminal. The son's condition seemed a likely candidate for the dream imagery. Since the rock had not disappeared beneath the water, it seemed likely that in spite of the son's terminal condition, he would still out-live his mother.

In another example of dreaming about a situation dealing with a loved one, the dream of a forty-something-year-old man seemed to indicate that the kitten he and his wife had obtained when it was only five-weeks old had reached maturity:

> *Dream of forty-something-year-old man:*
> I dreamt that my wife and I were in our bedroom when the kitten came in. However in the dream the kitten was a teenage girl and she proudly announced to the two of us that she was going to start dating. That was the end of the dream.

The man told his wife the dream and the two laughed about how attached they had become to the kitten in the nearly five months since they had adopted her. Neither thought anything more of the dream. Ironically, the couple had decided to have their kitten spayed just after its six-month birthday, as had been suggested by their veterinarian—a date less than a week away. Three days before the appointment the kitten went into heat. For several days the kitten endured much stress, crying, and intense biological drives. The dreamer felt that the poor kitten would not have had to endure such trauma had his dream been understood beforehand, prompting him to reschedule the veterinarian appointment for one week earlier.

As illustrated by the next two dreams, oftentimes whatever an individual is presently struggling with in life can become personified in dream imagery. When this is the case, the person attacking or threatening the dreamer is simply a symbolic metaphor of the challenging situation or problem. In the first example, a teenage boy raised in an extremely conservative and critical household had a dream that seemed to embody his worst fears:

Dream of teenage boy:
I saw the devil and he smiled and invited me to join with him. To tempt me, he said he would grant me one wish. I decide that my wish would be that all of his power be eliminated. However, as soon as I had the thought he knew it and trapped me in some kind of a glass sphere. He told me that I would never be able to destroy him. In the dream, I wanted to have the same power as the devil but to instead do good with it. Unfortunately, I was trapped in the ball. At the end of the dream, I suggest to the devil that he should try to do good with his powers instead of evil.

When helping an individual with his or her dream, it is important to use diplomacy when trying to relate a possible meaning. From the above imagery, one likely possibility is that the boy is feeling threatened by an overpowering and controlling male in his life—the boy's father being a likely candidate. However, stating that possibility to a young boy who still lives at home will probably not be helpful. For that reason, a better response could be: "It suggests that you are having some kind of a struggle within yourself about what you want to do with your life versus what others are saying you should do."

Essentially, the dream suggested that he was feeling trapped or imprisoned in some way (the glass sphere) and that he wanted the power to change things. All he really wanted was to be as powerful as the individual controlling him and to do something good with that power. The dream might also be a personification of the youth's self-criticism and not necessarily that of a controlling parent. With this in mind, another possibility was that in real life the boy was too hard on himself and that perhaps he was not being supportive of what he wanted to do because he felt like he could never do it anyway. Obviously, ultimately the dreamer has the power to become whatever he wants and that it is okay for him to pursue his own dreams. In the end, the boy seemed relieved that the devil was not really after him and he was surprised that the dream seemed to portray the feelings he had of being "trapped" by his present situation in life.

The second dream belonged to a fifty-something-year-old woman who wanted to become more established and gain a wider client base in her profession as a clinical hypnotherapist. She was also interested in lecturing and teaching. Self-certain and confident regarding the manner in which she felt her practice and work would grow, she was not at all open to listening to the advice of others:

> *Dream of fifty-something-year-old woman:*
> The dream began in a large room like a conference hall setting. I was there chatting informally with groups of people. It was the atmosphere of a cocktail party but there were no drinks. I realized that the people had gathered to hear me speak.
>
> Instead of speaking from the stage, I chose to walk among them in small groups, teaching and sharing. All of a sudden I heard the large double doors of the conference room open and several men and women entered—they were wearing dark business attire. They looked around, saw me and approached me.
>
> At first they were smiling—they handed me a small book. I thanked them and began looking at it. I observed that its colors were black and white. When I looked at it, I felt it was information belonging to some religious sect. I smiled at them and told them, "Thank you for sharing with me but I don't really believe the same." I wanted to return their book.
>
> They became angry and looked very evil. They started to chase the people that had come to hear me speak. They were trying to destroy them. They busted the windshield in their cars, stabbed their tires and killed those they could find. But I kept escaping from them.

They wanted to stop me from teaching holistic spiritual things. However, I kept going to teach in different areas and the same thing kept happening. The people in the business suits were always looking for me and would always try to destroy the people that came to listen to me.

My students asked if I was afraid they would kill me and I said, "No. Don't be afraid. They can only kill you but they can't destroy your soul." I said, "I am not afraid of dying or of them torturing me. I am only concerned that they keep me from being able to teach and share the truth. That is why I keep running and moving so I can teach and share as much as I can before they find out where I am."

The dream lends itself to a wide variety of possibilities. From the very first it appears as though the dreamer is very comfortable (or would like to become comfortable) speaking in an informal manner with her audiences and/or clients. She also feels as though she has something to say because people seem readily available to listen to her speak. Her desire to be informal is also picked up in the second paragraph when we learn that there is a stage available but the dreamer chooses not to use it, preferring instead to "walk among" her participants.

The people who interrupt her gathering are dressed in dark business attire. It is from them that the dreamer receives a black and white (right or wrong; appropriate or inappropriate, yes or no) booklet. They share their beliefs to which the woman responds, "Thank you for sharing with me but I don't really believe the same." One possibility suggested at this point is that someone or something is critical of how the woman has been trying to do her job, or that someone is critical of the woman herself. Another possibility is that the informal and even laid-back approach that the dreamer prefers in her work is being threatened by a more professional and "by the book" standards demanded by contemporary society. In addition to certain legal issues, the dream could pertain to insurance, licensing, professionalism and even marketing requirements. In dialoguing with the dreamer it became clear that these issues were very foreign to the "real work" with which the woman wanted to be involved.

In the fourth paragraph we learn that this intruders are "trying to destroy" what it is the woman hopes to accomplish. Busting out windshields could be symbolic of destroying a vision of where an individual is headed just as slashing tires can be representative of trying to impede progress that an individual is attempting to travel. It is also possible that the woman was doing herself in at one level as a means of escaping personal responsibility.

Essentially, the threat of these intruders is trying to prevent the dreamer from teaching things of a spiritual nature. No matter where she goes, there they are. Because of this dynamic, it is logical to ask the dreamer if she has been having a challenging time with her career pursuits. To this query, the fifty-something-year-old woman responded that it has been "very challenging" but that she felt driven to continue her efforts. In the end the dreamer gets to have her own fears put to rest by dialoging with her students. We learn that the dreamer really has nothing to be afraid of; she cannot really be killed. She will continue her work no matter what is trying to capture her.

It was suggested to the dreamer that by doing things a little differently it would not destroy the subject matter she was hoping to bring across to her clients. Perhaps she needed to be a little more traditional and professional in her approach. As it turned out, others had also recommended doing things more "by the book" but she had yet to heed their advice.

In the case of a young woman nervously considering her future and her career, family pressures suggested that she was not yet old enough to make a mature decision. The young woman was struggling with her family input and her own feelings regarding what she felt to be right. Finally, a dream set her fears at rest and told her that she really was headed in the right direction after all:

Dream of twenty-something-year-old woman:
I dreamt that I had a beautiful baby boy. He had the brightest blue eyes and was very young. I felt so close to my baby. I could feel a very intense love for him in the dream. Bridget (one of my classmates) lived across the street from me. She was

babysitting for me and when I came to pick my baby up, she wouldn't give him to me. Everyone seemed to think that I couldn't take care of him. However, I knew I could and they didn't know how deeply I loved him. I looked everywhere for my baby because some other people (I don't recognize them but in the dream I knew them) had taken him. I finally found him at a park in a clubhouse with these people. I got him back from them and I was so happy. The two of us got into my car. It was a little red Omni and we drove away. I had the car all packed up because I knew I had to go where no one would try to take him again.

To the dreamer, her classmate Bridget was a symbol of someone who always seemed confident, capable and decisive about what she wanted to do—qualities that the dreamer was trying to emulate in her own life. The baby represented a new beginning that was full of potential though not yet developed. The baby's blue eyes seemed to suggest that the dreamer was discovering something about her own personal spirituality in the process of pursuing her dreams. The young woman said, "I think the fact that I love my baby so much in the dream symbolizes the love of what I want to do. However, people trying to take the baby away from me represents my own fear of failure and not being able to hold on to this beginning. In the end of the dream, with my getting the baby back and driving away means that I will be able to hold on." Additionally, the red car can represent that the dreamer has the energy and the determination to succeed in this particular direction, one which may be very independent from what family members originally had in mind for her.

The importance of diplomatically exploring the possible meaning of a dream became clearly evident when another individual presented a dream that had been given to her for interpretation:

Dream of middle-aged woman:
I am standing on the front porch of a beautiful Victorian home, which is not my home in real life but seemed to be my home in the dream. Everything is beautiful! The home is covered

with ornate gingerbread trim. The porch has a couple of rockers and looks out over a gorgeous manicured lawn. Everything is in its place. The yard is surrounded by a quaint white picket fence. Even though I am not aware of where my husband is, I seem very happy.

I find myself thinking about how wonderful my surroundings are when I suddenly notice that a male deer is out on the edge of the yard all by itself. For some reason the deer seems very sad. Although it is in my yard, it stands next to the fence and seems to want to get out. It hangs its head and antlers over the fence and watches with wide-eyed attention as three female does run by the yard just on the other side of my fence.

The dream suggests that the woman's idealized image of her life is not necessarily realistic. At the very least, her sense of life and her relationship is not being shared by her male counterpart (the deer trying to get out of the yard). This is also represented by the fact that in the midst of the woman contemplating her own happiness, she becomes cognizant that she is not aware of what is occurring with her husband. Her husband seems discontent and even sad about his situation. As a result he may be looking for new relationship opportunities (three female does).

Certainly, it would not have been wise to respond to the dreamer with, "Your husband is thinking about having an affair." In the first place, it is possible that the woman's dream was simply portraying her husband dissatisfaction with his life and not necessarily a literal affair. In addition, since the subconscious mind only relates information to individuals in ways in which they can deal with it, people working with dream interpretation need to do likewise. For that reason, the communication that went back to the dreamer encouraged her to begin communicating with her husband more fully about their life together because the dream suggested that "Your idealized view of your life and your surroundings are not necessarily shared by your husband. The two of you need to talk about it." Because it was not possible to dialogue with the dreamer about her dream, coming to a clear understanding of why three does were present in the dream instead of one is speculative at best. Possibilities regarding the number three include the length of time of their marriage, the number of years her husband has been dissatisfied, the number of previous relationships with which he has been involved, or simply the fact that he is looking at several different opportunities.

In the final example of a dream exploring an individual's current situation, a twenty-something-year-old woman had gone to Jamaica with a girlfriend, leaving her boyfriend at home. Her dream occurred halfway through their vacation:

> *Dream of twenty-something-year-old woman:*
> I was in an underground cave that went on for miles and miles. While under the earth I came upon all of these trolls. The trolls were very happy to see me because the cave was filled with beautiful crystals that could only be energized by a human being and they wanted me to energize them. After I did, they gave me some stakes that they wanted hammered into the ground. I followed their instructions. Later, I was taken even deeper into the cave (below where we had been), and I was horrified to find that the stakes had gone through to a lower cave and impaled a man to death. I used the power of the crystals to destroy all of the trolls because of what they had made me do.

The symbol of an underground cave can represent the subconscious or it might correspond to an individual's "lower self" or sexual desires. A cave can also symbolize the womb and female sexuality. In the process of dialoguing with the dreamer, she admitted that one outstanding feature of her vacation had been that frequently "very good-looking" Jamaican males had been "hitting on" her. She admitted that she had been tempted to have an affair but decided against it because she really loved her boyfriend. This entire situation had become portrayed in her dream.

Trolls can be a symbol of something that diverts someone from his or her path. In literature, because they have been portrayed as interested in stealing children, trolls can also be symbolic of something that steals innocence. Therefore, the trolls represented the men that were hitting on the dreamer and trying to take her "innocence." Crystals can be associated with dreams or desires. However, in the dream these crystals can only be energized by a human being. The only thing that sets a human apart from the rest of Creation is free will. Therefore, the crystals can also be symbolic of the dreamer's own free will.

As is portrayed in the imagery, the dreamer can use her free will to hammer (a reference to a phallic image?) stakes into the ground. However that will only ground herself even deeper into her sexual feelings, resulting in the destruction of her relationship with her boyfriend (impaled a man to death). In the end, the dream showed the woman using her free will to destroy the trolls, suggesting that she rebuked their advances toward her.

Because dreams contrast and correlate the events of the day, primarily they serve as a means for the dreamer to wrestle with the issues, concerns, and feelings that have been on the individual's conscious mind. Dreams can provide an objective look at known facts, new insights, and even the possibility of potential solutions. This process enables individuals to come to terms with current events, make sense of their lives, or discover solutions to problems that they have been facing. This evaluation of current life events can address the dreamer's physical, mental or even spiritual wellbeing. It is a process that happens all the time and assists individuals even if they do not consciously work with their dreams. At the very least, this examination of one's life can prove extremely helpful to the subconscious mind. However, the process can become even more beneficial once individuals begin to decide that it is important to examine what their dreams are trying to tell them.

Chapter 5 Sample Dreams
See Appendix One for possible interpretations

Dream of fifty-something-year-old woman:
(Background information: Woman is in the midst of some life changes and the need to make decisions about her future.)

I dreamt that there was an elegant looking woman who was standing by herself. She appeared calm and collected. Suddenly I noticed that she was missing her entire right arm. There wasn't even a stub where her arm should have been. I was carrying a white shawl at the time and I took it over to the woman and draped it around her shoulders. I don't know if I was trying to cover her missing arm or help her stay warm. She seemed appreciative and thanked me.

Dream of twenty-something-year-old man:
(Background information: Twenty-year-old male has moved to a university town to attend school. He has not yet found a job to help support him and is worried.)

I am trying to take a picture of an awesome sunset down a road. It gets better and better. The sky gets very cloudy with bright orange colors. As I try to take the picture, a little boy gets in the way. I keep hoping he will move but when he does the sunset is gone.

Dream of nineteen-year-old woman:
(Background information: Young woman has begun to have romantic feelings for a male friend, Patrick, and is worried that the feelings will change their friendship.)

I had a dream that I was at a party. It seemed to be my house but it wasn't. I was outside and saw a snake in our neighbor's yard that looked like an anaconda. I went back in the house, found my friend, Patrick, and told him about the snake. When we went outside to look for it, it wasn't there. Afterwards, we walked through another

Chapter 5 Sample Dreams
See Appendix One for possible interpretations

room leading outside to the front yard because he had to leave. On the way to Patrick's car, we passed some friends playing cards. Before he left, he kissed me on the cheek, then we hugged and he kissed me on the lips.

The next thing I remember was being at another house with another guy who is a friend sitting on some monkey bars. Then I saw the snake again. This time it was winding itself around the pole and looping itself through the bars. I was scared but my friend told me it would be all right and wouldn't hurt me. Then Patrick came out (the other friend seemed to be gone) and we watched the snake go to the other yard.

6

Dreams for the Body, Mind and Soul

For years, many approaches to medicine simply addressed the physical needs of the body and whatever physical properties could be undertaken to treat an individual's illness. However, holistic medicine has found that addressing an individual's needs physically, mentally and spiritually is necessary in order to facilitate optimum healing because each individual is much more than simply a physical organism. With this same idea in mind, dreams can explore every area of an individual's life, physically, mentally, emotionally and spiritually. It does not matter whether an issue concerns an individual's health, feelings, aspirations, or spiritual values and beliefs, dreams can provide an exploration of whatever is facing the dreamer in waking life. Dreams that reflect and analyze the current life events of the dreamer can often be divided into one of three categories: dreams that relate to the body, dreams that provide psychological insights into life's events, and dreams that nurture the soul.

As mentioned previously, dreams can provide dietary recommendations and suggestions. However, dreams for the body are not limited to diet alone. In an example from the life of psychic Edgar Cayce, in real life he was suffering from a miserable cough and cold. Not able to find any relief from the cough that was bothering him, one night Cayce had a dream. In the dream he saw himself in the kitchen mixing a concoction made up of numerous ingredients including boiling water, honey, glycerin, simple syrup, horehound, benzoin, and whiskey. Upon awakening, he realized that the formula seemed to be a cough syrup made up of ingredients that could not harm him. As a result, the formula was prepared, ingested and the cough was finally relieved.

In another example from the Cayce files, a woman had a dream in which her mother (who was still alive) appeared to her and stated that the dreamer needed to see an osteopath. The mother said, "You should go to the osteopath. You ought to be ashamed of yourself! If your husband wants you to go to the osteopath, you should go!" When requesting an interpretation of the dream, Cayce told the woman that the interpretation was twofold: one to assure the woman that valid information could come to her through the dream state; and two, that she needed to see an osteopath!

In a contemporary example, a forty-something-year-old man developed chest pains and went to see a doctor about his condition. The doctor called in a couple of specialists who wanted to immediately perform a coronary bypass. However, the man was in great health. He ate a nutritious diet and had a good family history that did not indicate any predisposition to heart problems. For that reason the man felt that his chest pains might be more stress-related and he declined the operation. That night he had a dream:

Dream of forty-something-year-old man:
My dream that night was that a Model A Ford was sitting by the side of the road with its hood up. Two mechanics were working on the engine. I realized that the two mechanics looked like the two doctors I had seen the previous day, only in the dream they were wearing big, baggy pants like circus clowns.

In working with his dream, the man felt that the car represented himself and his body. He thought that the mechanics working on the engine corresponded to the doctors who had been looking into the situation with his heart. In spite of their diagnosis and their insistence regarding the need for surgery, essentially the dream was showing him that the two had been "clowns" and inappropriate for the occasion. Because of the dream, the forty-something-year-old man remained firm in his decision not to have surgery and instead focused on his need for stress reduction. Years later, the dreamer was still doing fine and he was grateful that he had not simply taken the doctors' advice for surgery he did not need.

In another example, a nineteen-year-old man had gone to a college located in the Rocky Mountains. It was the middle of the winter and the dormitory always seemed cold. During a phone conversation with his grandmother, the young man complained about never feeling warm at night. To his surprise, a week later his grandmother mailed him an electric blanket, which he began using immediately. Because he had been so cold, he left the blanket plugged in all night, causing him to feel warm "for the first time since coming to school."

Sometime later, the young man found himself feeling tired and very lethargic each morning upon awakening. Since he had always awakened feeling energized and refreshed, he decided that the condition must somehow be related to "Rocky Mountain weather." One night he had a dream:

Dream of nineteen-year-old man:
I saw myself standing in the bathroom in my Grandmother's house, looking in the mirror. I had my electric blanket draped over my shoulders and around my body. Suddenly, I opened up the blanket and stared in the mirror. I was horrified to see that my body was covered with hundreds of leeches.

The dream caused the young man to realize that the blanket was somehow draining his energy. The blanket was the cause of his feeling tired each morning and not the weather. From that day forward he plugged in the blanket about a half-hour before going to bed and unplugged it just before getting under the covers. After he had followed through on what he felt the dream was trying to tell him, he no longer felt exhausted each morning when he got up.

A sports injury from high school seemed to be the cause of a dream experienced by a businessman more than thirty years later. A football injury had resulted in some minor internal injuries to the young man's hip. He thought nothing more of the problem until thirty years later when he began having alternate "numb and throbbing" pains near the area of the injury. A dream provided the prognosis:

Dream of forty-something-year-old man:
A female surgeon is in a hospital room examining me. After examining me, she looks up, touches the area of my hip and says, "There's no longer any doubt, this has got to come out."

The dream prompted the businessman to make an appointment with his doctor, who referred him to a surgeon. After examining the hip, the surgeon recommended and then performed surgery to remove old scar tissue and the remnants of internal bleeding that had occurred decades previously. After the surgery and his recovery, the dreamer was no longer bothered by the pain in his hip.

A much more complicated dream scared the wife of a sixty-something-year-old man named Bob into changing the course of treatment that had been outlined for her husband. In real life, a lung problem had caused him to seek early retirement. However, apart from the lung condition Bob was healthy until he contracted pneumonia. Because of the pneumonia he was treated with antibiotics and had to briefly use oxygen. Although he was sent home from the hospital, he never fully recovered and was hospitalized a short time later with pneumonia and again he was put on oxygen. Bob was treated and released four days later but was readmitted to the emergency room a few hours later because of his breathing problems.

Again he was treated for his condition and new tests were performed before releasing him to go home, still on oxygen. Within two weeks the hospital called and informed the couple that the tests indicated that Bob had contracted tuberculosis. TB medications were begun immediately and Bob's condition deteriorated. It was only a short time until he had to be readmitted through the emergency room.

Further tests suggested that Bob's problem wasn't TB after all but a strain of pneumonia that was multi-drug resistant. While doing tests and waiting for a hospital bed, the couple was informed that Bob had to be transferred to another hospital for insurance reasons. Because the new hospital only recognized the TB diagnosis, even though they had been told otherwise, they continued with the treatment for TB. Bob's condition deteriorated even further while they waited for the "official" diagnosis of the strain of pneumonia. For days he had to work at every breath. Finally, they gave him the antibiotics he needed and Bob recovered well enough so that they could send him home, still on oxygen.

By this time, he was using four or five liters of oxygen a minute and was hooked to a fifty-foot lead, spending most of his time in a recliner where he could breathe. However, in spite of the various treatments he was still not well. Finally, a dream scared Bob's wife into finding a different course of action:

Dream of fifty-something-year-old woman:
I dreamed that Bob had awakened and his condition was worsened. We hurried to the doctor's to see if we could get him some help. Bob was driving to the doctor's and on the way he missed the turn. I told him he had missed it and he would have to turn around and go back. He kept driving and I was really irritated that he didn't turn around. Finally, after twenty blocks he turned around and went back.

When we entered the clinic, we separated so that each of us could try and find some help. I talked to the nurses at the desk and told them that Bob was worse and needed to see the doctor. They said they would squeeze him in. Bob returned and said that he hadn't been able to get an appointment and I told him not to worry that the nurses said they would take care of it. I pointed them out to him and they said that they would take care of Bob first since he was on oxygen. I realized that I should go out to the car and get an extra oxygen tank

in case he ran out. I left Bob and went out to the parking lot
to get a tank out of the car. I had difficulty locating the car and
I noticed two men in the parking lot. They seemed to be just
ordinary men, decently dressed. I became afraid that the car
couldn't be located but then I realized, "Oh, well, this is a
hospital and they will certainly have oxygen."

I went back in the building and saw Bob in the hallway. He
had collapsed and was flopping around the floor with uncon-
trollable movements. I went up to the nurses and asked what
had happened. They said he was having difficulty breathing.
The two men I had seen in the parking lot approached, said
they were doctors and that they would take care of him. They
got an assist chair with handles on either side to help carry him.

When they finally came by carrying Bob, he looked like he
was sitting Indian fashion. He said that his legs hurt and as I
looked closer I was shocked to find that his legs had been cut
off. I was very upset and asked how they had done it and they
said, "We did it with drugs." I was angry, "Can you do that
without our permission?" I asked to see the doctor who had
done it and they said he had already left. They offered to get
a public relations doctor to smooth things over and then the
dream ended.

Fearing that the continued course of treatment was going to make
her husband even worse, the woman related her dream to her husband. She told him, "It's true, they have cut off your legs. You are
immobilized and chained to the oxygen. The doctors are treating you
with drugs but you need more." As a result, the couple pursued a
more holistic approach and decided to admit him to a clinic that spe-
cialized in complimentary medicine. According to the woman, "That
experience led my husband being taken off the oxygen and a complete healing." In retrospect, the woman realized that the twenty
blocks that had been portrayed in the dream was symbolic of the
twenty weeks it had taken to turn Bob's illness around.

In addition to dreams that correspond to the physical condition of
the body, dreams can also provide psychological insights into life

events. In this regard, dreams can equip the dreamer with an examination of feelings, worries, thoughts and desires as well as a greater degree of self-understanding and even emotional healing.

In another example from the Edgar Cayce files, a dream occurred during a time when Cayce had been extremely worried about his personal finances. He was very concerned about whether or nor he could support his family. One night he had a dream in which he found himself walking along a street in Paris with the Duke and Duchess of Windsor and Jesus. They came to a sidewalk café serving drinks and Cayce invited his three companions to join him in a glass of champagne. The four travelers sat down and had a pleasant enough conversation. When the time came to leave and the Duke and Duchess got up, Cayce and Jesus were left alone at the table. To Cayce's horror, he realized that although he had invited everyone for drinks, he only had a few pennies in his pocket and would not be able to pay. When he pulled the change out of his pocket and showed Jesus, Jesus simply laughed and said, "Will I have to send you after a fish too?"

Because dream imagery can utilize personal symbols with which the dreamer is familiar, Cayce was very much aware of the reference to which Jesus was referring. In the book of Matthew, there is the story of the Apostles traveling to Capernaum and needing money to pay the tax of admittance to the city. Since they had no money, Jesus sent them to catch a fish. The first fish caught had a coin in its mouth—the very amount needed to pay the tax. With this in mind, the dream was simply the encouragement Cayce needed to have the faith that whatever he required to support his family would be provided.

In a second example, a couple was facing marital discord. During that time, the husband brought a dream to Cayce for interpretation. In the dream, he saw himself riding on a train with his wife sitting next to him. As he was watching the passage of scenery out the window, he noticed that his wife was trying to measure the window with a croquet mallet. The husband scolded her and exclaimed, "It can't be measured that way!"

Cayce told the man that the dream was an exploration of the different approaches the couple had taken in trying to measure the success of their relationship. Whereas the husband seemed content to measure success by how much material progress they made in their journey together, the wife was much more interested in measuring how much fun they were having. Apparently the couple needed to communicate about what it was they were trying to achieve in their life together.

In a contemporary example, a young woman's worries and feelings of financial inequality were portrayed in a dream while she was at college studying for her Ph.D.:

> *Dream of twenty-something-year-old woman:*
> I was on the main road in my hometown, where I am not currently living. On the road next to me were cars. It seemed that my body was my car and that everyone else had a real car. I was crawling around on the road with my blankets around me trying to keep up with the actual cars. I was extremely afraid and woke up just as I was trying to make a left turn into a mall.

At the time of the dream, the young woman was financially strapped and felt economically inferior to other people. Because of her lack of finances and her need to focus her time and energy into her studies and her schoolwork, her life seemed to lack any personal security or comfort. She believed that the dream imagery was trying to show her that she was overly concerned about material issues (turning in to the mall) or that she might have made a wrong career choice. In time, she did finish her Ph.D. and her finances did improve, but she never did choose to become a professor, which had been her career goal at the time of the dream.

In the case of a middle-aged woman, a dream reoccurred every year around Christmas, reflecting her worst fears about not being prepared for the holidays. The dream really bothered her because in spite of her hectic life and schedule, she really tried to make certain that Christmas was an enjoyable experience for every member of her family.

> *Dream of fifty-something-year-old woman:*
> Every year around Christmas I dream that it is Christmas day and I am with my family to celebrate. When it's time for gift

giving, I realize with horror that I have forgotten to buy any gifts for anyone. I scramble around trying to pull together anything to give to my family. I am so embarrassed and ashamed but my family doesn't seem to care.

Obviously, the dream portrayed the woman's own fears that because of her busy schedule she was not going to be prepared for Christmas day. However, at the same time the dream was trying to provide the reassurance that regardless of how much or how little she was able to accomplish, her family would still enjoy the holidays. In other words, she needed to stop worrying so much, do what she could without putting so much pressure on herself, and simply enjoy the season.

A fifty-something-year-old man who prided himself on his ability to serve as a peacemaker in family issues became frustrated when his diplomatic approach did not appear to be working in a situation involving one of his children. The child no longer seemed to be responsive to the rational and straightforward discussions that he had tried to emulate to his family. One night he had a dream that encouraged him to change his approach:

Dream of fifty-something-year-old man:
My car is broken down. I notice it is a Nash Ambassador, like the one I used to own years ago. Unfortunately, there is nothing I can do to make the car work.

Upon awakening, the man felt that the dream was telling him the diplomatic approach (the ambassador) was not working in some emotional situations. Because of the dream, the man felt it was appropriate to adopt a more assertive approach in the situation. The approach worked and the situation with his child was resolved.

A fifty-something-year-old woman, having ongoing marital difficulties was torn between leaving the situation or trying to make it work. Sometimes she felt that it was her responsibility to try and fix the problem, on other occasions she felt trapped by the situation and desperately wanted a way out. According to the woman, "I needed

my own space because I was feeling like a prisoner in my own home."
One day she finally made the decision that the time had come to move
out. However, that same night she began having second thoughts and
as she drifted off to sleep she thought to herself, "Perhaps I should try
and save this marriage one more time." That night she had a dream:

Dream of fifty-something-year-old woman:
I dreamt that I was trying to go back into a building that was
being destroyed. I was trying to save something. Everything
around me was crumbling and I suddenly realized that there
was nothing in the building worth saving. Saving my life was
more important.

She instantly knew what the dream was about. She was in danger
of destroying herself by remaining in the situation—it could not be
saved because there was nothing worth saving. The dream became
the final impetus the woman needed to get out of the situation: "I
needed to save myself and my sanity, both of which were crumbling.
I needed to be free."

A serious family argument prompted the dream of a seventy-something-year-old woman. During a vacation visit with her brother, her
brother became extremely angry over what appeared to be nothing.
During his outburst he made it very clear that he never wanted to see
his sister again. Heartbroken, the sister returned home and wondered
what she could do to help heal the situation. Because of previous inci-
dents involving the brother, other family members assured the
woman that there was nothing she could do. Still, she hoped to resolve the situation even though months had passed and her brother
remained steadfast in his resolve that he no longer wanted any ties
with the family.

Dream of seventy-something-year-old woman:
I had this dream that my brother and I were in a shoe store. I
wanted a pair of black patent leather Mary Janes, which I have
never liked. The clerk said he only had one pair but that he also
had a very pretty shade of brown in that same shoe. I looked

down at my feet and discovered that I had four feet!

I told the clerk that was fine, I could wear the brown ones on my back feet and they would not be too noticeable. My brother said that was ridiculous and was very disgusted and frowned.

The woman realized that the dream was showing her the confusion she was having about the direction she was supposed to take (four feet) in the situation with her brother. She was so upset about the problem that she was willing to settle for any solution, even if it did not seem appropriate. The dream was also suggesting to her that regardless of what she tried to do or how she tried to concede, her brother would remain angry and critical of her. When a family member discovered that the brother had disconnected his phone without telling anyone his new number, the sister realized that her brother alone controlled the situation and there was really nothing she could do about it.

In the final example of dreams exploring psychological issues, a fifty-something-year-old woman could not get a dream out of her head. The imagery seemed so clear and she felt so bothered by the experience that she sought assistance with interpretation.

Dream of fifty-something-year-old woman:

I was driving to my mother's house. When I got there, however, there was a mailman's truck in the driveway. I had to wait for him to move before I could pull in. When I finally pulled in the driveway, there were all these polar bears blocking the way. I had to park at an angle to get around them. When I started walking up the sidewalk to the door, there were more polar bears of all ages (babies, middle-aged, and old ones). I finally opened my mother's door and there was a bear rug lying on the floor. My mother was in the kitchen washing the dishes and I yelled in, "Mother, what are you doing with all these bears?" She yelled back, "They were on sale." That was the end of the dream.

When the dreamer was asked to describe her feelings for her mother, her reply was brusque. She stated that her mother was deceased, that she never got along with the woman anyway, and that she felt "nothing" after she had died. The dream seemed to be suggesting otherwise, however. In fact, it appeared that the issue between the dreamer and her mother could no longer be avoided.

In the act of driving to her mother's house—representing her relationship with her mother, the situation itself, or the fact that this was something she is headed for—there is a message (mailman in the driveway) that the dreamer has to deal with. From a thematic approach, something appears to be blocking someone—whether it's the mailman in the driveway or the bears scattered about the yard and house. This blockade is interfering with direct communication between the dreamer and her feelings or between the dreamer and her mother or both.

A polar bear is found in extremely cold climates, filled with ice and snow. Ice and snow can be suggestive of "frozen emotion"—or feelings that have been suppressed and held inside. In addition, a polar bear is one of the most aggressive creatures in nature. Therefore the emotion that the dreamer is suppressing has to do with the anger and aggression that she does not want to deal with. Rather than going at the situation directly, the dreamer may need to address the problem from a different angle than she has tried previously.

The polar bears of all ages are probably symbolic of all the repressed anger that the dreamer has felt because of the relationship with her mother during the various stages of her own life (child, teenager, adult). The fact that the dreamer discovers a bear rug right under her feet could indicate that this situation can no longer be avoided because it is underfoot and directly in front of her. The mother washing the dishes is suggestive of a couple of possibilities. Just as the plates are being cleaned, the relationship the dreamer has been served all of her life may be in the process of cleansing and healing. Another possibility is that the frozen emotion (ice) is beginning to melt as the healing process begins. It is also possible that the deceased mother was working on trying to heal the situation from the other side. The bears being on sale might represent the fact that this situation is going to be easier to deal with than the dreamer images, or that the dreamer might find it advantageous to deal with the situation even though she is not conscious of her desire to heal the relationship.

In spite of the fact that the dreamer claimed to feel nothing for her mother, the dream instead suggested that she had tremendous feelings about the relationship and had been seriously hurt by her interactions with her mother throughout her life. She could no longer repress the issue or let it go unresolved. With this in mind, it might be a good idea for the dreamer to find a counselor or someone with whom she could work through the situation.

In addition to dreams for the body and dreams for the mind, each individual also experiences dreams for the soul. Sometimes these dreams deal with spiritual issues and concerns and on other occasions the consciousness of the individual can literally come in contact with higher spiritual realities, experiencing what Edgar Cayce called "visions" in the dream-state. Dreams at this level can also explore past lives and precognitive information because the dreamer's consciousness is no longer limited to the normal confines of consciousness.

Perhaps more common than visionary experiences are dreams that simply explore spiritual issues with which an individual has been concerned. In the first example, a reoccurring dream reflected a young man's search to find spiritual information that would be personally meaningful for him:

> *Dream of twenty-something-year-old man:*
> It is in the mountains. I find myself on a high ridge where a bunch of pickup trucks are parked. People are sitting in chairs in the back of their pickups, fishing. They cast their lines far into the sky and hook these enormous trout! After catching the fish, they haul the fighting, flapping fish down and net them. It is a very clear dream.

Being in the mountains can be suggestive of exploring higher levels of the mind or it might represent the higher levels of spirituality. Generally a pickup truck is seen as a very informal, comfortable, rugged, or manly form of transportation. This indicated the young man's own desire to find something appropriate for himself spiritually with which he could be comfortable. Casting lines into the sky can be associated with exploring various spiritual ideologies, beliefs, or thoughts and trying to "hook" one appropriate to the dreamer. The fighting and flapping fish might be suggestive of the dreamer's own struggle to come to terms with a personal belief system.

In another instance, a fifty-two-year-old woman raised in a very strict, conservative and religious home, "with lots of 'Thou shalt not's'," felt driven to discover a spiritual meaning in life, however, at the same time she often found herself struggling with the punishing God she had been brought up with. A dream seemed to portray both her personal search and her struggle to free herself from the past:

Dream of fifty-two-year-old woman:
It is a reoccurring dream about climbing attic steps. I am trying to get to the top but the fear of shadowy figures along my path always scares me back down. I try to make the journey over and over again. Finally, I am able to get to the attic and find the interior of a church. It has lots of pews, stained glass windows, and a pulpit down front.

The dreamer took the dream to mean that she had finally faced and overcome the issues that had been in the way of her experiencing a meaningful spiritual life. Once she found the church in the attic, her waking life was no longer troubled by thoughts of the fearful God with whom she had been raised.

In terms of other kinds of dreams for the soul, there are also dreams regarding past-life experiences. Although it is common for individuals to have past-life dreams, generally a past-life dream always has a present-day significance. In other words, individuals do not randomly dream about the past. A past-life dream can be triggered by any experience or relationship in the present that is similar to one that occurred in the past. In other words, past-life dreams occur if an individual is literally revisiting a relationship or an issue in the present or whenever an individual is experiencing a similar life cycle to one that occurred in the long ago past. When these dreams occur, the subconscious mind is essentially looking for a similar experience or relationship to bring to one's awareness information that might be helpful in facing it again.

Historical places, clothing, people or events in a dream can all be suggestive of a past-life experience. Foreign cultures, international locales, and seeing one's self appear as a different person, a different sex or with a different skin color might indicate the same thing. Whenever individuals dream repeatedly of a historical period or a culture, they can feel confident that their subconscious mind is drawing upon the images of a past-life experience as a means of relating present-day information.

A fifty-something-year-old man who felt strongly drawn to Egypt—although he had never been to the country—had a dream in which he saw some kind of a ceremony being performed before thousands of people:

Dream of fifty-something-year-old man:
There was a great host of people going out to dedicate a tomb, that was being builded or prepared for someone, and they had seven days of entertainment with all sorts of dancing, prayer being made, and songs. Just before the last service was to be carried, I saw someone climb to the top of this pyramid or cone-like thing, and clang a big sheet of metal of some kind, or brass. There were camels, beautiful drapes and hangings, and costumes of the period.

In real life a psychic had told the dreamer that he was entering a period in his life when he would be drawn to many of the people he had once known in Egypt. Apparently, many of the relationships that he had encountered in the past were presenting themselves in the present. With this in mind, it came as no surprise to the man when he suddenly found himself surrounded by friends and associates who felt a similar attraction to Egypt. In addition to the imagery possibly having its basis in a literal past-life experience, it could have also symbolized an initiation or some kind of ceremony, indicating that the dreamer was now experiencing a similar life cycle in the present to one he had once encountered in the past.

Sometimes past-life dreams can utilize more contemporary imagery, as in the case of nineteen-year-old girl who seemed to dream about a past-life connection with a young man who was a friend in the present:

Dream of nineteen-year-old girl:
It was night and I was on a white horse with Daniel, riding out to a garden. We got off the horse, walked around, and found a place in the garden where we could lay down and look up at the stars.

The next scene I remember is riding the same white horse with Daniel on the beach. We came upon these rocks, got off the horse, and sat down to watch the dolphins play in the ocean. In the dream, my hair was much longer than it really is, my skin was a darker tan and I was wearing some kind of a dress that I don't own. Daniel looked pretty much the same but his skin was also darker.

In real life, the young woman had begun to have romantic feelings about Daniel who was a classmate at school. The dream suggested to her that her feelings toward Daniel had their basis in the past and that the two of them needed to "finish what was started back then." Shortly after the dream, the two began having a romantic relationship.

Precognitive dreams occur in a variety of ways, providing the dreamer with additional insights, warnings, or even a preview of things to come. In the case of a forty-something-year-old man, a dream provided him with an accurate depiction of an accident at work but unfortunately he did not realize it until after the accident had already occurred:

Dream of forty-something-year-old man:
I saw one of my female coworkers, working on top of a pallet-rack, as we occasionally did. For some reason, she must have lost her balance and I was helpless as I watched her fall to the ground.

The next day, the man watched as the dream played out before his eyes. At one point in the day his coworker was working on the pallet and she suddenly fell about eight feet from the top of the rack. Thankfully, she received only minor injuries. However, the dreamer became convinced that the fall might have been averted had he warned his coworker about his experience beforehand.

On another occasion, a thirty-something-year-old businessman had a dream that seemed to indicate a change in his company's table of organization. His boss had left the company, making him one of the applicants in line for the job opening which would have meant a promotion. While waiting for the decision to be made, he had a dream:

> *Dream of thirty-something-year-old man:*
> I saw the table of organization on the company president's desk. As if somehow watching over his shoulder, I saw the president use a pencil eraser to erase the entire division that had once reported to my boss and separate it into two different departments. Using his pencil, he then connected one of the departments to an already existing division within the company and then he connected the other department to another division.

Within a week, the company announced that the departing division director would not be replaced. Instead, as a cost-savings measure, the company had decided to break apart the division and separate its function between existing divisions within the corporation. As a result, the dreamer retained his job but ended up reporting to another division director.

A thirty-something-year-old woman had a dream in which she saw herself communicating with deceased family members. Even in the dream, she realized that there was something unusual about the fact that one of her friends was also present for the occasion:

> *Dream of thirty-something-year-old woman:*
> I saw myself traveling to (what I knew to be) the "other side."
> I landed at a beautiful seaport and saw members of my

deceased family assembled. We gathered at a table as if for a meal and seemed to be having a good time. I sat next to the ones I was closest to. My grandfather gave me a letter to read but I don't remember what it said. I suddenly realized that Edwin, a good friend and neighbor, was also at the table. I was surprised and wondered why he was there. After I gave a speech about the importance of families the dream ended.

A short time after having the dream, Edwin was diagnosed with terminal cancer and died at a very young age. The woman realized that somehow she had previewed a gathering on the other side of deceased individuals she had loved.

In the final example, a forty-something-year-old mother of two grown sons had a visionary experience that helped her through a horrible family tragedy. On vacation with her husband and baby granddaughter, for some reason the woman had been experiencing difficulty sleeping. However, the night of the experience she slept soundly:

Dream of forty-something-year-old woman:
A friend of mine who I associate with spirituality came to me in a dream. She was dressed all in white and she told me that she wanted me to meditate on three things upon awakening: 1) Death is never an accident; 2) there are no coincidences; and, 3) only love is real.

When she awoke, she told her husband about the dream and reflected upon the three messages off and on all day. The experience made her feel in touch with God and she felt very much at peace. Even later that day when the call came from the emergency room in the hospital that her eldest son had been killed in a freak explosion and fire, she was not thrown into a state of shock. At the hospital she found herself comforting the nurses. Through the entire experience, she was never in a state of shock and she did not need a sedative. She was also not in denial, for she felt everything. However, somehow the dream experience had prepared her for her son's passing.

The night after her son's death, as she lay drifting between sleep and wakefulness, she smelled fire and smoke. Suddenly she felt the presence of her deceased son who reached down "and gave me one of his bear hugs." The experience reinforced her belief that death was not an accident, that there was no such thing as coincidence, and that only love was real.

What is universally true about the human condition is that everyone dreams and that each individual's dreams can deal with physical problems or concerns, emotional or psychological issues and even matters of the spirit or soul. Dreams are important because they can provide the dreamer with an analysis of every area of her or his life and an examination of additional insights, unresolved feelings, possible solutions, unexpressed aspirations, potential outcomes, and even possible past-life situations. Ultimately, these dreams are prompted by the subconscious mind as a means of providing help and assistance to individuals as they meet the demands and issues of everyday life. Because dreams are not limited to what we think we know, they possess an unlimited source of information there for the asking if we simply begin to work with them.

Chapter 6 Sample Dreams
See Appendix One for possible interpretations

Dream of forty-three-year-old woman:
(Background information: woman is interested in personal spiritual development and in discovering her personal mission in life.)

I dreamed I was driving home in my Jeep. In real life, to get to my house on the mountain I have to drive up a very steep hill for about a half-mile, then wind around the mountain. On the steep hill, there were several boulders—all perfectly round and smooth. They were scattered randomly. I continued to drive. As I reached the first boulder I cautiously peered around it, saw the way was clear and continued on to the next boulder. There were one or two other cars on the hill that were stopped and couldn't go any further. I managed to weave around all the obstacles by driving up to them slowly, looking for an open path, finding one and continuing to drive. Eventually, I reached the top of the hill.

Dream of twenty-something-year-old woman:
(Background information: young woman wants to return to college and focus on her career. Husband is opposed to the idea and wants her to stay home with the kids.)

I dreamed that I was walking along and noticed that a snake was biting my arm. I had to struggle to turn it loose of my arm. Later, as I was walking, I noticed that a snake (could have been the same one) was biting my ankle.

Dream of forty-something-year-old man:
(Background information: man complained of feeling tired, lethargic and was having trouble concentrating.)

I dreamed that I was crazy and having problems thinking. Some-

Chapter 6 Sample Dreams
See Appendix One for possible interpretations

how I was able to look inside my head. With my skull open, I could see all kinds of gears and wheels spinning around in their proper place, except for one. One of the wheels had stopped running altogether because a particle of dirt or trash had gotten stuck in it.

7

Unusual Dreams, Personal Guidance, and What It All Means

There are as many different kinds of dreams as there are individuals who experience them. Unfortunately, individuals do not often take the time to reflect upon their dreams immediately upon awakening so the symbols and images become fragmented, dissipated and soon forgotten—if they were ever even brought to mind at all. For some individuals, however, there are occasions when a dream is so unusual and so memorable that it is not easily shaken from consciousness. There are also dreams that are capable of being molded and shaped by the dreamer, as if the dreamer actually had input regarding the substance of her or his dream once it was underway. In fact, taken a step further, most individuals do not realize that it is even possible to shape the direction and subject matter of one's dreams before going to sleep, obtaining answers to every imaginable question in the process.

A reoccurring dream had begun to terrify a thirty-something-year-old woman. She was so frightened by it that she dreaded going to sleep, often awoke in the middle of the night in a panic, and frequently awakened her husband in the process. Even discussing the dream gave the woman a sense of fear and foreboding:

> *Dream of thirty-something-year-old woman:*
> The dream is that I am alone in my house. Although I am inside, I know that it is dusk and I begin to feel apprehensive. The apprehension grows as shadows are cast through the windows. I can't really see out, but the shadows come in. I begin looking for someone to help me but there is no one and for some reason I cannot leave the house. I begin to hear whirling sounds as if something enormous is approaching overhead, like a helicopter. The sounds grow louder until the roof begins to shake and the ceiling begins to fall in because of the noise and the vibration. I become more afraid as I see the beams of the roof and then the sky and I panic when I realize that an enormous spaceship has come to get me. The spaceship hovers just over my head, a door begins to open, and a hideous creature comes out of the craft into my house. The creature approaches me and I am frozen with fear. Immediately, he begins to grope and touch me, putting his long, clammy fingers everywhere. I know I am going to be examined and raped. I go to scream but cannot make a sound. I usually wake up in a panic.

As the woman related her dream, she became fearful, fidgety, and visibly uncomfortable. She stated that she had even begun to wonder whether or not she was being abducted by aliens. Obviously, the imagery seemed to suggest that something over which she had no control was overpowering her. The woman wondered aloud, "Why do I keep having a dream like this?"

It is not uncommon for individuals who have unresolved life experiences to have those very same issues repeatedly come up in their dreams. When it was explained to the dreamer that anything unresolved that is associated with fear, regret, emotional trauma, abuse, or loss will be revisited by the subconscious mind in the dream state, the dreamer began to cry. She quickly volunteered, "I know what it's about." She then began to tell a horrendous story about the sexual abuse she had suffered as a child at the hands of her father. Clearly the dream was reflecting those very same issues: the fact that the darkness of evening brought a child's feelings of apprehension, the fact that there did not seem to be anyone who could rescue her, the fact that something continuously overpowered the girl as she stared up helplessly, and so forth. After telling her story, the dreamer admitted that she had thought all of the issues surrounding her childhood ordeal had been worked through but as it was apparent they had not she agreed to seek out additional counseling.

Another frightening dream occasionally occurred in the experience of a twenty-year-old young man who was extremely busy with college and work. Because of his hectic schedule, oftentimes he did not get sufficient sleep. The dream generally happened in the afternoon on those few occasions when he had found the time to take a short nap.

Dream of twenty-year-old man:
I am lying on my bed. Even though my eyes are closed, I feel like I am awake and I am conscious of everything in the room. I can even "see" and "hear" but I am still in bed. Suddenly I start to feel a very strong pressure on my chest, arms, and legs as if someone or something is pushing me into the bed. I try to say something but my mouth won't open and I am unable to move my body. Sometimes I can hear someone out in the hallway—and if I check with that person later, he or she was really there—but I cannot call out. I feel totally paralyzed and I become afraid. It takes a while before I am back to normal and able to really get up.

Although the dream can have many variations, this kind of experience is relatively common. However, rather than being simply a dream, it may be more accurate to describe the episode as an "out of body" experience. It is an experience that sometimes occurs just before or just after sleep when an individual is still in the hypnagogic state.

According to Edgar Cayce, consciousness is not limited to the confines of the physical body. Therefore, during the process of dreaming it is possible for one's consciousness to "leave" the body, sometimes hovering just above it. When an experience like this occurs, what has happened is that the individual somehow becomes conscious while she or he is out of body—generally that individual can still "see," "hear," "rationalize," and on occasion even "smell." But because the individual is no longer in her or his physical body, that person has absolutely no control over it. Until the consciousness of the individual returns to the body, the person will remain "paralyzed." According to individuals who have repeatedly had this kind of experience, by focusing their awareness on their foreheads, beginning to pray, or continually trying to move a body part (such as a finger), the duration of the experience can be significantly shortened.

Another type of dream that seems to suggest consciousness is not limited to the physical body is the process of lucid dreaming. Simply stated, lucid dreaming occurs whenever an individual becomes conscious of dreaming while in the dream-state and finds that he or she can mold, shape, change and direct the content of the dream. Rather than simply wasting this type of dream, individuals instead have the opportunity to have a very meaningful and enlightening experience in consciousness if they only chose to make it so. With this in mind, individuals having a lucid dream may want to do something spiritual in the midst of the experience.

A somewhat humorous lucid dream experience occurred in the case of a twenty-three-year-old young man from a Christian background. According to the dreamer, he often found himself flying in dreams and shortly thereafter would become lucid. Generally, he used the experience to feel the exhilaration of flight or to travel to some locale where he had never been in waking life. When he heard about the possibility of expanding consciousness in the dream state, he decided to do something spiritual the next time he had a lucid dream. A short time later the following lucid experience occurred:

Dream of twenty-three-year-old man:
I was flying in the clouds like I have done before. Suddenly, I became aware of the fact that I was dreaming. I was about to go flying again when I remembered I wanted to do something spiritual. Instead of flying I stopped in the air, looked around at the sky and said aloud, "I want to speak with Jesus."

All at once a shaft of light tore through the sky and began drawing the shape of a door. When the door was complete, a very bright light began to shine on all four sides of the door and some streams of light began pouring out from under it. Slowly, the door started opening, causing the brightest light I have ever seen to begin pouring out.

As I watched this I started to become very afraid. The door kept opening and I started to worry. Before the door could open any further, I screamed, "I changed my mind, I changed my mind!"

The dreamer awoke, still very apprehensive about what he had just witnessed. If instead of panicking the young man had been brave enough to continue the dream, he might have had a truly remarkable experience.

It is not uncommon for individuals to dream about disaster or tragedy and then wonder what those dreams are all about or be confused as to why they had the dream in the first place. A nine-year-old girl had the following dream and still wondered years later what she was supposed to do about it:

Dream of nine-year-old girl:
Two weeks before the spaceship Challenger blew up I had a dream that it did. When I saw the plume of smoke from the explosion on the TV, it looked the same as the plume of smoke in my dream. I was only in the third grade at the time and the experience really scared me. When I saw it on TV I felt like I could have done something to prevent it, but who is going to believe a little kid saying that the Challenger is going to blow up. The strangest thing about it was that Christa, the school-

teacher aboard had the same first name as I do.

In addition to their parents, children oftentimes connect with their teachers. It was apparently that connection that enabled the dreamer to pick up on a tragedy before it happened. The connection was further heightened by the fact that the dreamer and the school-teacher/ astronaut had the same name. Certainly a nine-year-old child would have never been able to prevent the tragedy. The dream obviously occurred as a result of the dreamer's intuition and her own feelings of having a connection with Christa McAuliffe.

Another memorable dream occurred in the life of a fifty-something-year-old woman who related a dream that occurred before the Oklahoma City bombing. Because the dream seemed to preview the destruction of the nine-story Alfred P. Murrah Federal Building, she felt guilty, confused, and overwhelmed because she had not done anything about the experience prior to the tragedy:.

> *Dream of fifty-something-year-old woman:*
> I was in some kind of a daycare center that was in an office building at least six stories tall. I was watching the children playing and everything seemed to be fine when suddenly there was a tremendous explosion. The blast ripped through the room, causing the children to be thrown against the wall. As the bodies flew, I knew most of them were dead. I turned to look at my own injuries which seemed to be mostly cuts and scrapes on my arms.

The dream occurred several days before the bombing, causing the dreamer to feel intense guilt after the incident: "Maybe I could have prevented it or warned someone somehow," she explained. Even though the dreamer lived near Atlanta and the dream had not specified any location for the bombing or given any details about the building, she still felt responsible because of her inaction. This same sense of guilt can occur whenever individuals have a dream that they believe somehow accurately forecasts an event and but they have no idea what to do about it. Sometimes these dreams are of disasters such as plane crashes or earthquakes and on other occasions they deal with a crime such as murder, robbery, or assault. The dreamer finds her or himself wondering why she or he experienced the dream in the first place as well as what was supposed to have been done to prevent it.

In terms of what was supposed to have been done, a dreamer can only be expected to follow through on those things that he or she is capable of accomplishing. In other words, there is quite a big difference between warning a friend to watch his or her driving and trying to discover what cities in the country have daycare centers in buildings with more than six floors. Individuals do not experience dreams of this nature because they are necessarily supposed to do anything about them. (As an aside, however, a dream of this nature can always be seen as a call to prayer—the dreamer praying for the situation and all those concerned.) Instead it occurs because something about the dreamer has become attuned to the situation in question. This attunement can occur because the dreamer has a heightened intuitive perception but generally it occurs because there is something about the situation that is somehow in sync with activities in the dreamer's own life. In other words, the innate psychic talent of the dreamer's subconscious mind looks for an external event to bring to conscious awareness the fact that something thematically similar is occurring in the dreamer's own life. To be sure, the dream and the external event are often more dramatic than the waking life experience but if they were not it is unlikely the dream would be recalled by the dreamer.

In terms of the dream that occurred prior to the Oklahoma City bombing, the dreamer stated that she was a schoolteacher who had served nearly thirty-years in elementary school education and was truly "burned out." Although part of her loved teaching and young children, she no longer felt strong enough to deal with the type and manner of children that were now a part of her classroom. "Children aren't the same as they used to be," she said, "and I'm just too old to deal with it." The woman also admitted her own sadness at having to consider retirement because for a long while she had truly loved her work.

The dreamer explained that after hearing about the bombing, she truly empathized with the children who had been killed and felt guilty that she could do nothing to help them. Upon further reflection, the woman admitted that she had the very same feelings about her current class of students: she empathized with them but felt guilty that she could not help them (or teach them) in the way they apparently needed to be reached. She felt totally ineffective in dealing with them, but she still felt guilty about leaving. Apparently that inability to help and the guilt that transpired because of her inability to help was the psychic thruway that enabled her to dream about the bombing.

Another precognitive dream that might have pertained to a major disaster occurred two days before the tsunami in Indonesia. A thirty-something-year-old woman and her daughter were living in Asia at the time:

> *Dream of thirty-something-year-old woman:*
> Two days before the earthquake and tsunami I had a dream, which disturbed me badly. It was all about my daughter and water; she is five. I saw her drowning inside the pool and I stretched out my hand to pull her up and saved her. I was standing nearby and the others who were inside the pool did not see her drowning. When I woke up it was difficult to think about the dream because of seeing suffering, but I was happy because I had saved her life. What does this mean?

Whether or not others would see the dream as a precognitive indicator of the tsunami, the dreamer was certainly convinced of the connection. In either event, the dream occurred not because of an upcoming tsunami but because the dream was personally relevant to the dreamer and her daughter. In other words, which is more likely: that the subconscious mind would randomly tap into global events over which the dreamer has no control; or, that somehow the subconscious mind is able to see external events and activities that are somehow relevant and thematically connected to activities occurring within the dreamer's own life?

In all likelihood, the dream was suggesting that there was an emotional situation occurring in the child's life (or in the dreamer's relationship to her daughter) and it was up to the dreamer to try and "save" she and her daughter from being overwhelmed by the experience..

Another "tragedy" dream occurred in the experience of a forty-something-year-old businessman who wondered whether or not his repetitive dream was a psychic premonition of upcoming terrorist attacks:

> *Dream of forty-something-year-old businessman:*
> I dreamed that I was in New York City, but I did not recognize it at all. I saw the Twin Towers and they were on fire again. Everyone was screaming but I kept moving towards the towers. I wanted to be near them as they fell. When they started to fall I tried to run to a basement type room with my friend and got only to the door. When I looked at myself, I wasn't covered in any debris, ash, or anything. Afterwards, the twin towers were still standing, and they kept collapsing, but were still there when I looked at them. On the fourth time collapsing, they were both gone.

When describing the dream, it was obvious that the businessman associated the dream with events outside himself over which he had no control. However, in further discussion, the dreamer admitted that at one time he had viewed the Twin Towers as essentially an icon of business success. In other words, if your office was in the Twin Towers, you were successful. He went on to elaborate that his company was experiencing a number of challenges due to changes in the market and the economy and that the company was currently going through another series of layoffs, as it had done on a number of occasions.

From this perspective, the dream is indicating the series of "tragedies" within the businessman's own company. Obviously, the dreamer is concerned about the future of his own employment. However, note in the dream: "When I looked at myself, I wasn't covered in any debris, ash, or anything," suggesting that the dreamer is not going to experience a layoff at this point in time. That said, however, the overall future of the company remains in doubt as the dreams ends with the office buildings collapsing for the fourth and final time until they are gone. It is likely that the dream is suggesting that the dreamer may need to begin looking for another source of employment for his long-term future.

Most individuals who work with their dreams would state that it is possible to get insightful and helpful guidance by working with dream interpretation. Unusual dreams can also provide guidance. The following two examples illustrate this point. The first is the dream of a young woman who averted a potential accident for one of her children and the second is that of a middle-age man who was finally able to break free from a dependent relationship.

According to the woman, when she became pregnant with her second child she told her two-and-a-half-year-old daughter, "Since the baby is going to sleep in your crib, you're now old enough to have a big bed." Shortly thereafter the woman and her husband purchased a full-size bed for their daughter and placed it up against her bedroom wall. That night she had a dream:

> *Dream of twenty-five-year-old woman:*
> The first night my daughter slept in her "big bed," my husband and I placed chairs against the open side of the bed in order to keep her from falling to the floor. That night when I was asleep I dreamed that she was calling for me. For some reason, she was in trouble. I immediately awakened and went to check on her.

When the woman entered her daughter's room, she found that the child had rolled out of the bed and was precariously hanging between the two chairs, still very much asleep. The dream had simply been a warning to go and help the child.

In the case of a middle-aged man, his wife of nearly twenty years had surprised him one day with the news that she no longer loved him and wanted a divorce. In addition to spending twenty years together, they were partners in business. He had also supported her emotionally and financially while she earned two degrees and eventually procured a very lucrative job. Just as the couple's marriage, future and financial wherewithal seemed better than ever, the wife requested a divorce. According to the husband, "I was devastated. I couldn't sleep and I couldn't eat. This was the closest I ever came to a nervous breakdown." Because of his depression and his emotional state, over the next few months he lost thirty-five pounds.

Even though his marriage had been far from perfect, he still wanted his wife back. His friends tried to help him through the emotional turmoil as best they could. Some even told him that he would probably look back on his divorce as a blessing. After all, there had been a number of things he had wanted to change about his life and now he had the perfect opportunity to start over. Still, the man was convinced that he needed to save his marriage. One night he gradually awoke from a dream with the awareness that getting back together with his wife would not change anything. While still in the hypnagogic state he had an unusual experience:

Dream of middle-aged man:
I knew that I was at a crossroads. It was a point of choosing. I seemed to be viewing things from a superconscious state. I was completely unemotional in this state and viewed the choices set before me. The story of "the Lady" or "the Tiger" seemed to be the choice. If I chose "the Lady" I was choosing "Lady Luck," taking my chances with what life had to offer and being free to do God's work. I knew this choice meant financial prosperity. It also meant joy and happiness.

However, if I chose "the Tiger," meaning my wife, it would mean many years of counseling and of working things out. An insight came to me that hanging on to my wife was hanging on to ego.

When the man completely awakened he no longer had any emotion about his wife's decision and knew that divorce was truly the best thing for him.

A very unusual example of dream guidance having to do with the Edgar Cayce information occurred many decades after Cayce's death. A middle-aged woman in New Zealand had been having a series of health problems. In addition to experiencing dizziness and fainting spells, she felt pain in her side and often complained of problems with her liver, kidneys, and bladder. Although her doctor had frequently examined her, the cause of her condition was never determined. Instead, the doctor began treating her for low blood sugar and an imbalance of red and white blood cells. Her symptoms persisted and she felt miserable. Finally, a friend suggested that she pray for guidance, which she did. One night she had a dream in which she saw herself looking at one of Edgar Cayce's readings. She could see that the case history number from the Cayce readings was number 1880.

She told friends about her dream and not knowing what else to do, they wrote Edgar Cayce's A.R.E. (www.EdgarCayce.org) in Virginia Beach, Virginia, requesting a copy of reading number 1880 for themselves. When several weeks passed and the copy finally arrived she was amazed to find that the individual who had requested the reading in 1939 had complained of the very same symptoms that she was experiencing in the present! In the 1939 case, Edgar Cayce told the individual that the cause of the problem was because of mercury poisoning. He then went on to outline a regimen of treatment.

After reading the information, the woman contacted her mother and asked if there had ever been a childhood incident in which she had been exposed to mercury. Surprised, her mother told her that as a child she had bitten off the end of a thermometer and swallowed its contents. Armed with this information, the dreamer went to her doctor and asked to have a test done for mercury poisoning. Unfortunately, the doctor did not respond favorably to the idea and refused to do it. Undaunted, the woman found another doctor who agreed to perform the test. It turned out that the test was positive. Although the second doctor did not believe that the mercury could be from the incident with the thermometer so many years in the past, he did think that it could have been the residual result of some of the medications she had been taking. Nonetheless, the woman began following the treatment that had been outlined in the Cayce reading and within a few months all of her previous symptoms had disappeared.

Individuals are often surprised to learn that rather than simply being receptive to dream guidance, they can also be proactive in obtaining it. But the truth of the matter is that it is possible to access the insights from one's subconscious mind simply by asking. All this entails is writing out a question just before going to bed, reading it once or twice before turning out the lights and drifting off to sleep, and then simply allowing one's own dreams to provide insights into virtually anything. The following are examples of this simple approach.

An individual who had been studying spiritual philosophies for a number of years wrote out the question, "What do I need to work on spiritually?" That night he had a dream:

> *Dream of middle-aged man:*
> I was walking next to some old buildings in a quaint little town. All at once I realized I was walking next to an individual that I considered to be very spiritual. I stopped, looked up at the person and asked, "So how am I doing?" as if to inquire about my spiritual progress. He looked at me, pulled his glasses down his nose a little, peered over the lenses and said, "Well, you know, you do spend more time watching TV then you do meditating."

The dreamer took the dream to mean that he needed to spend less time studying and reading about spiritual things and more time meditating and applying what he had been reading.

In another example, a middle-aged woman who asked about whether or not she should take a job that she had been offered had the following dream:

> *Dream of middle-aged woman:*
> I dreamed that I was looking at a shiny new car in the show room on a car lot. It was beautiful and I decided that I wanted it. I tried to get into the car but there was no key. When I finally found a salesperson with the key, the car wouldn't start. When the car was fixed and finally started, I couldn't get the car in gear—the car rolled backwards off of its platform in the showroom, crashing through the showroom window and into

> the parking lot. I quickly got out of the car and suddenly the hood opened and the engine rose out of the car and started heading towards me. I ran off in a panic.

Because of the dream, the dreamer did not take the job. She associated the new job with the shiny new car and decided that there were all kinds of unforeseen problems with the job that would cause her to wish that she hadn't taken it.

On another occasion, a twenty-something-year-old man who was tired of his current place of employment and was looking for a new job wrote out the question, "When will I get a new job?" After attempting the process for two nights, he had a memorable dream:

> *Dream of twenty-something-year-old man:*
> I am a waiter—like back when I was in college. I am standing next to my side station, where they keep the plates, glasses, and silverware, busily cleaning up my section. I know that I have to get everything in order because I will be starting a new job in six weeks. That was the end of the dream.

Taking the information at face value, the dreamer began putting all of his work affairs in order. He got caught up on tasks he had been neglecting, wrote out the new procedures for some of the functions he had changed while in the position, and simply "waited" to see what job might present itself. Three weeks after having the dream, the individual came across a new position that appealed to him. Although he had no previous experience in the line of work, he applied for it anyway. Several people had also applied for the job but he was not discouraged. He passed through the interview with flying colors, was offered the job, and gave two weeks notice at his old position. As had been indicated, he started his new job six weeks after having had the dream!

Another individual wanting to know why he was having certain challenging experiences in his life wrote out the question on a piece of paper, "What is the connection between this experience and my soul's purpose?" That night he had a dream:

Dream of middle-aged man:
I dreamed I was sitting at the breakfast table with my wife.
Suddenly, I notice a piece of paper sticking out of my pocket.
I reach down, open it up and see that it has one word written
on it: "enlightenment."

The dreamer took it to mean that his challenges were actually learning experiences, somehow helping him to become a better person by his having gone through them.

A final example of someone asking a question and getting an answer occurred in the case of a thirty-something-year-old woman whose three-year-old daughter, Terry, had been killed in a car accident. Depressed and completely devastated, the woman was uncertain about her beliefs in an afterlife. Friends had told her about the possibility of getting answers to any question in the dream state, so she wrote out the question: "How is Terry doing?" one night before going to sleep. That night she had a dream:

Dream of thirty-something-year-old woman:
I went to the cemetery and to the grave where Terry was
buried. When I got there, I saw Terry sitting all by herself on
top of the grave with a birthday cake and some lit candles. She
looked up at me, smiled and said, "Don't worry mommy, I'm
okay . . . I'm okay." I started crying, which woke me up.

She told her friends about the dream and then added: "It doesn't make any sense! Terry is not okay, she's dead!"

After hearing the dream, her friends explained that although her daughter was no longer physical, she was still very much alive. Although in the spirit world or on the other side, it appears that real communication had actually taken place between the two of them and the child was trying to reassure her mother.

Dreams are much more than fantasy, make believe, or the imaginative wondering of one's consciousness. They are more than simply the nighttime receptacle of an individual's thoughts, issues, experiences and concerns played out against the background of subconscious symbols and images. They are an exploration into the deepest recesses of our mind, giving individuals insights into repressed issues and desires, exploring current events and relationships, supplying them with practical guidance and straightforward advice, and providing a glimpse of the future or even alternative states of consciousness. Since the wealth of potential guidance and direction available in the sleep-state is apparently limitless, it is too bad that those same subconscious insights are not accessible by an individual during waking consciousness.

Or are they?

Dream of forty-something-year-old woman:

(Background information: Woman works at a bank in Norfolk, Virginia.)

I saw Norfolk, Virginia from the air. I could see the naval shipyard and downtown. Suddenly a missile descended from the sky and struck the ground near the waterside. Before anyone could realize what had happened, the city was annihilated and an enormous mushroom cloud rose high up into air.

Dream of thirty-year-old man:

(Background information: Grandfather with whom he was close died six weeks earlier.)

A few weeks after my Grandfather died, I kept have a reoccurring dream about him. In the dream there was some kind of a large family gathering like Thanksgiving. Everyone was gathering around the table in the kitchen for dinner. I happened to look through the door that led into the living room and saw my Grandfather who I knew was dead, sitting on the couch all by himself. I was the only one who could see him. I went and sat by him on the couch and started talking with him.

My grandfather told me that he was all right and doing just fine. He also thanked me and stated that he had really enjoyed being my grandfather. He gave me a hug and we talked some more. The experience was very uplifting and yet the whole time the rest of my family remained completely oblivious to my grandfather's presence and just went on about their dinner together.

Dream of sixty-something-year-old man:

(Background information: Individual wrote out the question, "What do I need to work on spiritually?" before going to sleep.)

Chapter 7 Sample Dreams
See Appendix One for possible interpretations

I dreamed that I was in the army (I have never been in the army) and I was some kind of a drill sergeant doing important paperwork. My desk was filled with important papers and things that were scheduled — everything was neatly organized and in it's proper place. Suddenly a younger man came into my office unannounced. He was singing and dancing and appeared to be having a very good time with himself. To my surprise, he jumped up on top of my desk and started tap dancing all over my paperwork. Everything that I had neatly organized was in disarray. After making a thorough mess, the man continued to sing and dance and danced right out of my office. Immediately, I picked up the phone and called security and yelled into the received, "I want that man arrested, and I want to know who he is!" I slammed the phone down, very angry for the interruption. Suddenly, security came into my office bringing the man who had caused the disruption. They announced that they had caught him and that he was "the company clown."

8

Conscious Dreamplay: Obtaining Personal Guidance and Intuition in the Waking State

Individuals are much more aware of themselves, their surroundings, and their challenges, skills and weaknesses then they may be consciously aware. Like a complicated radar system, the human mind is constantly collecting data and information that can be drawn upon in any situation at any time. To be sure, most of this acquired information is never brought to conscious awareness. Instead it remains within the subconscious and becomes the basis for such things as feelings, hunches, insights, and even intuition. Although the human mind utilizes, at least subconsciously, all of the information coming to it, some studies have suggested that of all the data collected by an individual's mind, less than five percent ever truly becomes conscious.

This might sound low but how often do we become cognizant of everything in our surroundings? How often do we hear the sounds of our heating and air conditioning systems? Do we always feel the touch of our clothing against our skin or do we have to move our awareness in that direction? Do we ever become aware of the sounds of breathing made by someone who is standing or sitting near us? Do we become conscious of the feeling of the seat upon which we are sitting, the weight of our glasses upon our nose or the fit of our shoes against our feet? How often do we drive to work and then have no conscious knowledge of the trip that actually took us there? Do we ever even hear the rhythmic sounds of the tires beneath our vehicles? Most often, all of this information is observed by the mind but never comes into conscious awareness. The question we might ask is "What happens to it?" The answer is that all of the data, information, and sense perceptions that are acquired by the mind become stored in the subconscious. It is for this reason that individuals who witness a crime scene are often able to remember more details under hypnosis then they might have recalled consciously. No information is ever forgotten. It is just stored in a place we do not normally know how to access.

In addition to its seemingly limitless storage capacity, the subconscious mind is also a primary facilitator of personal intuition. Because consciousness at this level is not limited by physicality, there are no boundaries to block personal awareness. Things we often refer to as "hunches," "gut feelings," or some kind of special "knowing" can all originate at this level. In this same manner, professional intuitives are somehow able to tap the resources of their subconscious mind and provide answers to questions of which they had no consciousness knowledge.

Because of the wealth of information stored within the subconscious mind, no wonder dreams can provide an abundance of insight, guidance and personal direction. But what if this information was not limited to the sleep-state? What if these insights were not just available to professional intuitives but to regular individuals in waking life? What if an individual could somehow bypass the limitations of her or his conscious mind and access information directly from the subconscious? To be sure, the information would be in the form of symbols, the language of the brain, but could it be accessed and would it be helpful?

This question has led a number of individuals to develop various approaches to something called "intuitive imagery," "creative imagery," a "psychic game," or simply the "imagination game."[3] Essentially, the various approaches of this game simply entail creating a real question that the individual desires answers or insights to, providing the conscious mind with a decoy focus, and then accessing valid symbolic insights regarding the real question from the subconscious mind of the individual doing the imagining. Because the end result of the process is very much like a dream that needs to be interpreted, we might call the process "Conscious Dreamplay."

This game has countless variations and can be played alone or with others. Just like a dream, it can provide insights into an individual's life, work, relationships, challenges and potential future. The actual process is simply to become relaxed and then to begin imagining whatever the conscious mind has been asked to focus upon. (A sample relaxation exercise can be found toward the end of this chapter.) For ease of explanation, what follows is one woman's experience with the process at a workshop:

> *Dreamplay experience of fifty-something-year-old woman:*
> A fifty-something-year-old woman wanted to know if the time had come to leave her present employer. She wrote out the question, "Is it time to leave my job?" on a small piece of paper. She folded it so that no one could see the question and handed it to another member of the conference. Her question became the "real" question to which she wanted her partner's subconscious mind to provide insights.
>
> When everyone else had written their question, folded it so that no one could see it, and traded the question with a partner, everyone was taken through a short relaxation exercise and then asked to imagine the following:

---

[3]Proponents of intuitive imagery include: Magaly del Carmen Rodriguez, consultant to *Fortune 100* companies, and her work with creative imaging; Annie Gottlieb and Slobodan D. Pesie, authors of *The Cube . . . Keep the Secret;* and, John B. Pehrson and Susan E. Mehrtens, authors of *Intuitive Imagery: A Resource at Work.*

1) *"See a scene, a place of any kind, it can be a scene that you make up or one that truly exists—what do you see?"* This became the question for the conscious mind to focus upon. What occurs in the process is that the subconscious (the place where symbols arise) will provide a symbol that answers the real question.

2) Next, participants were told: *"Meet someone wonderful, who do you see? How do you feel about this person?"*

3) Finally, after a few moments, participants were told to imagine: *"This person has something to give you, what is it?*

After the three statements had been provided, individuals were asked to write down what they had seen for each of the questions on the piece of paper they were holding: 1) where was the scene; 2) who was the wonderful person; and, 3) what were you given.

One at a time, participants unfolded their questions and tried to interpret the images they had seen in relationship to their partner's question. For example, the partner of the fifty-something-year-old woman who had asked about her job had seen the place, Quito, Ecuador, met the person, Walt Disney, and had been handed Walt's watch. In the process of interpreting these images, the partner stated that he associated Quito, Ecuador, as the location where the equator had been measured. In Quito, there is a place where an individual can stand with one foot in the Southern Hemisphere and the other in the Northern Hemisphere. While discussing this fact, the woman asking about her job admitted that she often felt as though she had her "feet in two different worlds" (e.g. I should leave my job; I should stay).

The partner felt that Walt Disney was suggestive of "creativity and imagination." Both of these elements were lacking in the woman's present job, prompting her to seek new employment. She admitted that she felt like she was working on an "assembly line with no creativity." She obviously did not feel that her talents and abilities were being put to use. The symbolism of the watch appeared obvious as a symbol for time. In response to the woman's original question, "Is it time to leave my job?" the answer was, "It's time!" Another interesting insight occurred when both the woman and her partner realized what the first four letters of Quito spelled: Q—U—I—T. Obviously, the conscious dreamplay game suggested that it was time to find a new job. All of the above insights prove especially amazing when it is remembered that the woman's partner had no knowledge of the real question!

In terms of step-by-step instructions, the process for playing the psychic game with others is simply as follows:

Conscious Dreamplay with Others

1) Formulate a question you would like an answer to. Write out the real question so that only you can see it. You can ask it anyway you wish, but a question phrased, "What is the energy (or possibilities) surrounding the new job offer?" will be easier to interpret than "If I get the new job, will I like it and will it allow me to utilize my talents?"

2) Create a decoy question that the conscious mind of the "imaginer" (the person trying to visualize the image) can focus upon. This question should be something easy to imagine, such as "See a package," "See a structure," "See a person," "See a painting," "See a movie," "See a scene," etc. This question becomes the "decoy question" receiving the attention of the conscious mind of the individual doing the imagining. Because intuition originates at the subconscious, that same individual's subconscious mind will be tuning into the real question, providing symbols and images that correspond to it.

So in the case of the real question, "What is the energy surrounding the new job offer?" You might plan to ask the individual doing the imagining a decoy question such as "See a structure . . . what do you see?" As the game progresses, you can add additional decoy questions for greater insights into the real situation. Examples are as follows: "See a structure . . . what do you see?" "Something is going on inside the structure, what is it?" "How do you feel about this structure and what you see?" "If you could rate this picture from one to ten (ten being the best), how would you rate it?" etc. All of these addi-

tional images can be interpreted in relationship to the real question
after the conscious dreamplay experience has been completed.

3) After the conscious dreamplay imagination questions have been
asked, it is time to work with your partner to interpret any images
received against the real question.

On another occasion, a twenty-something-year-old woman wanted
to know if a job prospect she had been told about was worth pursuing. Using the same decoy questions that involved seeing a scene,
seeing a person, and being given something, what follows is her experience with the exercise:

> *Dreamplay experience of twenty-something-year-old woman:*
> I wrote out the question, "Is the job in Houston worth looking
> into?" I folded my piece of paper and handed it to my partner,
> who had no idea what I was asking. After the imagination
> exercise, my partner told me that she had seen a scene in
> which two ornate double doors opened onto a beautiful
> garden. The person she met was an old boyfriend that she had
> broken up with a long time ago and he handed her a ring.
>
> In interpreting the images, my partner and I decided that
> the double doors indicated that the job was worth pursuing.
> The doorway meant that this job could be the doorway to
> some beautiful experience, where I'll be able to use my
> talents, indicated by the garden. After discussing it for a little
> while, she told me that she had really been attracted to this
> boyfriend but he had never wanted to make a commitment to
> her so they had broken up. We decided that since the boy-
> friend in her image had offered her a ring, it symbolized one
> or two possibilities. Either this job will be ideally suited for me,
> like a marriage, or not only will I really like the job but it might
> lead to a new relationship for me.
>
> I think the job is definitely worth pursuing!

A forty-something-year-old employer in the travel business used
another variation of the conscious dreamplay exercise when a prob-

lem occurred at work. Vicki, one of his travel agents, came into his office expressing concern that Darlene, the twenty-two-year-old staff person assigned to accompany the tour to Egypt, had suddenly been forbidden to go on the tour by her father. Apparently Darlene's father was concerned about political events in the country. Since the tour was scheduled to leave in four days, the employer had a problem. Who was he going to send on the tour? His own schedule did not allow for a last minute tour of such duration. As a result, without explaining anything more to Vicki, he told her that he wanted to play an "imagination game" to help solve the problem. What follows is a discussion of the conscious dreamplay game that he used:

Dreamplay experience of forty-something-year-old employer:
I told Vicki that we should play an "imagination game" to see if we could come up with the answer to the problem. I instructed her to sit down, close her eyes, and take a deep breath so that she could begin to relax. I encouraged her simply to become relaxed.

While she was relaxing, I wrote out my real question at the top of my page, "Who is going to Egypt?" Logically, I thought that there were only three choices. Since I couldn't go, the options were Darlene, Vicki, or Angela, another woman in the office. I figured that I might be able to call Darlene's father and convince him that the trip was safe. Another option was Vicki, who had a lot of previous experience traveling on very short notice. The final logical choice was Angela, who had told me several times that one day she wanted to see the pyramids.

On my piece of paper beneath my real question, I decided to draw three doors, one right next to the other. Beneath each of the doors I wrote a name: Darlene, Vicki, and Angela, in that order.

When Vicki was relaxed, I told her, "I want you to see three doors." I waited for a moment and then said, "Describe the first door to me." The *real* question I was thinking is, "How about sending Darlene to Egypt?"

Vicki explained that she could see a wooden door that was

bolted shut with an enormous chain across it. I asked her to try and open the door and see what was behind it, and she replied, "The room is empty. There's nothing there."

Next, I asked her to see the third door, to open it, and to describe what was behind it. The *real* question I was thinking is, "How about sending Angela to Egypt?" She said, "I see a very attractive door. It's a very rich looking color, like royal purple. I really like this door. Behind it I can see a rolling countryside. There are beautiful trees and meadows." When I asked her to rate it from one to ten, the rating she gave the image was a seven.

Finally, I asked her to describe the middle door and what was behind it. The <u>real</u> question I was thinking is, "How about sending Vicki to Egypt?" She replied, "The door is the color of alabaster, like an old column in a temple. Behind it I can see brilliant sunlight, beautiful palm trees, and stretches and stretches of sand. The rating I give it is a nine-and-a-half."

Since the employer associated the first door that was locked and had nothing behind it to Darlene, he decided that the imagery was suggesting that Darlene's father had made up his mind (it was locked) and there was "nothing" the employer could say to get him to change it. Although the third door, associated with Angela, appeared very attractive at first, it was not as impressive as the center door, corresponding to Vicki. The imagery seemed to suggest that is was best to send Vicki to Egypt. Because of the experience, the employer decided that Vicki was the one to accompany the tour. As a result of the exercise, Vicki went to Egypt with the tour and she and the group had a wonderful experience.

Interestingly enough, back home halfway through the tour, Angela's mother was taken unexpectedly to the hospital for emergency open-heart surgery. The employer decided that was the reason why it was more attractive for Vicki to go to Egypt rather than Angela. Somehow Vicki's subconscious mind had known that Angela would need to remain behind to be with and help her mother.

It is also possible to play the conscious dreamplay exercise alone.

Since the questioner and the individual doing the imagining are the same, the conscious mind has to be given several decoy questions so that it does not impose its feelings, thoughts, and desires on any symbolism for the real question. One possible approach to playing the game by one's self is as follows:

Conscious Dreamplay with Self

1) Formulate a question you would like an answer to. Place three 5 x 8 cards (or identical pieces of paper) on the table in front of you. On one of the cards write out the real question for which you are interested in receiving insights. Because part of the process is not allowing the conscious mind to know what the real question is, on each of the other two cards write out an additional question. Additional questions can be things that you really want an answer to, or simple questions such as, "What is the energy surrounding this weekend?" "How will I feel about this particular movie?" etc. When each of the cards has a question written on it, fold them or turn them all upside down so that you are no longer able to see what question is on which card. Mix all of the cards on top of the table so that you don't know where any question has ended up.

2) Now that each card has a question, create a decoy question that your conscious mind can focus upon. As when doing this exercise with others, this question should be something easy to imagine, such as "See a door," "See a structure," "See a person," "See a package," "See a movie," "See a house," etc. This question becomes the "focus question" receiving your conscious attention. Your subconscious mind will be able to tune into the hidden real question, providing symbols and images that correspond to it.

Place your hand on one of the cards and begin to focus on the decoy question. During the process you can add additional decoy questions for greater insights into the real situation. Examples are as follows: "See a person . . . who do you see?" "This person has just finished a particular project, what is it?" "If this person could give you a message, what would it be?" "If you could rate this picture from one to ten (ten being the best), how would you rate it?" and so forth.

3) When you have completed the imagination experience for one card, write down all of the images you saw on the back of that card. Move on to the next card, repeating the imagination game for each of the cards. [Note: you can ask the same question for each card, e.g. "See a person," or a completely different question for each card; e.g. 1) "See a person," 2) "See a structure," 3) "Open a package."] Do not turn over any of the cards until you have completed this process for each of your questions, one real question and two phony questions.

4) After the conscious dreamplay imagination experience is complete for all three cards, it is time to interpret each of the images received against the questions written on the other side of the card.

Using the above exercise, a thirty-something-year-old woman wanted to know about her job prospects. Currently a part-time consultant, she was in need of a larger income and had started looking for full-time work. She wrote out three questions on the back of three different cards. Although we could certainly interpret the imagery associated with each of her three questions, two of them were relatively unimportant. The real question she wanted answered was "What are the chances of my getting a new job soon?" This was her experience:

> *Dreamplay experience of thirty-something-year-old woman:*
> My real question was "What are the chances of my getting a new job soon?" I wrote out two other questions having to do with my week and my family. Afterwards, I turned each of the cards over, shuffled them in front of me, relaxed, and closed me eyes.
>   I decided to imagine seeing someone for each of the cards. One at a time, I imagined seeing an individual, describing that person, sensing how I felt about that individual, and having the person give me something. When the experience was over, I went through and tried to interpret each of the images.

> The image that corresponded with my real question was Mr.
> Magoo. I saw Mr. Magoo standing and squinting unable to see
> in front of him. I felt like I really liked him even thought he was
> not able to clearly see me. When I imagined him giving me
> something, it turned out to be a big sack of money. I rated the
> image an eight.

After the experience, the woman decided that the picture of Mr.
Magoo suggested that there was something right in front of her but
she was unable to see it. That something was going to become very
lucrative (sack of money) and she was really going to like it (rating =
eight). As a result of the image, she tried to put her worries to rest and
to instead keep her "eyes open." A few weeks after the imagination
experience, one of the companies that she had been a consultant for
called her and offered her a full-time job. The money was good, even
more than she had been looking for. Apparently the job had been open
for quite some time but neither the employer nor the woman had been
able to immediately "see" that she had been a perfect fit for the position.

On another occasion, a thirty-something-year-old man was trying
to decide whether or not the purchase of a particular stock would be a
good investment. As in the preceding example, he wrote out three
questions, the real one dealing with the stock purchase. He decided to
"See a building" as his decoy question and had the following experience:

> *Dreamplay experience of thirty-something-year-old man:*
> My question was ""Is _____ stock a good investment for
> me at this time?" I wrote this question on one card and two
> additional questions on two different cards. I turned all the
> cards over and rearranged their order so that I would not know
> where any of the questions were.
>
> I imagined that I could "See a building" for each of the
> cards. My secondary decoy question was "Something is occur-
> ring in the building what is it?" When the imagination part of
> the game was complete and I had written some notes about
> my visualization on the back of each card, I turned all of the
> cards face up.

> On my real question, the building I had seen was the World Trade Center, which I associate with business success. [Note: someone who associated the World Trade Center with a disaster or tragedy would obviously have an entirely different interpretation of this image.] The activity that was occurring inside the building was a big party, involving hundreds of employees within the building. I could see balloons and streamers; some of the employees even had noisemakers like a New Year's Eve party. It was a real celebration.
>
> I decided that the image was showing me that the stock would be met with a great deal of success and that I would truly celebrate my having purchased it. I went ahead and bought the stock.

The conscious dreamplay exercise can be played with any number of variations. For example, one variation is to have several individuals sitting around a table and on identical cards or pieces of paper writing out their real questions. The pieces of paper are then folded (so that no one can see the real questions), collected, and shuffled. Each person around the table then draws one of the papers without looking at the question. It does not matter if an individual gets her or his question, because the consciousness mind will not know and the subconscious mind will be able to access appropriate insights regardless of which question is being answered.

After each individual has drawn a question, one member of the group can ask a series of generic decoy questions for everyone. "See a place," "Meet someone," "See a painting," "Describe a scene," etc., are all examples of questions that might begin the process. As before, additional decoy questions can be asked to acquire further insights into the real question. Rather than having one person ask the decoy questions, another option is to have each individual think of a series of decoy questions to ask him or herself. Regardless of which approach is used, when the exercise is over, each individual will take turns reading the real question she or he drew aloud. After reading the question, the individual will then discuss what was seen in response to the decoy question. Afterwards, everyone around the table can work together to interpret the imagined images in terms of the real question.

One example of playing the conscious dreamplay game in a group is the case of a fifty-something-year-old woman who wanted to inquire about her father's health. The father had been widowed and was living alone but was in relatively good health. However, recently he had been talking about his desire to die and rejoin his wife. One fall, when the woman was with some friends, the four of them decided to play the imagination game. She wrote out the question, "How much longer will my father be with me?" The questions were then shuffled and each person drew one. This was her experience:

Dreamplay experience of fifty-something-year-old woman:
I did not know whose question I had drawn, but the first thing we imagined as a group was, "See a painting." The painting was supposed to give us insights into what the real question was all about. All at once, I saw a painting of a beautiful Christmas tree with lights. In order to discover some additional insights into the question, we each imagined that we 'snapped' our fingers and watched what happened to the painting. Suddenly, the Christmas tree became real and was covered in brilliant white lights. The next image was to imagine an individual who could help us solve the question. All at once I saw my deceased mother who stood there smiling at me lovingly. The final decoy image was to imagine that this individual handed me something—again as a means of solving the question. In response to the question, my mother reached out and handed me an angel ornament, like you would take off a Christmas tree.

When it came time for the woman to read aloud the real question she had drawn she was amazed to see that she had picked her own question. The woman told the group that she loved Christmas and always considered it to be a special time of year. In addition to her mother being deceased, she also associated her mother with love. In addition to Christmas, the angel was a symbol of spirituality and heaven.

After comparing the images to the real question, "How much longer will my father be with me?" the group decided that one possible meaning of the symbolism was that the questioner's father would die shortly after Christmas. The rationale was because the Christmas tree corresponded to the holiday season, one of the things that the mother was associated with was death, and the ornament had been taken off of the tree—just as occurs after Christmas. For that reason, the woman was encouraged to make Christmas with him a very special occasion. Several months passed until the holiday season arrived. Christmas came and went without incident and the woman did all that she could to make the season a joyful experience for her father. Nothing about his health had changed from the fall. However, the first week of January the woman called all of her friends to tell them the surprising news: her father had died suddenly and peacefully in his sleep!

When working with a group or leading a workshop, another variation is for the individual guiding the participants through the process to decide ahead of time what the real question is going to be for everyone. Although he or she will ask decoy questions aloud, there can be an unspoken real question that the individual may be interested in assisting participants in discovering for themselves. This approach can be helpful in order to have a group discussion regarding a particular topic that everybody has been focusing upon (although unknowingly), or it might enable a therapist or a counselor to help a client work through certain issues where there may be some kind of a block.

One example of this is the following conscious dreamplay exercise, which is designed to enable participants to see some aspects of their current life and to imagine symbolic representations of their own strengths and weaknesses. The decoy questions are the questions that are spoken by the leader and heard by the participants; the real question is kept in mind by the leader and is not revealed to participants until after the imagination portion of the exercise has been completed:

Conscious Dreamplay Exercise[4]
*(Can help participants view their life and
their own strengths and weaknesses)*

1a) Decoy question spoken by leader: "In your imagination, see a book and describe it and your feelings about it. What does this book mean to you?"

1b) Real question, kept in mind by leader and/or written on a piece of paper: "See a book that symbolizes what the individual's life has been all about."

2a) Decoy question spoken by leader: "Open the book to a section. What is it you see, hear, feel, experience, or just somehow know?"

2b) Real question, kept in mind by leader and/or written on a piece of paper: "Let the individual have a personal message appropriate for her or him at this time."

3a) Decoy question spoken by leader: "See a structure. What do you see? This structure has a story to tell . . . what is it?"

3b) Real question, kept in mind by leader and/or written on a piece of paper: "Let the individual see a symbol of the thing that is most *challenging* in his or her life at this time."

4a) Decoy question spoken by leader: "See another structure. Now what do you see? This structure also has a story to tell . . . what is it?"

4b) Real question, kept in mind by leader and/or written on a piece of paper: "Let the individual see a symbol of the thing that is most *exciting* in his or her life at this time."

---

[4]Based on an exercise formulated by Magaly del Carmen Rodriguez.

After being led through this exercise, a nineteen-year-old woman had the following experience:

> *Dreamplay experience of nineteen-year-old woman:*
> The image that corresponded to my life story was a big blue fairy tale book that I had when I was a child. For me, the symbolism meant that my life story has been the unfolding tale of innocence, spirituality and achieving expectations. I also have a great deal of optimism and hope for the future.
> The section I turned to was a beautiful picture of the forest. My message is that I have a great deal of potential and possibilities. It can also suggest that I need to pay more attention to the small details in my life—being able to see the trees and the forest.
> The first structure I saw was a large Japanese house with a heavy curved style roof. It was beautiful and serene. Since this is a challenge, it seems to mean that right now I am trying to learn a lot of foreign or new information and ideas (Japanese roof). I am in school and much of what I am studying is challenging, new and requires a lot of thought. At the same time, however, it has been a very serene and beautiful time of my life.
> The second structure was a glass greenhouse. One of the things I may be most excited about is giving structure to the world of my hopes, dreams, imagination and potential. I am also excited about showing my strengths and ideas to others.

A fifty-something-year-old woman was led through a variation of the above exercise. In her experience, participants were asked to see a book (life story), to turn to a section (personal message), to meet someone (an individual who can help answer the question), and to receive something from that someone (a talent that the individual could utilize to solve his or her question). Her experience and what she got out of it follows:

Dreamplay experience of fifty-something-year-old woman:
The book I imagined was the Bible. That seemed appropriate since much of my life has been the search for spiritual insights that are relevant to me. The section I turned to was a picture of being inside a castle with no windows and no doors. This describes my life perfectly. I have material possessions but I often feel imprisoned in a relationship (my marriage) that does not give me anything emotionally. As a couple we don't even have a dream for the future—we're just stuck in the "now" and don't see a way out.

I was really surprised to see my sister. In many ways I envy her life, her personality, even her marriage. She is such a special person. To me this might mean that I have all of those same ingredients inside myself that my sister has. Somehow I just need to cultivate them in my own life.

When we were asked to imagine that this person gave us something, my sister handed me a picture of her smile. Quite simply, I think it means that I need to have more joy in my life. Definitely true!

Maybe the whole thing is suggesting that I have been stuck in a rut and I need to find a way out. I certainly need more joy. Maybe I can just imagine what my sister would do in my circumstance (or even ask her), and do likewise.

As a final example, a twenty-something-year-old woman was faced with an imminent choice that she needed to make. She had gone to school in Virginia Beach, Virginia, more than 700 miles away from her home and family in Michigan. Two weeks prior to graduation she had met a young man and wondered if he was in fact "the one." The choice she had to make was whether or not she was supposed to remain in Virginia Beach in order to give the relationship a chance, or to move back to Michigan to be with the family that she missed. This was her experience:

Dreamplay experience of twenty-something-year-old woman:
I took two identical pieces of paper. On one I wrote "Virginia

Beach" and on the other I wrote "Michigan." I folded the pieces of paper into fourths and mixed them up so that I wouldn't know which one was which.

I held the first piece of paper in my hand and imagined myself somewhere. I saw myself in Rome at the Coliseum. I associated the Coliseum as a place with a lot of history but with a lot of conflict because of all of the battles that had been fought there for sport. I wrote what I had seen on my piece of paper.

I took the second piece of paper and imagined myself somewhere else. I saw myself at the beach on the Chesapeake Bay. It is one of my favorite places in Virginia Beach; it is a place I have even called "my heaven." I wrote down what I had seen on the second piece of paper.

When I unfolded the pieces of paper, the one associated with Michigan was in fact the image of Rome. And, honestly, my home is a place with a lot of history but a lot of conflict. The idea of being in Virginia Beach with my boyfriend did sound like heaven to me.

As a result of the exercise, the twenty-something-year-old woman decided to remain in Virginia Beach to be with her boyfriend—a decision she claimed had truly been the right choice six months later.

Conscious dreamplay accesses the subconscious mind's insights and intuition through the use of imagery and imagination. Just like a dream, the symbols and images will need to be interpreted, but in the process of their interpretation all manner of information can suddenly become available to the individual. The uses of conscious dreamplay are limited only by the imagination. In the same way that an individual can work with her or his dreams, obtaining countless insights into every area of life, the conscious dreamplay exercise can be helpful for accessing the mind's subconscious wisdom without even having to go to sleep. Whether as a tool for personal guidance, as a means of clarifying an issue, as a method of obtaining information about one's self, or even as a technique for perceiving a precognitive glimpse of the future, the imagination game is a unique method of self-discovery and obtaining personal insight.

Note: for ease of working with the conscious dreamplay exercise, what follows is a sample relaxation reverie and additional exercises that can be utilized to play the imagination game.

Relaxation Exercise
(A relaxation reverie is spoken at about ⅓ʳᵈ the normal rate of speech)

Become comfortable and relaxed and begin focusing your attention on your breathing. Let your awareness begin to notice how cool the air feels as you inhale and how warm it feels as you breathe out. After a few moments, bring your attention to your feet and ankles. Breathe in relaxation to your feet and ankles, and breathe out any tension.

Next, breathe in relaxation to your legs and knees, breathe out any tension to the same area. Breathe in relaxation to your hips, thighs, and buttocks, breathe out any tension.

Move up to your back, stomach and chest. Breathe in relaxation to these areas, and breathe out any tension. Next, breathe in relaxation to your shoulders and neck, breathe out any tension.

Breathe in relaxation to your head and forehead; let go of any tension to the same areas. Take a deep breath and simply relax.

Conscious Dreamplay Exercise I
(**Note:** In this exercise, individuals would either be holding the "real" question in their hands or the questioner leading the exercise will have the real question in his/her mind while the following is being spoken.)

1) Decoy question: "Imagine a package or a present of any kind." [Pause.] "How does this package appear to you?"

2) Decoy question: "Unwrap your package and see what's inside."

[Pause.] "How do you feel about what you see?"

3) Decoy question: "Snap your fingers and what happens to the contents inside?" [Pause.] "Now, how do you feel about what you see?"

Conscious Dreamplay Exercise II

(Note: In this exercise, individuals would either be holding the "real" question in their hands or the questioner leading the exercise will have the real question in his/her mind while the following is being spoken.)

1) Decoy question: "Imagine a door." [Pause.] "What does it look like to you?"

2) Decoy question: "Open the door and see what's behind it." [Pause.] "What do you see and how do you feel about it?"

3) Decoy question: "Imagine it is six months from now?" [Pause.] "What happens to the image behind the door?"

Conscious Dreamplay Exercise III

(For a group leader to guide participants in perceiving their life over the next twelve months)

1a) Decoy question spoken by leader: "In your imagination, see a building." [Pause.] "What is it you see, hear, feel, or experience?"

1b) Real question, kept in mind by leader and/or written on a piece of paper: "See a building that symbolizes the theme of the individual's next twelve months."

2a) Decoy question spoken by leader: "There are people inside the building. What are they doing?"

2b) Real question, kept in mind by leader and/or written on a piece of paper: "Give a visual representation of what activities will be occupying most of the individual's time."

3a) Decoy question spoken by leader: "Someone in the building seems to stand out to you. Who is this individual and what is that individual doing?"

3b) Real question, kept in mind by leader and/or written on a piece of paper: "Is there an activity that the individual should make certain to incorporate into daily life?"

4a) Decoy question spoken by leader: "There may be something wonderful just around the corner from the building." [Pause.] "If so, what is it?"

4b) Real question, kept in mind by leader and/or written on a piece of paper: "Does the individual have some kind of unexpected surprise coming to her or him? If so, picture it."

Chapter 8 Sample Dreamplay Images
See Appendix One for possible interpretations

Dreamplay experience of twenty-something-year-old woman:
[Background information: Woman was asked to imagine a book (life story), a section (personal message), a first structure (challenge) and a second structure (something exciting).]

I saw a brown-colored book like a diary. It was large and thick and seemed like it had been read a lot because it was worn.

When I opened the book to a section, I saw a sailboat. There were no words, just a beautiful scene with the boat sailing smoothly on the water.

The first structure I saw was the Tower of Babel and the second structure was a beautiful secluded beach house made of stucco (my boyfriend works with stucco).

Dreamplay experience of forty-something-year-old man:
[Background information: Man was trying to decide between two vacation possibilities for his family. In order to get insights into the question, one door represented a camping trip and the other corresponded to a beach vacation. When doing the imagination exercise, he did not know what door symbolized which question.]

The first card I touched had the image of a very bright, white door. It had a gold doorknob and seemed very attractive. When I opened the door, I saw a mall with lots of different stores and people doing all kinds of activities. There were movie theaters and restaurants. Everyone seemed to be having a good time. I rated the picture as an eight.

When I touched the second card, the door appeared to be the same at first. The door and the doorknob were just as attractive. However, when I opened the door I saw a gray concrete building. It was empty and stark and felt cold inside. I gave it a one.

Chapter 8 Sample Dreamplay Images
See Appendix One for possible interpretations

When I turned over the questions, the first door corresponded to the beach vacation and the second door corresponded with the camping trip.

Dreamplay experience of fifty-something-year-old woman:
(Background information: Woman was asked to imagine a building (theme for next twelve months), people doing something in the building (activity occupying her time), a person standing out from the crowd (what individual should be personally involved with) and something just around the corner (unexpected surprise).)

There was a big office building. It was very tall with lots of windows. When I looked inside the building I could see that it was actually one of the largest Laundromats I had ever seen. People were busy washing and dry cleaning and pressing all kinds of clothes. I noticed that this one woman was sitting and sipping a cup of coffee while everyone else was working. For a minute she turned to look at a stack of dirty clothes, but she picked up a book and began to read it instead. When I imagined myself outside the building to see what was around the corner, I could see an amusement park.

Conclusion

Perhaps more than anything else, the wondrous insights available from the subconscious mind suggests that there is much more to us than a physical body. Obviously, consciousness is not limited to the body or to our perceptions of what we think we are. During the sleep-state, the mind becomes open to information from all space and time. This information ties into activities and events occurring in waking life and can be extremely helpful if only the dreamer will attempt to use it. This same type of information can be accessed through imagi-nation games, intuitive imagery, or conscious dreamplay—tools that utilize the limitless boundaries of the imagination within the helpful parameters of personal insight and intuition.

For the most part, dreams contrast and correlate the events of the day, providing the individual with another look at the very issues with which he or she is concerned. They can provide an objective look at known facts, process potential solutions, or acquire information and guidance not known or available to the conscious mind. Dreams address everything about an individual's life and wellbeing: physically, mentally, emotionally and spiritually—they can relate to the health of the body, explore psychological issues, and even nurture the soul.

The most important element individuals can use in working with dreams for themselves can be stated in one word: practice. For that reason, you should start writing down your dreams immediately upon awakening. Although you may only remember a color, a scene, or a feeling, write it down. Even if you only have the feeling of a good night's sleep the next morning, write it down. If you remember seeing the face of someone you know, *write it down*—let the subconscious mind know that you are serious.

As you begin to write something down each morning, you might be surprised at how many dreams begin coming to mind. It's not so much that you have to remember an entire story rather the process is one of re-experiencing the experience. If you wake up in the middle of the night, keep a "dream notebook" near your bed and write down a few scenes so that they can help prompt you to write down the entire dream upon awakening the next morning.

In addition to writing something down, other individuals have found different approaches for remembering their dreams in the morning. Saying something like, "I will remember my dreams" when falling to sleep, or purposefully drinking a big glass of water in order to awaken in the middle of the night, or setting the alarm five to ten minutes early in the morning, can all be helpful for dream recall. The important thing is simply to start practicing.

Whether an individual happens to be working with dreams or the exercise of conscious dreamplay, remembering the meaning of a lot of symbols is not all that important. To begin with a good dream dictionary or even an unabridged dictionary can be just as helpful as a list of memorized symbols. A dream or imagery's theme and overall feeling is also every bit as important as any symbols.

Since each individual is most aware of the activities and events occurring in his or her waking life, ultimately, each one of us is our own best dream interpreter. Our personal symbols take precedence over whatever anyone else might think of them. For that reason, in time we may also wish to begin a "personal dream dictionary" and watch for reoccurring symbols, characters, themes, and emotions within our own dreams. Even when using conscious dreamplay to answer another individual's question, all symbolism should first be interpreted in terms of what the individual doing the imagining personally associates with that symbol.

Because other characters often become the subject of our dreams and imaginings, it is important to keep in mind that most often they symbolize something about the self. Even animals, nature, and inanimate objects can oftentimes be symbolic of something in relationship to one's self. Since most dreams deal with the dreamer, we do not generally dream *for* other people unless we have specifically and consciously decided to attempt to do so—and even then a dream will invariably have personal relevance.

Rather than thinking that there is only one way to interpret a dream or conscious dreamplay exercise, any of the following approaches (or combinations thereof) might be helpful:

A. *Work with the theme first and any symbolism second.* Try describing the dream in no more than one or two sentences in terms of "What is happening to whom?" For many individuals, creating a possible story line for the images being portrayed can be one of the easiest ways to decipher the meaning of a dream or imagery experience.

B. *Explore the emotional content of the dream or image.* Does it feel like a positive dream? A frustrating dream? A frightening dream? Or, an inspiring dream? Just what does it feel like? The most important thing to remember in regards to interpretation based upon emotional content is that whatever emotion is being aroused by the dream or image generally corresponds to a situation or experience in the individual's life that evokes a similar feeling or emotion.

C. *Consider whether the dream is literal or metaphorical and then interpret the symbolism accordingly.* Most dreams deal with personal not global events. Most dreams contrast and correlate the events of the day. What about the images being portrayed remind the dreamer of his or her real life? A literal dream deals with some aspect of exactly what is being portrayed in the imagery. Conversely, a metaphorical dream symbolizes something else. Dreams can be both metaphorical and literal.

D. *Attempt to analyze the dream against life's current happenings.* Dreams may serve primarily as a means for the individual's subconscious to wrestle with issues, concerns, or feelings that have been on the dreamer's conscious mind.

E. *Work with symbol interpretation.* Buy a good dream dictionary (there are bad dictionaries, as well) or an unabridged dictionary. When looking through a dictionary look up symbols that you already know and see whether or not the dictionary makes sense or agrees with you. Remember there has got to be some logical connection between a symbol and what it is supposed to mean. In other words, a dream does not mean something simply because someone says it does.

Using these approaches, anyone can begin working with her or his dreams immediately. Individuals might also wish to begin playing the conscious dreamplay exercise for personal insights into virtually any question imaginable. Potentially, dreams, symbols, imagination and the intuition can all work together to bring to the consciousness of individuals whatever they need to know in order to learn about themselves and to become all that they were meant to be.

As you begin to explore the depth of your own consciousness, finding insights into yourself, your life, and your relationships, you will be amazed at the depth of wisdom that has always been available to you—you just never knew where to look for it. In addition, you will make your own contribution to a day somewhere off in the future when each and every individual is encouraged to work with dreams so that the wonderful worlds of symbolism, dreams, the imagination and intuitive imagery become a normal part of everyday life.

Appendix 1

Possible Solutions to End-of-Chapter Dreams and Imagery

Chapter 1:

Dream of fifty-year-old woman:

(Background information: Woman has been extremely busy; her shelties have actually been dead several years.)

I dreamed that I was inside my house and all of a sudden I remembered that I hadn't watered or fed my shelties in quite some time. For some reason, I had put them in a shed out back of the house and never went back to check on them. Suddenly, I was in a panic and tried to go and check on them but a neighbor showed up and kept interfering with me trying to go see my dogs. Finally, when the neighbor left I was able to go out to the shed. I was horrified to find that the dogs were gone!

The fact that the dream occurs within the woman's house suggests that the dream is related to a current situation or experience with which she is dealing. Her shelties can represent something she loves about herself or something she loved about having the dogs in her life. Because the shelties have been put in back of the house and essentially forgotten, it suggests that the woman has put something important to her either in the background or in the past. The something she has been ignoring comes to mind in her life but it appears as though external demands keep vying for her attention. When she finally makes the time to attend to what is truly important to her, it seems like it is too late.

In real life, the woman was extremely busy with work, family and school obligations. She admitted that the thing she had been most neglecting was herself. She didn't take the time or feel that she had the time to do the things she loved. She realized that the dream was encouraging her to rethink some of her priorities.

Dream of forty-something-year-old woman:
(Background information: Woman works in an office where there is a lot of backstabbing that really bothers her.)

I was speaking to the office receptionist about the fact that I was being promoted. I had decided that from now on there would be a new dress code that everyone would be wearing. I had on a smart-looking business-type pantsuit to show her what I was talking about.

The act of being promoted suggests that the dreamer is going to become more prominent in a situation, probably dealing with work. The office receptionist can correspond to the act of communication. A dress code is symbolic of one's outer appearance as well as one's demeanor and the way an individual presents her or himself to others. The fact that the woman is wearing what will become the company dress code can indicate that the dreamer knows how to interact with others in a way that does not contribute to the problems she associates with work. In addition to suggesting that the dreamer knows how to be helpful in regards to fixing the problem, an additional possibility is that the dreamer is literally going to be promoted and will be able to further address some of the problems in her new position.

Dream of middle-aged man:

(Background information: Man does not get along with his mother.)

I dreamed that I was speaking to my mother and as I was speaking my two front teeth kept falling out. I'd push them back in but they kept falling out. The funny thing was, I don't think my mother noticed. It made me feel uncomfortable to be around her.

Teeth falling out of the dreamer's mouth seem to indicate that he either does not feel comfortable speaking to his mother and does not really know what to say or that things are coming out of his mouth that shouldn't (gossip, for example). His mother not seeing the problem could suggest that either or both of them continue to be oblivious to the communication problem or it might represent the fact that the only time he speaks about his mother is behind her back. In real life, the dreamer felt that both possibilities were accurate.

Chapter 2:

Dream of eighteen-year-old woman:

(Background information: This is a reoccurring dream. The woman stated, "I do occasionally chew gum but only regular size pieces." She has been trying to make changes in her life.)

In the dream I am chewing a really big piece of gum. When I'm ready to take out the gum, it will not come out. In my attempt to remove the gum, it becomes stringy and sticks to my teeth. The gum never comes out!

A possible theme is that "Someone is having a hard time doing something." Another could be "Something is difficult to remove or change." Because the "sticky situation" is in the young woman's mouth, it is possible that she is biting off more than she can chew in regards to her current activities or she might be having a difficult time communicating. The dreamer admitted to being very frustrated with her life and with the fact that she was continually trying to make personal changes without success.

Dream of forty-something-year-old woman:

(Background information: Woman's husband has asked for divorce.)

I was working in a hospital. A man's wife was dying of lung disease. He and his son came to me and asked me to steal some meds for her. They kept telling me how she was suffering. I told them that I of all people understood but I could not steal drugs or bring in herbs that would interfere with her treatment. I also said there was a lot of security and I just couldn't do that. I reached over and got my stuff to leave and I was crying saying that I couldn't help them. I woke up crying.

The imagery is that "Someone or something is dying and apparently nothing can be done about it." Since the dreamer states that her husband has asked for a divorce, obviously the marriage is what is dying and that is why the dreamer can understand the pain and the suffering that the man and his son are going through. The woman dying of a disease related to her chest probably symbolizes the fact that the dreamer herself is suffering from a broken heart and there does not appear to be anyone who can help. Because the dreamer is unable to provide medication in the dream, it may indicate that in real life the woman has perhaps thought about "medicating" herself and changed her mind or she has come to realize that even such things as tranquilizers and alcohol will not help ease her pain.

Dream of fifty-something-year-old woman:

(Background information: Woman expresses concern about her friend.)

I dreamed about going into a big house with one of my female friends. To our horror, in walking through the house there were all of these disembodied heads that we had to walk around just to get through to where we were going.

Simply stated, "Someone is losing his or head over something." Since the dreamer expressed her worry regarding a friend, the dream suggests that either the dreamer is losing her head in the situation, her friend is losing her head, or that both women are losing their heads. The house is symbolic of the current situation. Because the two women are walking around disembodied heads as they move through the house, it suggests that the dreamer is having a challenging time trying to figure what direction to move in regards to helping her friend with the problem.

Chapter 3:

Dream of thirty-something-year old woman:

(Background information: Dreamer complained of relationship with her aggressive mother, a woman prone to critical comments.)

I was going home and being followed by a Velociraptor dinosaur. I had reached home and the Velociraptor had followed me inside. I raced up the stairs and went into one of the rooms and shut and locked the door. Although the door was shut I knew the dinosaur would be breaking through the door at any moment. Afraid, I climbed out of the window and crawled out onto the roof of the porch that was below the window. I was kind of hanging below the roof so it wouldn't see me. It finally went away but I knew it would be back.

Next, my family was packing our belongings: the pets, the food, and the things that we needed quickly so we could leave and be safe from the dinosaur. The dream ended with my being able to watch the car, all packed up and loaded, with all of us inside, driving away.

The mother's biting and aggressive temperament is represented by the Velociraptor dinosaur. The fact that the dinosaur has come inside the home suggests that the dreamer is either unable to escape from her mother's criticism or her mother's criticism has become a part of the dreamer, making the dreamer critical of herself or others. In the dreamer's attempts to escape from the creature, it becomes clear that the woman is unable to get away. This may suggest that even if the dreamer is successful in avoiding her mother physically, the issues remain a part of her and in all likelihood need to be dealt with. Even if the dreamer shuts out her mother, there is the danger that the problem will break into the dreamer's private thoughts. The dreamer being near the roof (thoughts) suggests that she has given some thought to dealing with this issue and has partially been successful ("It finally went away but I knew it would be back"), but there is still work to be done.

By driving away with her family, the dreamer is able to either escape from her mother's criticism or she can get so caught up in her family's life that the issue does not seem to be as prominent. However, overall the dream seems to be suggesting that issues related to this relationship cannot be suppressed or avoided, something still needs to be done to resolve the effect the mother had and still has upon her daughter.

Dream of teenage boy:
(Background information: Middle-aged man recalls reoccurring dream that he often had growing up.)

The dream is that I am at home in my parent's home where I grew up. All at once I look out the window and am frightened to see that a number of tornadoes are heading right for the property. Although afraid, I suddenly remember that this is something I have been through many times before. The thought comes to me that just as I have survived previously, I'll probably be able to survive this most recent storm. The last thing I remember is being afraid and simply hoping that I will be okay.

Since the dream reoccurred in childhood only, we can assume that it dealt with an issue that was relevant at the time. If the dream repeated itself in the present, it would probably indicate a similar situation or experience occurring in the man's life rather than it being simply an unresolved issue related to that previous experience.

The parent's home represents his life, his surroundings, and perhaps even his personal security. Looking out the window at tornadoes suggests that he is observing some kind of volatile emotional upheaval (tornadoes). These arguments or outbursts seem to be occurring around him and are either something he is participating in or something he is subjected to. However, since these storms have occurred previously without injuring him, we can assume that it is more likely that he has witnessed them rather than having been physically involved.

In real life, the dreamer admitted that his parents were always fighting during his youth. He stated that even though they fought behind their closed bedroom door, he could still hear the shouting coming through the walls. The shouting between the two of them really bothered him as a teenager and naturally he wished it would stop. He wanted things to be okay and for his parents to learn to get along. Eventually, however, his parents ended up divorcing.

Dream of forty-something-year-old woman:
[Background information: Woman lives out of state from the rest of her family. Elderly parents are still alive.]

I was driving back to Iowa (where we use to visit my grandparents) with my Dad. We were going back to honor my great, great grandfather. We finally drove into a dinky town in Iowa and drove up to a large house that looked almost like an office building or a courthouse. A crowd of people scattered about the lawn just staring. For some reason the scene seemed eerie.

I went into the house and was confronted by an angry lady who seemed to resemble me. She was irate and screamed at me for failing to visit my dying great great grandfather. She said that I could not see him *anymore and then she proceeded to abruptly escort me out of the house.*

After a little reflection, I was determined to see him anyway because I had come a long way for that very purpose. I went back in the house and insisted on seeing him. Finally, the angry woman relented and led me back into the bedroom.

My great great grandfather was so old and aged and frail that I could hardly believe his condition. He was curled up in a fetal position and was as tiny as an infant. As I stood there looking at him in sadness, he opened his eyes as if to speak.

Suddenly, my alarm clock went off and I was awakened. I found myself desperately sad from the feeling of the dream and from my desire to know what he would have said to me.

One possibility suggested by the dream is that the dreamer is worried or concerned about a family issue or relationship. It is an important issue (office building/courthouse) that the dreamer does not know how to deal with (people just standing around). She may also be worried or scared about the situation ("the scene seemed eerie").

Obviously, the angry woman is the dreamer herself who seems to be upset that she has not been participating in or dealing with something. In actuality that something is her father: a man (the dream suggests) that she considers to be a great, great, even grand individual. The dream suggests that she is feeling guilty about something related to her relationship with him. The dream portrays the symbol representing her father as being very sick, very old, and even curled up in a fetal position. If he is ill or worried about something, then she feels guilty that she cannot spend more time with him, or she doesn't know what to do to help him, or both.

In real life, the dreamer expressed concern for her father and some measure of frustration that she did not get to spend as much time with him as was her desire.

Chapter 4:

Dream of forty-something-year-old woman:

[Background information: Female Accountant expresses dislike for male co-worker, "Bob."]

I dreamed that I came to the office, and where my desk had once been, there was now a bed. Although I didn't seem surprised about it in the dream, Bob was waiting for me in bed. I smiled at him, took off my clothes and crawled in next to him and we started to kiss. I woke up feeling very confused and alarmed as to why I had done such a thing.

Although there might be some unresolved sexual or romantic feelings that the dreamer is suppressing, a more likely scenario is that the dream is about the dreamer's and Bob's work relationship. A bed being where her desk had been suggests that some kind of a partnership or cooperative venture is about to become a part of her work life. When this activity occurs, the dreamer may find herself working in cooperation with Bob on a project. The project seems to go well and, to the dreamer's surprise, the two may end up having a positive experience with one another and perhaps even like each other.

Dream of forty-something-year-old woman:
[Background information: Woman's daughter, with whom she is "very close," is about to attend college out of state.]

I was in the house and got a phone call that Amanda had been killed. The police were calling to tell me about her death. When I heard the news I screamed and dropped the phone. I ran through the house calling out to my husband, needing him to help me. I was horrified and sick to my stomach.

Although a dream of this nature might have some precognitive imagery associated with it, in dialoguing with the dreamer we discover that the woman is about to "lose" her daughter to college. With this in mind, the dream is most likely about a mother's sadness and loss related to a child growing up and leaving home. Because the two had been very close, having the daughter go away to school may seem like a death—the old relationship is no longer alive. The woman's own higher self (police) is trying to make her deal with the changes that are occurring, indicating that perhaps the woman has been hesitant to talk about her fears, concerns, and sadness with anyone. The dream is suggesting that the dreamer needs to open up to her husband and release some of the anxiety and sadness that is making her sick to her stomach.

Dream of thirty-something-year-old woman:
(Background information: Husband is frustrated with business partner about finances; wife is frustrated with husband about marriage. This is the wife's dream.)

I dreamed that I was standing in the dining room next to my husband, looking at my husband's business partner. I said to the partner that I didn't want *anything* to do with him because of how he had treated my husband. I no longer wanted to eat with him or be in the same room with him.

Before we decide too quickly that the dream is simply about the dreamer's relationship with her husband's business associate, it is important to keep in mind that most dreams have a component about one's self. With that in mind, from a marital perspective the dreamer is also her husband's "business partner." Being in the dining room suggests that there is an issue she has been dwelling upon (digesting) for quite some time. The dreamer states that she no longer wants to have anything to do with the partner (literal business partner or marriage relationship?).

In discussing the dream, the woman admitted that just as her husband was sick of dealing with his partner in business, she was sick of dealing with her husband. Rather than simply holding her thoughts within herself, the dream may have been suggesting that the woman needed to deal with her husband face-to-face, enabling the two of them to come to some resolution.

Chapter 5:

Dream of fifty-something-year-old woman:

(Background information: Woman is in the midst of some life changes and the need to make decisions about her future.)

I dreamt that there was an elegant looking woman who was standing by herself. She appeared calm and collected. Suddenly I noticed that she was missing her entire right arm. There wasn't even a stub where her arm should have been. I was carrying a white shawl at the time and I took it over to the woman and draped it around her shoulders. I don't know if I was trying to cover her missing arm or help her stay warm. She seemed appreciative and thanked me.

Oftentimes, every character in a dream can be symbolic of the dreamer. The elegant woman standing by herself suggests that the dreamer appears regal and alone in real life. Although she may come across to others as being "calm and collected," something has happened that has caused her to feel as if she is missing a limb (suggestive of divorce or abandonment or great loss). Because it is her right arm and possibly symbolic of the future, it might suggest that something related to the woman's future appears to have been taken from her. In spite of how stable, self-certain and self-sufficient the woman appears to others, whatever has happened has really affected her. In the dream, the woman or her higher self is trying to comfort her self and tell her that in spite of how things appear in the present, everything will be okay.

In response to the above analysis the woman replied, "That's it exactly!"

Dream of twenty-something-year-old man:

(Background information: Twenty-year-old male has moved to a university town to attend school. He has not yet found a job to help support him and is worried.)

I am trying to take a picture of an awesome sunset down a road. It gets better and better. The sky gets very cloudy with bright orange colors. As I try to take the picture, a little boy gets in the way. I keep hoping he will move but when he does the sunset is gone.

Looking back down a road and taking a picture of a sunset might represent reflecting back upon one's present journey and enjoying the memories that are now fading (sunset). On the other hand, taking an opposite approach could suggest that something one has long-awaited has now been set before the dreamer and can be cherished and enjoyed if only it is not blocked by something else.

Orange can be the color of creativity or sexuality. Because of current events in the dreamer's life, in this case the color probably has something to do with a creative solution. The little boy might be symbolic of the dreamer's new life or of his childish fears related to his present situation. In either case, the dreamer's thoughts (clouds) are being blocked or interfered with by the present situation. Because the child does not get out of the way, the dreamer is having a difficult time coming to terms with the fact that his life has changed or he is having difficulties effectively facing his problems in the present.

The dreamer stated that because of his inability to find work, he had begun "to worry about everything." He added, "To me, the picture represented memories, experiences and relationships. The sunset suggested the closing period of my life, a death. The dream seemed to say that childhood fears are either holding me back or I am not moving past something."

Dream of nineteen-year-old woman:

(Background information: Young woman has begun to have romantic feelings for a male friend, Patrick, and is worried that the feelings will change their friendship.)

I had a dream that I was at a party. It seemed to be my house but it wasn't. I was outside and saw a snake in our neighbor's yard that looked like an anaconda. I went back in the house, found my friend, Patrick, and told him about the snake. When we went outside to look for it, it wasn't there. Afterwards, we walked through another room leading outside to the front yard because he had to leave. On the way to Patrick's car, we passed some friends playing cards. Before he left, he kissed me on the cheek, then we hugged and he kissed me on the lips.

The next thing I remember was being at another house with another guy who is a friend sitting on some monkey bars. Then I saw the snake again. This time it was winding itself around the pole and looping itself through the bars. I was scared but my friend told me it would be all right and wouldn't hurt me. Then Patrick came out (the other friend seemed to be gone) and we watched the snake go to the other yard.

Being at a party can be suggestive of having fun. In the process of having fun (in real life probably with her friend Patrick), the dreamer notices a snake, which can be symbolic of a male relationship or male sexuality. Because the snake is not in her yard, it might suggest that the dreamer really does not need to deal with it. Since she tells Patrick about the snake, it suggests that she has had sexual feelings about him and may even have discussed the fact that her feelings are becoming more than simply a friendship. However, when they look for the snake it wasn't there, perhaps indicating that her feelings are not shared by Patrick or that the two of them will have difficulty maintaining a sexual relationship. The fact that Patrick has to leave and that the couple pass by other friends playing cards may both suggest that the dreamer and Patrick's ideal relationship is simply that of friends.

After the dreamer kisses Patrick she meets another friend. This might indicate that the dreamer has tried to find romantic relationship in other male friendships previously. This possibility is further reinforced because she and the friend are sitting on monkey bars, suggesting that they have been "monkeying around." As she monkeys around with her friend, the sexuality presents itself again. Once she and Patrick get together, the snake leaves.

In dialoguing with the dreamer, it became very clear that she was planning to pursue a relationship with Patrick regardless of what the dream seemed to suggest. Because of the dream imagery, a strong possibility was that the romance would be short-lived and the two of them would simply return to their friendship. Since both were afraid of ruining their friendship another possibility was that there was nothing to be afraid of because everything would work out okay— regardless of what transpired between them. In this case the snake might represent fear of sexual expression and the fact that it leaves the yard once the two of them got together could indicate that the fear dissipates once they are romantically involved or that the romance is over as soon as it begins.

Chapter 6:

Dream of forty-three-year-old woman:

(Background information: woman is interested in spiritual development and in discovering her personal mission in life.)

I dreamed I was driving home in my Jeep. In real life, to get to my house on the mountain I have to drive up a very steep hill for about a half-mile, then wind around the mountain. On the steep hill, there were several boulders—all perfectly round and smooth. They were scattered randomly. I continued to drive. As I reached the first boulder I cautiously peered around it, saw the way was clear and continued on to the next boulder. There were one or two other cars on the hill that were stopped and couldn't go any further. I managed to weave around all the obstacles by driving up to them slowly, looking for an open path, finding one and continuing to drive. Eventually, I reached the top of the hill.

Since it is the dreamer who is driving her Jeep up the mountain to her house, it could represent the fact that the dream is about the woman's life journey, her search for spirituality, or both. The presence of boulders in her path are suggestive of obstacles or difficulties she will encounter (or has encountered) during her journey. The fact that the boulders are rounded and smoothed could indicate that these are issues with which the dreamer has dealt for a long time, wearing them down in the process. Continuing her travels and cautiously planning her next move is perhaps symbolic of the dreamer's methodical and well-thought-out approach to whatever it is she decides to do. Passing other cars on the road could represent leaving behind earlier problems, difficulties, or belief systems, or it might indicate surpassing family (or her personal) expectations. Reaching the top of the hill is associated with the dreamer achieving her personal and spiritual goals. Whether it's enlightenment or personal fulfillment, it appears that the woman is going to be successful.

Dream of twenty-something-year-old woman:
(Background information: young woman wants to return to college and focus on her career. Husband is opposed to the idea and wants her to stay home with the kids.)

I dreamed that I was walking along and noticed that a snake was biting my arm. I had to struggle to turn it loose of my arm. Later, as I was walking, I noticed that a snake (could have been the same one) was biting my ankle.

A snake in a dream is often associated with a male energy or it might correspond to temptation. Because of current events in the woman's life, it appears as though in the process of trying to travel her life's journey (walking along), a snake begins to bite her arm. The arm can be symbolic of the self or it can be associated with free will. Biting can correspond to negative words being spoken. The imagery suggests that a male energy is trying to interfere with her free will, either physically or verbally. The snake biting her ankle is also suggestive of a male energy trying to impede her path.

In real life, the woman decided that the dream was showing her what was happening in her relationship with her husband. She decided that both a family and a career were important to her and she ignored her husband's attempts to stop her from returning to college.

Dream of forty-something-year-old man:
(Background information: man complained of feeling tired, le-

thargic and was having trouble concentrating.)

I dreamed that I was crazy and having problems thinking. Somehow I was able to look inside my head. With my skull open, I could see all kinds of gears and wheels spinning around in their proper place, except for one. One of the wheels had stopped running altogether because a particle of dirt or trash had gotten stuck in it.

Because of the imagery of the head, the dream suggests that either the dreamer's thoughts or some kind of a physical blockage may be the cause for his condition. Corresponding thoughts that might cause lethargy and problems with concentration include depression, repressed anger, hopelessness, or somehow feeling "stuck" by routine. The dream may be purely physical, showing how some kind of a physical blockage is at the root of his feeling tired and having problems thinking. If this is the case, then the logical assumption is that the dreamer is having problems with his physical elimination processes (particle of trash getting stuck) and toxins are building up in his system, causing both the lack of energy and the slow thought-processes.

Chapter 7:

Dream of forty-something-year-old woman:
(Background information: Woman works at a bank in Norfolk, Virginia.)

I saw Norfolk, Virginia from the air. I could see the naval shipyard and downtown. Suddenly a missile descended from the sky and struck the ground near the waterside. Before anyone could realize what had happened, the city was annihilated and an enormous mushroom cloud rose high up into air.

Because of the national importance of Norfolk as a shipyard, the woman feared that the dream was precognitive and wanted to know how she could warn the city. She also wondered aloud how far away from the city people would have to evacuate in order to be safe. During the process of dialogue it was discovered that she worked in Norfolk. Other possibilities might have been that her husband was in the armed services (he was not), or that she associated her family with Norfolk (she did not). Since she most closely associated Norfolk with her job, it is very likely that something was about to destroy the job she had known.

Although no follow-up was ever received from the dreamer, as an interesting aside, several months after the dream several bank mergers and acquisitions occurred in the Norfolk area, affecting a number of banks and their employees.

Dream of thirty-year-old man:
(Background information: Grandfather with whom he was close died six weeks earlier.)

A few weeks after my Grandfather died, I kept have a reoccurring dream about him. In the dream there was some kind of a large family gathering like Thanksgiving. Everyone was gathering around the table in the kitchen for dinner. I happened to look through the door that led into the living room and saw my Grandfather who I knew was dead, sitting on the couch all by himself. I was the only one who could see him. I went and sat by him on the couch and started talking with him.

My grandfather told me that he was all right and doing just fine. He also thanked me and stated that he had really enjoyed being my grandfather. He gave me a hug and we talked some more. The experience was very uplifting and yet the whole time the rest of my family remained completely oblivious to my grandfather's presence and just went on about their dinner together.

Since consciousness is not limited to the confines of the physical body, it is very likely that real communication occurred between the dreamer and his grandfather. In other words, the grandfather was simply trying to reassure his loved ones that he was doing well, even though he was no longer physically alive.

In dialoguing with the dreamer, it became clear that he was the only one out of his entire family who ever paid any attention to his dreams, shedding possible light on the repetitive nature of the dream. In all likelihood the grandfather was trying to reassure every member of his family that he was doing fine—all the individuals at the dinner table were probably contacted in the dream-state. However, since only the thirty-year-old paid any attention to his dreams, the rest of the family remained completely oblivious to the presence of the grandfather or the conversation that the two of them were having.

Dream of sixty-something-year-old man:

(Background information: Individual wrote out the question, "What do I need to work on spiritually?" before going to sleep.)

I dreamed that I was in the army (I have never been in the army) and I was some kind of a drill sergeant doing important paperwork. My desk was filled with important papers and things that were scheduled — everything was neatly organized and in its proper place. Suddenly a younger man came into my office unannounced. He was singing and dancing and appeared to be having a very good time with himself. To my surprise, he jumped up on top of my desk and started tap dancing all over my paperwork. Everything that I had neatly organized was in disarray. After making a thorough mess, the man continued to sing and dance and danced right out of my office. Immediately, I picked up the phone and called security and yelled into the received, "I want that man arrested, and I want to know who he is!" I slammed the phone down, very angry for the interruption. Suddenly, security came into my office bringing the man who had caused the disruption. They announced that they had caught him and that he was "the company clown."

Although the dreamer had never been in the armed services, he had a very regimented way of doing things. In spite of being retired, his entire schedule was structured hour-by-hour and he frequently made "to be done" lists that were adhered to completely. Repeatedly, the dreamer's wife had encouraged him to relax and to be less structured, but to no avail. It was only after receiving the above guidance in response to his query that the dreamer even realized he had a problem. The dream finally convinced the individual that he needed to learn how to have fun—something that he obviously had been stifling in himself because he was taking things far too seriously.

Chapter 8:

Dreamplay experience of twenty-something-year-old woman: *(Background information: Woman was asked to imagine a book (life story), a section (personal message), a first structure (challenge) and a second structure (something exciting).)*

I saw a brown-colored book like a diary. It was large and thick and seemed like it had been read a lot because it was worn.

When I opened the book to a section, I saw a sailboat. There were no words, just a beautiful scene with the boat sailing smoothly on the water.

The first structure I saw was the Tower of Babel and the second structure was a beautiful secluded beach house made of stucco (my boyfriend works with stucco).

Even though the woman was unaware that she was imagining a book that symbolized her "life story," she saw a diary. The color brown is suggestive of practical and down-to-earth, perhaps being descriptive of the woman herself. The book being thick and worn could be associated with the fact that the woman may have already had many life experiences in spite of her age.

The sailboat corresponds to a personal message for her at this time. This suggests that either her present experience is a beautiful, serene time for her, or that she needs to try and incorporate such a time into her life right now. The imagery of the sailboat can also be associated with being on a spiritual journey.

The Tower of Babel is a phallic symbol, suggesting a male energy. Because of the Biblical account, it also symbolizes having problems with communication. It is interesting to note that in real life the woman and her boyfriend were having a hard time communicating—especially, when it came to deciding their future together.

Since the woman also associated the stucco with her boyfriend, it suggests that one of the things she is most excited about is the future (one filled with serenity and perhaps even spiritual interests) that she is planning with him.

Dreamplay experience of forty-something-year-old man:
(Background information: Man was trying to decide between two vacation possibilities for his family. In order to get insights into the question, one door represented a camping trip and the other corresponded to a beach vacation. When doing the imagination exercise, he did not know what door symbolized which question.)

The first card I touched had the image of a very bright, white door. It had a gold doorknob and seemed very attractive. When I opened the door, I saw a mall with lots of different stores and people doing all kinds of activities. There were movie theaters and restaurants. Everyone seemed to be having a good time. I rated the picture as an eight.

When I touched the second card, the door appeared to be the same at first. The door and the doorknob were just as attractive. However, when I opened the door I saw a gray concrete building. It was empty and stark and felt cold inside. I gave it a one.

When I turned over the questions, the first door corresponded to the beach vacation and the second door corresponded with the camping trip.

Since both doors appeared identical at first, it might suggest that both vacations looked just as fun to begin with. However, obviously the image behind the first door is much more appealing. The mall imagery might correspond to the fact that there will be plenty to do at the beach (lots of activities) and every member of his family will have a good time. Conversely, the second door might indicate such things as boredom, the lack of excitement, or the fact that there will be weather problems during the camping trip—after all, it was "cold" in the building.

Dreamplay experience of fifty-something-year-old woman:
(Background information: Woman was asked to imagine a building (theme for next twelve months), people doing something in the building (activity occupying her time), a person standing out from the crowd (what individual should be personally involved with) and something just around the corner (unexpected surprise).)

There was a big office building. It was very tall with lots of windows. When I looked inside the building I could see that it was actually one of the largest Laundromats I had ever seen. People were busy washing and dry cleaning and pressing all kinds of clothes. I noticed that this one woman was sitting and sipping a cup of coffee while everyone else was working. For a minute she turned to look at a stack of dirty clothes, but she picked up a book and began to read it instead. When I imagined myself outside the building to see what was around the corner, I could see an amusement park.

The imagery could correspond with the woman being very busy putting things in order or "cleaning up" something related to her home, her work, or her life in general. The woman sitting and relaxing might suggest that the woman imagining this scene needs to take time to relax and enjoy herself, even in the midst of having so many things to do. The need for relaxation and personal enjoyment is further reinforced by the image of the amusement park. It could be that something fun is just around the corner.

Appendix 2

More Than 500 Common Dream Symbols and Their Possible Interpretation

Symbol/Image:	Possible Interpretations Include:
Abortion	1. Associated with that which is abandoned, forgotten, or ending. 2. Could be a miscarriage of justice. See also **Death**.
Accident	1. Suggestive of a problem or a dangerous situation. 2. Could correspond to a warning.
Actor/Actress	1. The part one is currently playing. 2. May represent aspects of self. See also **Self**. 3. Whatever we associate with that individual. See also **People**.
Advisor	1. Can correspond to one's higher self. See also **Higher Self**.

	2. May be associated with personal advice or counsel. See also **People**.
Airplane	1. May be associated with a spiritual journey. 2. A lofty idea or project. 3. Might correspond to one's present direction or journey. See also **Journey**.
Akashic Records	1. Associated with the record of all that exists. 2. Can be connected to soul memory (e.g. past lives), future probabilities, and intuition. 3. Corresponds to the divine mind, God, or one's higher self. See also **God** and **Higher Self**.
Alarm Clock	1. Corresponds with timing, and may relate to the end of something or the beginning of something. 2. May be associated with a warning or a message.
Alien	1. That which is a foreign idea, experience or circumstance. 2. Depending on the imagery, might be associated with one's higher or lower self, or one's dreams or fears. See also **People**.
Alligator	1. Might represent biting/critical words or a rough exterior. 2. See also **Animals**.
Ambulance	1. Suggestive of an emergency situation. 2. Could represent a serious concern or message. 3. See also **Automobile**.
Amusement Park	1. Associated with joy, fun, happiness or relaxation. See also **Places**. 2. Could be suggestive of the need to relax and have fun, or that one is not taking something seriously.

Angel	1. A heavenly or spiritual messenger. 2. Might correspond to one's higher self. See also **Higher Self**. 3. See also **People**.
Animals	1. Animals are generally suggestive of whatever one most associates with that animal. 2. Can be symbolic of the creature's most outstanding trait or appearance (e.g. a lamb could indicate innocence or purity; a giraffe might represent a strong will because of the animal's neck; a turtle a long life or slow and methodical; an elephant could be suggestive of memory or being nosey; a baby animal could indicate a new beginning, that which is cute, etc.)
Antique	1. Often associated with the past, or a past life. See also **Karma** and **Historical Clothing/Settings**. 2. Might be indicative of that which is valuable or conversely that which is no longer useful.
Ants	1. That which is biting or bugging me. See also **Bugs**. 2. Could represent a busy worker or someone who feels insignificant.
Arm	1. Associated with self. See also **Self**. 2. May be symbolic of free will. See also **Body**. 3. Metaphorically, to keep at arm's length = to keep at a distance; she is my right arm = she is indispensible. 4. The left arm might correspond to the past; the right arm could indicate the future. See also **Direction**.
Army	1. Corresponds to whatever one most associ-

	ates with the army (e.g. career, war, aggression, etc.). 2. Might be indicative of the need to fall in line. 3. Could correspond to one's working environment. See also **Work**.
Athlete	1. Often associated with one's performance in the game of life. See also **People**. 2. Depending upon the imagery, can be symbolic of strength, agility, positive performance, etc. See also **Sports**.
Arrow	1. Can correspond to a weapon or a message. 2. Might symbolize a male energy. See also **Phallus**.
Atomic Bomb	1. A dangerous or an explosive situation. 2. Something which may cause a problem or annihilation. 3. Might be associated with an emotional experience.
Attic	1. Could indicate the higher mind, the higher self or one's own thoughts. 2. May correspond to memories or the subconscious. 3. See also **House**.
Attire	1. Associated with one's outer self, physical body or identity. 2. The type of clothing is often symbolic of what is being portrayed (e.g. a hat = ideas, shoes = direction, overcoat = emotions, business attire = work, etc.) 3. See also **Historical Clothing/Settings**.
Audience	1. Can correspond to those who are witnessing

	an activity or experience at home or at work. See also **People**. 2. Might be associated with that which is in public view, or one who craves attention.
Automobile	1. Often associated with one's direction or one's present journey. See also **Journey**. 2. Might be symbolic of the physical body or one's health (e.g. engine = heart; exhaust = eliminations, etc.). See also **Body**.
Baby	1. Associated with a new beginning, project, idea or relationship. 2. May represent a literal pregnancy. 3. Might be symbolic of the childlike aspects of self or another. See also **People**.
Back	1. Metaphorically, it's in back of me = behind me; to turn one's back = to ignore. See also **Body**. 2. Can correspond to one's past. See also **Direction**.
Backyard	1. Could represent a present situation or experience. See also **Yard**. 2. Can be associated with that which has been put behind self or that which is in the past. See also **House**. 3. Might be symbolic of that which is hidden from public view. 4. Metaphorically, in my own backyard = in my own life or experience.
Balloons	1. Can be symbolic of a celebration or the attainment of an accomplishment. 2. Could be associated with a lofty idea of journey.

	3. Might correspond to that which is full of hot air.
Banana	1. Can be symbolic of a literal dietary suggestion. See also **Food**. 2. Might be associated with male sexuality. See also **Phallus**. 3. Might correspond to one who monkeys around. See also **Monkey**.
Bank	1. Symbolic or money, finance or success. See also **Building**. 2. Metaphorically, you can bank on it = you can depend on it.
Barbecue	1. May be symbolic of whatever one associates with barbecues (e.g. family, friends, relaxation, socializing, etc.) 2. Can correspond to food, diet or health. See also **Food**.
Barefoot	1. Not being prepared for something, being exposed, or being vulnerable. 2. Could indicate relaxation. 3. May be symbolic of whatever one associates with being barefoot. See also **Feet**.
Basement	1. May be associated with the unconscious, sexuality, or repressed feelings and desires. 2. See also **House**.
Basket	1. Associated with one's personal belongings, talents, or that which one controls or can draw upon. 2. Might correspond to receptivity or female energy. See also **Womb**.
Bathroom	1. Corresponds with eliminations or the need to eliminate something.

	2. See also **House**.
Beach	1. Corresponds to whatever one most associates with the beach (e.g. relaxation, vacation, reading, etc.). 2. See also **Places**.
Bear	1. Can be angry, ferocious, overprotective, overbearing or dangerous. See also **Animal**. 2. Metaphorically, a real bear = a difficult person; a bear market = stocks in decline.
Bed/Bedroom	1. Associated with a relationship or sexuality. 2. Metaphorically, to be in bed with something = to be involved. 3. See also **House**.
Bee	1. That which biting or stinging (e.g. words spoken). See also **Bugs**. 2. Metaphorically, busy as a bee = extremely productive.
Beetle	1. That which is irritating. See also **Bugs**. 2. An Egyptian scarab corresponds to good luck or fortune.
Bible	1. Associated with spiritual truths or insights. See also **Book**. 2. Could represent a spiritual journey. See **Journey**. 3. Corresponds to the book of life. 4. Might correspond to one's soul or Akashic Records. See also **Akashic Records**.
Bicycle	1. A solitary journey or experience. 2. A balancing act. 3. Could represent one's physical body.

Bird	1. May represent a message or a messenger. The type of bird can symbolize the type of message (e.g. a dove= peace or love; a raven = warning or death; a rooster = sexuality or a new beginning, etc.). 2. See also **Animals**.
Birth	1. Generally corresponds to a new beginning. 2. That which is fresh, innocent and renewed.
Bite/Biting	1. Might correspond to criticism or aggressive expression. See also **Teeth**. 2. A situation with which one is connected or involved. 3. Metaphorically, have a bite = go ahead and try the experience.
Birdcage	1. Can be symbolic of a message or a messenger of confinement. See also **Bird**. 2. May represent one's personal association with birdcages. 3. Might symbolize that which has one confined or imprisoned. See also **Prison**.
Black	1. Corresponds to the unknown. See also **Colors**. 2. Might be symbolic of depression or death. See also **Death**. 3. Metaphorically, one who sees things as black and white = one who is extremely focused in perspective seeing only yes or no, right or wrong, etc.
Blanket	1. Can be associated with personal security or warmth. 2. Depending on the imagery, might indicate protecting one's self emotionally.

	3. Could represent sexuality or a relationship. See also **Bed/Bedroom**.
Blue	1. Can correspond to spirituality or higher wisdom. 2. Metaphorically, feeling blue = feeling sad or depressed. 3. See also **Colors**.
Boat	1. Most often associated with a spiritual or an emotional journey. See also **Water**. 2. May indicate one's present situation or experience.
Body	1. Associated with the self. See also **Self**. 2. May symbolize whatever we associate with that body part (e.g. one's feet could indicate direction; one's face may be associated with identity or self-esteem; one's mouth could represent words spoken or communication; reaching for something with one's fingers or arms could symbolize free will, etc.)
Bomb/Bombing	1. An explosive or volatile situation. 2. Could be a warning of a possible problem or a negative situation. 3. Metaphorically, she dropped a bomb = she said something that had major repercussions.
Book	1. Can represent whatever we most associated with that book, story, or source of information. 2. Corresponds to knowledge or insight. 3. Might symbolize one's soul or Akashic Records. See also **Library** and **Akashic Records**. 4. Metaphorically, by the book = according to regulations.

Boulders	1. Symbolic of difficulties, obstacles, problems or life's stumbling blocks. See also **Rocks**. 2. Can represent hardened emotions or stubborn immobility.
Boy	1. Can correspond to an idea, project, or activity in one's own life about the same age. See also **Children**. 2. Might be symbolic of one's own inner child. 3. See also **Phallus**.
Boyfriend	1. May be representative of whatever we most associate with that individual. See also **People**. 2. Could be symbolic of the masculine aspects of self. See also **Phallus**.
Box	1. Associated with a self-contained experience or idea. 2. That which one has under control. 3. Could represent female sexuality. See also **Womb**.
Brakes	1. Corresponds with the need to stop or slow down. 2. Might literally be associated with brakes. See also **Automobile**.
Bread	1. May be symbolic of personal sustenance or food. See also **Food**. 2. Metaphorically, bread = money.
Breath	1. Associated with life and personal being. See also **Body**. 2. Metaphorically, she takes my breath away = she takes away my personal control. 3. Might be indicative of the breath of life or spirit. See also **God**.

Bridge	1. That which allows a transformative passage. 2. Associated with bridging a new experience, understanding or insight.
Briefcase	1. Corresponds to one's personal identity or occupation. 2. Might be related that which is "in hand" (e.g. that with which one is already involved). 3. Could be symbolic of work. See also **Work**.
Broadside	1. That which is unexpected or comes out of nowhere. 2. An unexpected detour.
Brother	1. Most often represents the individual or whatever trait or character we most associate with that person. 2. May be associated with an aspect of our relationship with that person. See also **People**.
Brown	1. Corresponds to the material, the earthy and the practical. 2. See also **Colors**.
Buddha	1. Can be associated with faith or spirituality. 2. Generally corresponds to whatever we most associate with that individual. See also **People**.
Bugs	1. May be symbolic of whatever is associated with that bug (e.g. mosquitoes suck one's life, a butterfly corresponds to transformation, etc.) 2. That which is biting, irritating or bugging me.
Building	1. Corresponds to whatever we associate with that building (e.g. a post office = a message; places of worship = spirituality; an office building = work, etc.).

	2. May be symbolic of self or one's present situation or experience. See also **House**. 3. A tall building could correspond to male sexuality. See also **Phallus**. 4. An open or a receptive portion of a building might correspond to female sexuality. See also **Womb**.
Bull	1. That which is stubborn or aggressive. See also **Animals**. 2. Metaphorically, it's bull = it's nonsense; a bull market = stocks on the rise. 3. May represent primal urges and desires.
Bus	1. Can correspond to a group journey, project, situation or experience. 2. See also **Automobile**.
Butterfly	1. Often associated with personal transformation and change. 2. Might correspond to a spiritual experience or journey. See also **Bugs**.
Cage	1. That which is confined or limited by self or another. 2. Could be associated with personal ownership or self-imposed thoughts.
Cake	1. Corresponds to a celebration or recognition. 2. Metaphorically, to have your cake and eat it too = to get everything you desire.
Camping	1. Corresponds to whatever one most associates with camping (e.g. relaxation, vacation, getting away from it all, etc.). 2. Might correspond to a temporary situation or experience.

	3. See also **Places**.
Cancer	1. A problem situation or something that is eating at self. 2. Might indicate the need to see a doctor. 3. Might be a literal warning.
Candle	1. Can be symbolic of celebrations or the indication of certain events. 2. Might be associated with personal prayer and meditation. 3. Metaphorically, burning the candle at both ends = having too many activities and personal demands.
Candy	1. That which is sweet, tempting or desirable. 2. Might be indicative of the need to change one's dietary habits.
Cannibal	1. That which feeds off of or sucks the life from another. 2. Could be associated with one who is taking advantage of another.
Canyon	1. May correspond to a separation, a divide, or a disagreement in an experience or a relationship. 2. Might be symbolic of female sexuality. See also **Womb**.
Captain	1. Associated with a higher authority or power (e.g. God, one's boss, one's father, one's spouse, etc.). 2. See also **People**.
Car	1. Often associated with one's direction or one's present journey. See also **Journey**. 2. Might be symbolic of the physical body or

	one's health (e.g. engine = heart; exhaust = eliminations, etc.). See also **Body**.
Carpet	1. Symbolic of one's foundation. See also **House**. 2. Metaphorically, being called on the carpet = getting into trouble.
Cartoon	1. Can correspond to a creative, unbelievable, humorous, or unreal situation. 2. Might be associated with one's present experience.
Cashier	1. Associated with the payment and/or the receipt of something. See also **Money**. 2. Might correspond to one's personal karma (e.g. payment on that owed).
Castle	1. Can correspond to one's personal experience, situation or physical body. See also **House**. 2. Associated with protective walls from the outside world (e.g. insulated by one's own emotions).
Cat	1. Corresponds to whatever one may associate with cats. See also **Animals**. 2. Depending upon personal association may be symbolic of independence, love, contentment or allergies. 3. A black cat can symbolize bad luck.
Catastrophe	1. Generally corresponds to a personal challenge, struggle, hardship or obstacle. 2. Might be symbolic of a literal forthcoming experience.
Cave	1. That which is hidden, concealed or unconscious.

	2. Could be indicative of female sexuality. See also **Womb**. 3. Might correspond to the lower self.
Chair	1. One's present situation, understanding or station. 2. Might indicate a comfortable situation (e.g. something one is used to – a job, a relationship, a behavior, etc.). The type of chair could indicate the type of situation.
Champagne	1. Generally corresponds to whatever one most associates with champagne (e.g. a celebration, wealth, romance, etc.). 2. Might indicate the launch of a new direction or journey. See also **Journey**.
Chew/Chewing	1. That which one is contemplating or in the process of saying. See also **Teeth**. 2. Metaphorically, chew on it for a while = think about it for a while; biting off more than you can chew = taking on more than one is able.
Chicken	1. Metaphorically, to be a chicken = to be afraid. See also **Animals**. 2. Depending upon imagery, cold be associated with a group at home or work. 3. Might be a literal dietary suggestion.
Children	1. A young project, experience or idea. 2. Associated with one's inner child or younger self. 3. Could correspond to whatever one most associates with his or her children. See also **People**.
Christmas	1. Generally corresponds to whatever one

	most associates with the holiday. 2. Might be symbolic of the fact that one is about to receive something. 3. May be associated with personal spirituality. 4. Could correspond to the timing of an event.
Church	1. Often represents spirituality or faith. 2. Can be associated with whatever one has previously experienced with churches. See also **Building**.
Circumcision	1. Could correspond to feeling emasculated or personally challenged. See also **Phallus**. 2. Might represent coming of age. 3. Can be symbolic of a promise or a covenant.
Cliff	1. Symbolic of a dangerous precipice or situation. 2. Could be indicative of that which is beyond control in one's current experience.
Cleaners	1. Associated with that which needs to be cleaned. 2. See also **Places**.
Clock	1. Suggestive of timing for a situation or an experience. 2. Could indicate the present, past or future. 3. See also **Akashic Records**.
Clothing	1. Associated with one's outer self, physical body or identity. 2. The type of clothing is often symbolic of what is being portrayed (e.g. a hat = ideas, shoes = direction, overcoat = emotions, business attire = work, etc.)

	3. See also **Historical Clothing/Settings**.
Clouds	1. Can correspond to thoughts, ideas, emotions or the weather. See also **Sky**. 2. The imagery of the clouds may have a great deal to do with their symbolic meaning (e.g. gray clouds may indicate depression or confusion; white buoyant clouds may indicate an uplifting experience or idea). 3. Metaphorically, it is a little cloudy = it is a little uncertain.
Clown	1. Often corresponds to whatever one associates with a clown (e.g. humor, joy, foolishness, frivolity, or fear). See also **People**. 2. Might represent the display of one's emotions. 3. Metaphorically, he's a clown = he's foolish or inept.
Clubhouse	1. Generally symbolic of whatever one most associated with clubhouses (e.g. relaxation, meals, socializing, etc.). 2. See also **Places**.
Coat	1. May be associated with that which insulates self from the world (e.g. emotions). 2. Could indicate present situation or experience. See also **Clothing**.
Coffee	1. May be symbolic of whatever one associates with coffee/caffeine (e.g. energy, relaxation, the start to a new day, etc.). 2. Might correspond to the need for more energy.
Coffin	1. Corresponds to great change or the end of something.

	2. Associated with death. See also **Death**.
Cold	1. That which is unfeeling, uncomfortable or unappealing. 2. See also **Weather**.
Coliseum	1. Corresponds to whatever one most associates with the Coliseum (e.g. conflict, history, the Roman Empire, etc.). 2. Might be indicative of a past-life experience. 3. See also **Places**.
Colors	*Black* = May be associated with unconsciousness, negativity, or depression. *Blue* = Often associated with spirituality or higher wisdom. Metaphorically, feeling blue might represent feeling sad. *Brass* = Can represent a false or tarnished truth. *Brown* = Corresponds to the material, the earthy and the practical. *Gold* = Can correspond to that which is invaluable (spiritually or materially), or that which is of the Divine. *Gray* = Related to confusion, depression, or that which is cloudy or unclear. *Green* = May be symbolic of healing, growth, or envy. *Indigo* = Often associated with the higher mind or the soul. *Ivory* = Somewhat clouded from the truth; may relate to detachment and aloofness. *Orange* = Associated with creativity, energy or sexuality. *Pink* = Symbolic of higher or divine love, health ("in the pink"). *Purple* = Can be related to spiritual development or a regal nature.

	Red = Symbolic of sexuality, anger or rage; can also be associated with base creativity. *Silver* = Often associated with material value or intuition. *Violet* = Corresponds to great spirituality or spiritual dedication. *White* = Associated with purity, innocence, and holiness. *Yellow* = Represents intelligence or personal power.
Compass	1. Associated with direction. 2. Could symbolize one's life journey. See also **Journey**.
Compost	1. That which is rotten or decaying. 2. Could symbolize the need for or the act of something being recycled.
Computer	1. May be associated with work. See also **Work**. 2. Can be symbolic of memory and soul memory (e.g., Akashic Records). See also **Akashic Records**. 3. Might be an extension of one's self and self's abilities.
Condom	1. Could correspond to being vulnerable, or the need for personal protection (sexual, emotional, or otherwise). 2. Associated with male sexuality. See also **Phallus**.
Conference	1. Can be symbolic of a group activity, project, or a learning situation. 2. Might correspond to the act of listening or being heard. 3. Depending upon imagery, see also **People**.

Confusion	1. Corresponds to the unknown and the undecided. 2. See also **Emotions**.
Cook/Cooking	1. Associated with the creation of a project or idea, or one's personal responsibility with a project. See also **Work**. 2. Metaphorically, too many cooks in the kitchen = too many people in charge; to cook the books = to create fraud and deception; something is cooking = something is in the works. 3. May correspond to dietary needs/habits.
Coral	1. Can be symbolic of creativity, growth, color, and personal talents. 2. See also **Water**.
Counselor	1. Can represent one's higher self. See also **People**. 2. Indicative of personal counsel.
Court/Courthouse	1. Associated with a higher authority or power. 2. Could represent feeling judged, tried, criticized or condemned. 3. Might indicate that which is important and/ or that which needs to be judged.
Cowboy	1. Can correspond to whatever one may associate with cowboys (e.g. independence, freedom, warfare, manliness, cockiness, etc). See also **People** and **Phallus**. 2. Metaphorically, he's a real cowboy = he's really independent, or he's really cocky and unmanageable.
Crayon	1. Associated with creativity and personal talent.

	2. See also **Colors**.
Crochet	1. Can be indicative of personal creativity. 2. That with which one is presently involved. 3. Might be a metaphor for the passage of time—e.g. a stitch in time.
Crucifix	1. May be symbolic of faith. See also **Jesus**. 2. Can correspond to that which is crucifying self or causing self to suffer. 3. Might indicate the need to relinquish one's personal will in the situation.
Crying	1. Associated with loss, regret, sadness and personal release. 2. See also **Emotions**.
Crystals	1. Corresponds to clarity or insight. 2. Could represent one's dreams, ideals, talents, or goals. 3. Might be associated with that which is valuable.
Cup	1. Can be symbolic of one's present experience. 2. Might be indicative of a personal mission or life journey. See also **Journey**.
Dancing	1. A joyful or harmonious journey. See also **Music** and **Journey**. 2. Might represent a relationship or a cooperative venture.
Daughter	1. Most often represents the individual or whatever trait or character we most associate with that person. 2. May be associated with an aspect of our relationship with that person. See also **People**.

Dawn	1. Can correspond to a new beginning, a new start, or a new understanding. 2. See also **Sun**.
Day	1. Might be indicative of a fresh start or a new beginning. 2. Metaphorically, as different as night and day = that which is opposite; it's a new day = it's a fresh start.
Death	1. Generally associated with change, transition or the end of an experience. 2. Could indicate feelings of being over-whelmed by a situation. 3. Might represent a literal death. 4. Dreams of the dead can correspond with real communication.
Deer	1. Generally symbolic of whatever one most associates with a deer (e.g. gentle, the outdoors, hunting, innocence, etc.). 2. See also **Animals**.
Defecate	1. To eliminate, dispose or release something. See also **Bathroom**. 2. To spoil or ruin. 3. Can symbolize that which is crap.
Dehydration	1. May indicate that emotional, spiritual or physical sustenance is being withheld from self or another. 2. Associated with the need for water. See also **Water**.
Destruction	1. That which is in danger of being destroyed or left behind. 2. Might be a personal warning of some kind.

Devastation	1. Can be symbolic of the complete loss of something. 2. A major change upon one's life journey.
Devil	1. Corresponds to temptation, hidden desires, one's shadow or evil. See also **People**. 2. Might be symbolic of one's own fears. 3. Could symbolize a negative male energy. See also **Phallus**.
Diary	1. Represents one's life story. 2. Could correspond to one's soul or Akashic Records. See also **Akashic Records**.
Dinosaur	1. Can correspond to anger and aggression See also **Animals**. 2. Because of the angry mouth, could correspond to biting criticism. 3. Metaphorically, he is such a dinosaur = he is outdated and past his prime. 4. Might be indicative of that which is in the past and no longer relevant.
Direction	1. Corresponds to one's personal path and/or life direction. See also **Journey**. 2. Each direction might also symbolize issues related to the self (e.g., west or going left can be indicative of the past; east or going right can correspond to the future; north can be associated with thoughts/ideas or spirituality; and, south can represent the unconscious or sexuality).
Dirt/Dirty	1. Can be associated with that which is unclean, immoral, challenging or labor intensive. 2. Depending upon imagery, dirt can correspond to that which is grounded or of the earth.

Dishes	1. That which is being presented (e.g. ideas or experiences). 2. The personal situation within one's own hands. 3. Washing dishes could symbolize cleansing a situation.
Doctor	1. Can be associated with physical, emotional or spiritual health. See also **People**. 2. Could indicate a higher authority or power. 3. Metaphorically, to doctor something = to change or take care of it.
Doe	1. A doe can be symbolic of whatever one most associates with a female a deer (e.g. vulnerability, nature, innocence). See also **Animals**. 2. Could correspond to the feminine aspects of self or another. See also **Womb**.
Dog	1. Corresponds to whatever one may associate with dogs. See also **Animals**. 2. May represent friendship, love or companionship. 3. Depending upon imagery might represent that which is important to one's self, an extension of family, allergies, or even anger/aggression.
Dolphin	1. Can be associated with spirituality or higher intelligence. Although a mammal, see also **Fish**. 2. Because of "New Age" association, might be indicative of new thought, holism, or evolutionary spirituality. See also **Animals**.
Donald Trump	1. Associated with whatever we most think of that individual. See also **People**.

	2. Might be symbolic of personal wealth, successful business, arrogance, etc.
Door/Doorway	1. Can correspond to new opportunities or directions. See also **House**. 2. The location and appearance of the door will have a great deal to do with its possible symbolic meaning (e.g. front door = something coming to face you; a locked door = that which doesn't want to be dealt with, etc.).
Dove	1. A messenger of peace and tranquility. 2. May represent whatever one associates with doves. See also **Animals**.
Dress Code	1. Often corresponds to that which is appropriate, proper, or personally required. See also **Clothing**. 2. Generally associated with work. See also **Work**.
Drill Sergeant	1. Associated with extreme control, regimentation and exacting procedures. 2. Metaphorically, he is such a drill sergeant = he is a control freak.
Drink	1. Associated with that which can quench one's thirst. 2. That which takes into one's self. 3. Depending upon imagery, see also **Water**.
Driveway	1. Might be associated with one's present situation or experience. 2. The place where one is currently "parked" (e.g. at home or work). See also **Home** or **Work**. 3. May be indicative of one's present direction or a pending situation.

Driving	1. Can be symbolic of traveling the journey of life. See also **Journey**. 2. If someone else is driving your car, it may indicate that you have relinquished control to another or may need to take control. See also **Car**.
Drugs	1. Depending upon personal association, might be associated with personal healing or personal escape. 2. Might correspond to an illegal undertaking.
Eagle	1. Associated with a message of idealism or strength. See also **Animals**. 2. May be symbolic of the United States and whatever one associated with the United States (e.g. freedom, independence, military power, etc.). See also **Places**.
Ear	1. Corresponds with listening or the need to be heard. 2. See also **Body**.
Earth	1. Represents one's current situation or experience. 2. Associated with that which is grounded, stable or earthy. 3. Might correspond to that which is practical.
Earthquake	1. May correspond to a major shakeup in one's personal journey. See also **Journey**. 2. Can be symbolic of personal or emotional instability. 3. Might be a precognitive event.
East	1. Generally associated with whatever one thinks of the east (e.g. government, the rising sun, etc.)

	2. Could be indicative of the left and be suggestive of the past. See also **Direction**.
Eating	1. Associated with choices or decisions made (e.g. free will and what one puts in one's mouth). 2. That which one takes into one's self. See also **Food**.
Egypt	1. Corresponds to whatever one associates with Egypt (e.g. the pyramids, the Middle East, vacation, a foreign idea, the desert, etc.). 2. See also **Places**.
Eiffel Tower	1. May be symbolic of love, romance, passion or travel. 2. Can represent a male figure or energy. See also **Phallus**. 3. See also **Tower**.
Eight	1. May correspond to balance, good judgment, infinity, great strength or great weakness. 2. See also **Numbers**.
Elephant	1. Can be symbolic of memory, age, wisdom or power. 2. Could represent that which is "nosey" or that which is "thick-skinned." 3. Can be symbolic of whatever one most associates with elephants. See also **Animals**.
Elevator	1. Corresponds to different levels of consciousness. 2. The ups and downs of one's present experience. 3. Ascending might signify that which is a promotion whereas descending might indicate a demotion.

Eleven	1. Represents mastery in the physical dimension; might also be indicative of two. 2. See also **Numbers**.
Emotions	1. Whatever emotion is being portrayed is often indicative of a real-life situation in which the dreamer feels the very same emotion. 2. Generally associated with one's feeling in a current situation or experience. See also **Journey**.
Enemy	1. Represents that from which one is running or avoiding in self or in others. 2. Can be symbolic of something that causes one to be fearful. 3. See also **People**.
Engaged	1. Might be indicative of a literal engagement or relationship. 2. That with which one is presently involved or connected. 3. Depending on imagery, see also **People**.
Engine	1. Can be symbolic of that which gives power and vitality. 2. Might be associated with one's literal heart or with one's feelings about something. 3. Depending upon imagery, see also **Automobile**.
Eyes	1. Associated with vision or insight. 2. An aspect of self. See also **Body**. 3. Might be indicative of the all-seeing Eye (e.g. God). See also **God**.
Face	1. Corresponds to the self. See also **Body** and **Self**.

	2. How self may be viewed by others. 3. That which one is currently facing. See also **People**.
Fairy	1. Associated with magic or enchantment. 2. Could represent a spiritual messenger. See also **People**. 3. Metaphorically, a fairy = a person who is gay; a fairy tale = an untruth.
Falling	1. Symbolic of a situation that is out of control or overwhelming. 2. May indicate a fear of failure or a loss of personal power/will.
Fangs	1. Corresponds to that which sucks the life out of self or another. 2. May be associated with the loss of personal energy, enthusiasm or will. 3. Depending upon imagery, see also **Teeth**.
Father	1. Most often represents the individual or whatever trait or character we most associate with that person. See also **People**. 2. Associated with a higher authority or power (e.g. God, one's boss, one's father, one's spouse, etc.). 3. Can be symbolic of some aspect our relationship with that person.
Feet	1. Associated with one's direction or life's journey. See also **Body**. 2. Could indicate one's personal foundation or understanding.
Fence	1. A barrier which confines, keeps out, or protects.

	2. May be associated with one's current situation or experience. 3. Metaphorically, on the fence = being undecided.
Fetal Position	1. Can be indicative of that which is vulnerable. 2. Associated with that which is developing or immature. See also **Baby**. 3. Metaphorically, she crawled into a fetal position = she was scared, nervous or overwhelmed.
Fiancé/Fiancée	1. Most often represents the individual or whatever trait or character we most associate with that person. See also **People**. 2. Corresponds to a cooperative venture or a relationship. 3. Could indicate personal integration.
Field	1. Often associated with one's current situation or experience. See also **Work** or **Home**. 2. The issue which has been presented to you.
Fight	1. Symbolic of a personal struggle with self or others. 2. That with which one is at war. See also **War**.
Fingers	1. Represents choice or free will. 2. An extension of self. See also **Body**.
Fire	1. Can represent strong emotions, anger or volatility. 2. That which destroys or purifies. 3. Metaphorically, playing with fire = taking a big risk.

Fish	1. Often associated with spirituality or faith. See also **Animals**. 2. Metaphorically, something's fishy = something's not right; a fish out of water = that which is out of place or inappropriate for the situation. 3. Can correspond to whatever one most associates with fishing.
Fishbowl	1. Associated with one's spiritual belief system. See also **Fish**. 2. May be associated with one's present situation or experience. 3. Metaphorically, I live in a fishbowl = others see and know everything about me.
Five	1. Can correspond to the earth, materiality, service, stability, or human love. 2. See also **Numbers**.
Flag	1. A signal, a message or an affiliation. 2. Associated with whatever country or image is being portrayed. 3. Can correspond to patriotism.
Flood	1. Represents an overwhelming emotional experience or situation. See also **Water**. 2. Can indicate personal transformation and change.
Flowers	1. Symbolic of one's talents or abilities. 2. That which is about to blossom or bloom. 3. Different types of flowers are often associated with different meaning (e.g. a lily can correspond to rebirth; a rose is suggestive of love, etc.).

Flying	1. Can be associated with great joy or euphoria. 2. May correspond to an elevating experience or spirituality. 3. Suggests personal mastery or the ability to rise above an experience.
Flying Saucer	1. That which is a foreign idea, experience or circumstance. 2. Depending on the imagery, might be associated with one's dreams or fears. 3. See also **Airplane**.
Fog	1. Symbolic of personal confusion or doubt. 2. Might be suggestive of conflicting emotions.
Food	1. Sometimes dreaming of food can indicate a literal dietary suggestion (e.g. something one needs to eat or something one needs to stop eating). 2. That which one takes into one's self. 3. Can be associated with free will. 4. Associated with physical, mental or spiritual sustenance.
Forehead	1. Associated with an idea, thought, or decision in the forefront of one's mind. See also **Head**. 2. Could correspond to the third eye or the higher self. See also **Higher Self**.
Forest	1. One's present situation or experience. 2. Can indicate growth and stability or overgrowth and confusion. 3. Metaphorically, can't see the forest for the trees = getting caught up in details. 4. You may also wish to see **Trees** or **Woods**.

Fountain	1. Associated with spiritual knowledge or insight. See also **Water**. 2. The fountain of youth represents youth and vitality. 3. Could indicate the bursting forth of talents, emotions, ideas or sexuality.
Four	1. Can correspond to the earth, materiality, service, stability, or human love. 2. See also **Numbers**.
Four Leaf Clover	1. Associated with good luck or good fortune. 2. You may also wish to see **Four** and **Grass**.
Friend	1. Corresponds to the individual's outstanding character, talent or trait. See also **People**. 2. An aspect of self in relationship to that individual. 3. Can be symbolic of our relationship with that person.
Front	1. Metaphorically, it's in front of me = ahead of me; to be up front = to be direct. See also **Body**. 2. Can correspond to one's future. See also **Direction**.
Front Yard	1. Could represent present situation or experience. See also **Yard**. 2. Can be associated with that which is in the future. 3. Might be symbolic of that which is being shown to or seen by others. 4. See also **House**.
Funeral	1. Corresponds to great change or the end of something. 2. Associated with death. See also **Death**.

	3. In portions of South America, dreaming of a funeral often symbolizes that someone is about to get married.
Games	1. Corresponds to a team event or a competition. See also **Work**. 2. The game one is currently playing on the journey of life. See also **Journey**. 3. Any type of game or sports event can also correspond with what one literally associates with that game or event (e.g. relaxation, specific seasons, family activities, etc.). 4. Metaphorically, the game is up = it is over or there is no longer the possibility of a successful outcome; playing the game = to act in accord with what one should be doing.
Garage	1. May be associated with that which is unused or that which is in personal storage (e.g. memory). 2. Can represent one's self. See also **Automobile** and **House**.
Garbage	1. That which has been discarded or needs to be discarded. 2. Might correspond to something worthless or immoral.
Garden	1. Can correspond to one's talents and abilities. 2. Might be symbolic of whatever one associates with the garden.
Genie	1. The magical or limitless part of one's self. See also **People**. 2. Associated with magic, power or boundless creativity. 3. Could represent a wish or a lucky situation.

Ghost	1. May symbolize the past, one's shadow, or that which is haunting you. 2. See also **Death**.
Giant	1. That which appears large, threatening or immense. See also **People**. 2. Might correspond to an obstacle or a challenge.
Giraffe	1. May be symbolic of one's neck (e.g. sticking one's neck out) or will power. 2. See also **Animals**.
Girl	1. Can correspond to an idea, project, or activity in one's own life about the same age. See also **Children**. 2. Might be symbolic of one's own inner child. 3. See also **Womb.**
Girlfriend	1. May be representative of whatever we most associate with that individual. See also **People**. 2. Could be symbolic of the feminine aspects of self. See also **Womb**.
Glass	1. As a substance can be associated with insight or fragility. 2. A glass (for drinking) generally is dependent upon whatever is in the glass but in general it can correspond to the situation within one's own hand or it might be indicative of a personal mission or life journey. See also **Journey.**
Glasses	1. Corresponds to vision, comprehension or insight. 2. That through which one perceives. See also **Eyes.**

Gloves	1. That which covers one's hands. See also **Hands**. 2. Metaphorically, to handle with kid gloves = to be careful with.
God	1. Associated with the Creator, the ultimate spiritual source, the impetus behind all that exists, and that which is Divine. 2. Might correspond to personal spirituality or one's higher self. See also **People** and **Higher Self**.
Gold	1. Might symbolize spiritual wealth, insight or information. 2. Associated with one's own potential talents or resources.
Gold (color)	1. Can correspond to that which is invaluable (spiritually or materially), or that which is of the Divine. 2. See also **Colors**.
Goldfish	1. Can be symbolic of personal faith or a spiritual journey. 2. See also **Fish**.
Grand Canyon	1. That which is separated and apart (e.g. a big divide). 2. May correspond to whatever one associates with the Grand Canyon (e.g. vacation, honeymoon, danger, etc.) See also **Places**.
Grandfather/ Grandmother	1. May represent the individual or whatever trait or character we most associate with that person. See also **People**. 2. Often can correspond with wisdom or insight. 3. Might be symbolic of an aspect of our

	relationship with that individual.
Grass	1. Can represent one's current situation or experience. See also **Yard**. 2. Depending on the imagery, might be associated with growth and vitality. 3. Metaphorically, grass = marijuana.
Grave	1. Corresponds to great change or the end of something. 2. Associated with death. See also **Death**. 3. Could represent that which one has buried, repressed, or that which is extremely serious (e.g. "grave').
Gray	1. Related to confusion, depression, or that which is cloudy or unclear. 2. See also **Colors**.
Green	1. May be symbolic of healing, growth, or envy. 2. See also **Colors**.
Grocery Store	1. Can correspond to the act of making personal choices and decisions (e.g. choosing things to put in one's cart). 2. May be associated with something occurring in one's present experience. 3. Might correspond to diet and health.
Ground	1. Associated with that which is grounded, stable or earthy. 2. Might correspond to that which is practical.
Gum	1. Can be associated with that which one is currently contemplating or communicating. See also **Chewing**. 2. See also **Teeth**.

Gun	1. Can represent violence, aggression or dominance. 2. Might be symbolic of a male energy or sexuality. See also **Phallus**.
Hair	1. Often related to thoughts, ideas or insights. See also **Body**. 2. Metaphorically, a hair-raising experience = a scary experience; splitting hairs = to argue about the trivial.
Hammer	1. Can correspond to a powerful or driving force. 2. That which builds or creates. 3. Might be associated with a male energy. See also **Phallus**.
Hand	1. Associated with the self or one's free will. See also **Body**. 2. Metaphorically, to give a hand = to congratulate; to force one's hand = to push someone into action.
Hat	1. Often related to thoughts, ideas or insights. See also **Hair**. 2. Might indicate one's occupation or that with which one is involved.
Hat Pin	1. Can correspond to thoughts, ideas or insights. See also **Hat**. 2. Might be associated with something that is stuck or pricking at one's thoughts.
Head	1. Can correspond with the self or one's thoughts. See also **Body**. 2. Metaphorically, losing one's head = not thinking something through; using one's head

	= giving something much contemplation.
Heart	1. Generally symbolic of love and relationships. 2. Metaphorically, her heart was not in it = she was not really interested. 3. See also **Body.**
Helicopter	1. May be associated with a spiritual journey. 2. A lofty idea or project. 3. Might correspond to one's present direction or journey. See also **Journey.**
Herbs	1. Can be associated with diet, health and personal healing. See also **Food.** 2. Might be a literal health or healing recommendation.
Hero	1. May represent one's inner talents or higher self. See also **People** and **Higher Self.** 2. The qualities we associate with the ultimate human being. See also **Phallus** and **Womb.**
Higher Self	1. Corresponds to one's soul or divine self. See also **God.** 2. Can be associated with personal guidance and direction. See also **Message.**
Hill	1. A small challenge, obstacle or goal. See also **Mountain.** 2. May be associated with levels of ability or consciousness. 3. Metaphorically, over the hill = past one's prime. 4. Going over a hill can be a warning related to one's personal lifestyle or journey.
Historical Clothing/ Settings	1. Often corresponds with whatever an individual associates with that clothing or setting.

	See also **Clothing**. 2. May be indicative of a past-life memory pattern that is similar to a present-day experience. 3. See also **Places**.
Home/ Rooms in Home	1. Representative of one's personal experience or current situation. 2. Rooms in a house can correspond to whatever is associated with that room (e.g., Master Bedroom = relationships or sexuality; kitchen = diet or home and family; basement = repressed desires; bathroom = eliminations, cleanliness). 3. A house can also represent one's physical body (roof or attic = thoughts, basement = unconsciousness, etc.). See also **Self**. 4. Could be symbolic of what is occurring in the life experience of a member of one's family.
Horizon	1. Often associated with the future and/or that which is about to enter into one's present experience. 2. See also **Journey**.
Horse	1. Can be associated with a message or a messenger. See also **Animals**. 2. Might represent one's sexuality or desire. 3. Metaphorically, to horse around = to not be serious. 4. A white horse can be associated with a hero; a black horse might correspond to death or the end of something.
Hospital	1. Symbolic of a problem, situation or health concern requiring immediate attention. See also **Building** and **Places**. 2. That which needs to be healed or is in the

	process of being healed. See also **Doctor**.
Hot	1. That which is appealing, stimulating, or sexually exciting. 2. See also **Weather**.
Hot Dog	1. Can correspond to whatever one most associates with hot dogs (e.g. a picnic). See also **Eating**. 2. Metaphorically, "hot dog!" = that's wonderful!
Hotel	1. Associated with a temporary experience or situation. See also **House** and **Building**. 2. Can correspond to whatever an individual associates with hotels.
House/ Rooms in House	1. Representative of one's personal experience or current situation. 2. Someone else's house can be symbolic of whatever you most associate with that person. See also **People**. 3. Rooms in a house can correspond to whatever is associated with that room (e.g. Master Bedroom = relationships or sexuality; kitchen = diet or home and family; bathroom = eliminations. 4. A house can also represent one's physical body (roof or attic = thoughts, basement = unconsciousness, etc.). See also **Self**.
Hurricane	1. Often symbolic of emotional turmoil. 2. Can correspond to verbal arguments and aggression. 3. Can be associated with a challenging experience or situation over which one has no control.

Husband	1. Might correspond to a partnership or a co-operative venture. See also **Marriage** or **Wedding**. 2. May represent the individual or whatever trait or character we most associate with that person. 3. Can be symbolic of our relationship with that person. See also **People**.
Ice	1. Associated with frozen, chilly or repressed emotion. See also **Water**. 2. Metaphorically, on thin ice = on dangerous ground.
Indian	1. Might correspond to nature, the earth, or whatever one associates with Indians. See also **People**. 2. Could symbolize a spiritual journey or quest.
Indigo	1. Often associated with the higher mind or the soul. 2. See also **Colors**.
Insects	1. May be symbolic of whatever is associated with that bug (e.g. mosquitoes suck one's life, a butterfly corresponds to transformation, etc.) 2. That which is biting, irritating or bugging you.
Internet	1. Often associated with whatever one most does while on the internet (e.g. socializing, shopping, surfing specific sites, gaming, etc.) 2. Can correspond to personal communication. 3. Might be symbolic of the Akashic Records. See also **Akashic Records**.

iPad	1. May be associated with work. See also **Work**. 2. Can be symbolic of memory and soul memory (e.g., Akashic Records). See also **Akashic Records**.
iPhone	1. Generally associated with communication at home or work. See also **Home** and **Work**. 2. Can correspond to whatever one associated with iPhones (e.g., social networking, extension of self, etc.). See also **Message**.
Island	1. Can correspond with one's present situation or experience. 2. Symbolic of an emotional or spiritual experience. See also **Water**. 3. Might represent one who is isolated or set apart.
Ivory	1. Somewhat clouded from the truth; may relate to detachment and aloofness. 2. See also **Colors**.
Jail	1. That which has one caged or captive (e.g. work, a situation or a relationship, etc.). 2. Represents a confining experience. See also **Building**.
Jaws	1. Might be associated with words spoken. See also **Teeth**. 2. A clenched jaw could be indicative of something being held inside. 3. Might correspond with one's self and image. See also **Face**.
Jeep	1. Often associated with one's direction or one's present journey. See also **Car**. 2. Can correspond to one's personal independence.

Jesus	1. Can be associated with faith or spirituality. 2. Generally corresponds to whatever we most associate with that individual. See also **People**.
Jewels	1. Symbolic of one's talents or abilities. 2. Might be associated with truth, wisdom, healing or insight. 3. Metaphorically, a real jewel = something valuable.
Job	1. Associated with one's work. See also **Work**. 2. Could correspond to one's talents, abilities, duties, etc. 3. The image of an old job could symbolize one's present employment.
Journey	1. Generally associated with one's personal mission, life experiences and/or journey in life. 2. The imagery of what is occurring upon one's journey is often associated with present experiences and relationships, especially at home or work. See also **Home** and **Work**.
Jungle	1. Could represent one's present situation or experience. 2. That which is lush, overgrown or filled with life and potential. 3. Metaphorically, it's a jungle out there = the situation is wild and uncontrollable.
Key	1. Associated with the solution or the answer. 2. Metaphorically, to hold the keys = to hold the answer or the power.
Kidnapped	1. Corresponds to that which is taken or stolen. 2. Associated with something being out of one's control.

Kill	1. Can correspond to overt aggression, control or suppression of self or another. 2. Might be symbolic of loss or the death of something. See also **Death**.
King	1. Associated with a higher authority or power (e.g. God, one's boss, one's father, one's spouse, etc.). 2. See also **People**.
Kiss	1. Suggestive of affection, passion, sexuality or friendship. 2. May correspond to a cooperative venture or situation. 3. Metaphorically, kiss and make up = to make amends; giving someone the kiss off = to brush someone aside.
Kitchen	1. Associated with diet or home and family. See also **House**. 2. That which one is preparing or taking into one's self.
Kitten	1. Generally symbolic of whatever one associates with kittens (e.g. playfulness, innocence, etc.). See also **Animals**. 2. See also **Cat**.
Kleenex	1. Associated with sadness or one's personal health. 2. Depending upon imagery, see also **Nose**.
Knife	1. Can represent anger, aggression or power. 2. Might be suggestive of that which cuts or divides. 3. May symbolize a male energy. See also **Phallus**.

Ladder	1. Corresponds to different levels of consciousness. 2. The ups and downs of one's present experience. 3. Ascending might signify that which is a promotion whereas descending might indicate a demotion. 4. Walking under a ladder could represent an unlucky situation or experience.
Lady Luck	1. Associated with luck and person gain. 2. Might indicate financial gain or personal success.
Lake	1. Can correspond to a spiritual or an emotional source. See also **Water**. 2. That which is at peace or tranquil. 3. Might be associated with meditation.
Lamb	1. Represents purity, innocence or meekness. See also **Animals**. 2. Metaphorically, as innocent as a lamb = extremely gentle. 3. Biblically, might represent the Christ. See also **People**.
Lamp	1. Can be symbolic of light or illumination. 2. Might correspond to placing focus or insight on a situation or experience. 3. A genie's lamp is symbolic of good luck. See also **Genie**.
Laughter	1. Associated with joy, happiness, attainment and personal release. See also **Emotions**. 2. Might indicate one who is hiding behind true feelings.
Laundromat	1. Associated with that which needs to be cleaned.

	2. See also **Places**.
Lawn	1. Can represent one's current situation or experience. See also **Yard**. 2. Depending on the imagery, might be associated with growth and vitality. 3. Metaphorically, grass = marijuana.
Leaves	1. Associated with growth, possibilities or new ideas. 2. Blowing leaves may indicate that which is being discarded or the passage of time.
Leeches	1. That which drains one's energy or life force. 2. Could correspond to an individual who is using another.
Left	1. Associated with the past, open-mindedness, being liberal, and the west. See also **Direction**. 2. Might correspond to the left brain or logic.
Legs	1. Often symbolic of one's direction or present standing. See also **Body**. 2. Could represent one's foundation or support system. 3. You may also wish to see **Journey**.
Letter	1. Represents a message or a communication. 2. Information from another source (e.g. one's intuition, another person).
Library	1. Can be associated with knowledge, learning or insight. See also **Building**. 2. Could correspond to one's own soul or Akashic Records. See also **Book**.
Light	1. Associated with a flash of insight or a new idea.

	2. Can correspond to spiritual truths or insight. 3. Might represent God or one's higher self. See also **Higher Self**.
Lightning	1. An emotional storm or outburst. 2. Symbolic of a warning message. 3. Might indicate vivid flashes of insight or ideas.
Limb	1. Can correspond to an extension of one's self. See also **Arm** or **Leg**. 2. Missing a limb may be symbolic of loss, abandonment, divorce, or missing that which is integral to the situation.
Lion	1. Represents personal power or vitality. See also **Animals**. 2. The king of the forest (e.g. the boss, one's higher self, etc.). 3. Might be symbolic of a play on words and one who is lying. 4. Depending upon imagery, could indicate anger and aggression.
Lips	1. Can correspond to communication, romance, or personal identity. See also **Mouth**. 2. Metaphorically, to give someone lip service = to say what someone wants to hear.
Liquor	1. Can be associated with over-indulgence or the loss of personal inhibitions. 2. Might be symbolic of "the spirits" (e.g. spirituality or emotion).
Living Room	1. One's present situation or experience. See also **House**. 2. The environment in which one finds herself or himself (e.g. work, home, a relationship, etc.).

Lottery	1. Often associated with good luck or good fortune. 2. Might be literal and symbolic of chance and one's personal timing.
Luggage	1. Associated with one's own baggage (e.g. feelings, beliefs, talents or problems). 2. Could represent a literal or a metaphorical trip (e.g. a vacation or traveling between thought, ideas, or goals). 3. Might correspond to soul memory.
Lungs	1. Associated with life and personal being. See also **Body**. 2. Metaphorically, she takes my breath away = she takes away my personal control. 3. Might be indicative of the breath or life or spirit. See also **God**.
Mail/Mailman	1. Represents a message or a messenger. 2. Information from another source (e.g. one's intuition, another person). 3. If a mailman is being portrayed, you may also wish to see **People**.
Mall	1. Symbolic of choices, opportunities, decisions, or personal activities. 2. Can correspond to whatever one may associate with a mall. See also **Places**.
Man	1. Can indicate the masculine side of one's self or another. See also **Phallus**. 2. Could be associated with masculine traits (e.g. strength, courage, stubbornness, etc.). 3. See also **People**.
Mansion	1. Can correspond to one's present situation or

	experience. See also **House** and **Work**. 2. Might be associated with a lofty goal or a successful outcome.
Map	1. Can be associated with personal direction and guidance. 2. Might be indicative of one's mission or journey. See also **Journey**. 3. Could correspond to one's present life and experience.
Marriage	1. Represents a partnership, a new venture, or a relationship. See also **People**. 2. Could indicate a cooperative situation or experience. 3. Might be literally symbolic of that which is to come. 4. Associated with coming to terms with another.
Meat	1. Depending upon imagery, might be indicative of personal dietary advice. See also **Eating**. 2. Suggestive of whatever one most associates with meat (e.g. protein).
Mechanic	1. Corresponds to whatever one associates with a mechanic (e.g. tune-up, repairs, etc.). See also **People**. 2. May be symbolic of one's personal automobile. (e.g. journey or physical body). See **Car** and **Journey**.
Medicine	1. May be associated with the need for personal healing. See also **Doctor**. 2. Might correspond to literal healing advice.
Meditation	1. Associated with spirituality, attunement and the divine. See also **God**.

	2. Could be related to divine communication.
Menorah	1. May represent faith or spirituality. 2. A seven-branched candlestick. See also **Candle**. 3. Might be associated with the seven spiritual centers. See also **Seven**.
Message	1. Can be associated with personal guidance, needed information, intuitive assistance or information from one's higher or soul self. See also **Higher Self**. 2. May be either a literal or a symbolic message related to one's life, personal journey, relationships, work or home. See also **Journey**, **Work** and **Home**.
Milk	1. Might indicate a literal dietary suggestion. See also **Food.** 2. That which nurtures or feeds one's self. 3. May be associated with one's own mother. See also **Mother.**
Mirror	1. Reflective of the self or one's current situation. See also **Self**. 2. Could frame things in an alternative perspective. 3. Might be associated with memory and personal reflection. 4. Breaking a mirror might correspond to an unlucky situation or experience.
Mohammed	1. Can be associated with faith or spirituality. 2. Generally corresponds to whatever we most associate with that individual. See also **People**.
Money	1. Symbolic or money, finance or success.

	2. Could represent energy or personal power.
Monkey	1. Might correspond to one who monkeys around. See also **Animal**. 2. May represent foolishness or pranks.
Monster	1. Can represent one's fears or problems. See also **People**. 2. That from which one is running.
Moon	1. Associated with the emotions and the intuition. 2. Can correspond to the feminine aspects of one's self. See also **Womb**.
Moses	1. Can be associated with faith or spirituality. 2. Generally corresponds to whatever we most associate with that individual. See also **People**.
Mother	1. Most often represents the individual or whatever trait or character we most associate with that person. 2. Associated with a higher authority or power (e.g. God, one's boss, one's mother, one's spouse, etc.). 3. May be symbolic of our relationship with that person. See also **People**.
Mountain	1. Represents a goal, a challenge, a destination or an accomplishment. 2. May be associated with higher mental or spiritual states of awareness. 3. Ascending a mountain might indicate a promotion; falling off a mountain might indicate a failure or a warning related to one's personal lifestyle or journey.

Mouth	1. Corresponds to words spoken or that which takes into one's self. See also **Body**. 2. Metaphorically, having a big mouth = speaking too much. 3. You may also wish to see **Teeth**.
Movies	1. Can correspond to one's life story, present situation or soul's journey. 2. Could be symbolic of whatever one associates with that movie. See also **Actor/Actress**.
Mud	1. An emotional or unclear situation or experience. 2. A hindrance, an obstacle, or that which has created a problem (e.g. a muddy situation).
Mushroom Cloud	1. Can correspond to a dangerous or problematic situation. 2. May be indicative of a volatile temper in self or another.
Music	1. Associated with a harmonious situation or experience. 2. See also **Dancing**.
Musical	1. A harmonious situation with which one is presently involved. 2. Often associated with the role one is presently playing. See also **Actor/Actress**.
Nail	1. Symbolic of that which holds things together. 2. Could correspond to personal projects and/or work. See also **Work**. 3. Might be associated with personal crucifixion. See also **Crucifix**.

Naked	1. Can correspond to showing off or personal vulnerability. 2. Might represent the act of becoming completely exposed.
Neck	1. Often corresponds to the personal will. See also **Body**. 2. Metaphorically, putting one's neck out = taking a chance; to wring one's neck = to punish.
Neighbor	1. Most often represents the individual or whatever trait or character we most associate with that person. 2. May be associated with an aspect of our relationship with that person. See also **People**.
New	1. That which is fresh, new, or unused. 2. Could be associated with something which has yet to be explored or taken advantage of.
Newspaper	1. A message or communication. 2. Associated with knowledge, insight or information.
New Year's Eve	1. Symbolic of whatever one most associates with New Year's Eve (e.g. a celebration, a change, etc.). 2. Can be indicative of the timing of an event or experience (e.g. in the New Year; next year).
New York City	1. Corresponds to whatever one most associates with New York (e.g. business, work, finance, or the theater). 2. See also **Places**.
Nightmares	1. A situation or experience from which one has been running.

	2. May be associated with that which one has been ignoring or neglecting. 3. Can correspond to fears or personal anxieties.
Nine	1. Can represent fulfillment, completion, transformation or wholeness. 2. See also **Numbers**.
Noisemakers	1. Can be associated with a celebration, an achievement, or a major event. 2. Might correspond to someone or something making a lot of noise without substance.
North	1. Generally associated with whatever one thinks of the north (e.g. liberalism, business, etc.) 2. Could be indicative of the mind or the higher self. See also **Direction**.
Nose	1. Associated with the self or one's personal identity. See also **Self** and **Head**. 2. Can correspond with a sense of smell. 3. Metaphorically, led by the nose = easily manipulated; being nosey = being involved where one shouldn't. 4. Might be symbolic of a drug habit.
Numbers	In addition to the possibility of symbolizing whatever we most associate with that specific number, numbers can correspond to the following meanings: *Zero* = Symbolic of nothing, that which is absent or the all-encompassing. *One* = The first, the beginning, individuality; personal survival. *Two* = Can symbolize duality, opposites, relationships; sexuality.

	Three = Represents body, mind, spirit; the trinity; great strength or personal power. *Four* = Can correspond to the earth, materiality, service, stability, or human love. *Five* = Associated with change, the five senses, new beginnings, or will power. *Six* = Can indicate symmetry, beauty, and harmony; human dominance or Christ-mindedness. *Seven* = Might be associated with spirituality, sacredness, perfection, or the seven spiritual centers/chakras. *Eight* = May correspond to balance, good judgment, infinity, great strength or great weakness. *Nine* = Can represent fulfillment, completion, transformation or wholeness. *Ten* = Can suggest completeness and strength; or, the same as one. *Eleven* = Represents mastery in the physical dimension; might also be indicative of two. *Twelve* = Can correspond to cosmic order, the circle of life; or same as three. *Thirteen* = Bad luck; same as four. *Twenty-two* = Mastery in the mental/emotional dimension; same as four. *Thirty-three* = Mastery in the spiritual dimension; same as six. *Forty* = Associated with cleansing, purification, trial, or transformation; same as four.
Nurse	1. Can be associated with physical, emotional or spiritual health. 2. Might represent one's higher self. See also **People**. 3. Metaphorically, to nurse something = to take care or it.

Ocean	1. An emotional situation or experience. See also **Water**. 2. Associated with a spiritual journey. 3. Might represent one's own unconscious or subconscious mind.
Office	1. Symbolic of work. See also **Building**. 2. One's present situation or experience. 3. A duty or an obligation.
Old Person	1. Generally corresponds to wisdom or one's Higher Self. See also **People**. 2. The imagery related to whatever is occurring with and around the old person will have a great deal to do with the symbolic meaning.
One	1. The first, the beginning, individuality; personal survival. 2. See also **Numbers**.
Opossum	1. Can correspond to whatever one most associates with opossums. See also **Animals**. 2. Might be indicative of "hanging out" or personal laziness.
Orange (color)	1. Associated with creativity, energy or sexuality. 2. See also **Colors**.
Orange Juice/ Oranges	1. Might indicate a literal dietary suggestion and the need for vitamin C. 2. See also **Food**.
Osteopath	1. Corresponds to the spine, literally or metaphorical (e.g. the need for a physical adjustment or one's personal power and self-esteem).

	2. Can be associated with health. See also **People**. 3. Could indicate a higher authority or power.
Over	1. Suggestive of being out of, beyond, superior to, or not affected by that which one is over. 2. Depending upon imagery, might be indicative of a literal out of body experience, or an experience in consciousness. See also **Flying**.
Owl	1. Associated with wisdom. See also **Animals**. 2. Metaphorically, a night owl = one who stays up late.
Oxygen	1. Corresponds to that which facilitates life. 2. Might be symbolic of spirit. See also **Spirit**.
Painting	1. Generally corresponds to one's present experience or situation. 2. Might be indicative of a creative talent or personal mission. 3. See also **Picture**.
Pants	1. Can correspond to one's direction. See also **Legs**. 2. Might be associated with one's personal identity or belief system. 3. Metaphorically, wearing the pants in the family = being the boss.
Paper	1. Blank paper can be symbolic of a new beginning or something which has yet to be undertaken. 2. A message or communication. See also **Newspaper**.
Parachute	1. Symbolic of escaping, deserting or the need

	to abandon a situation. 2. Can indicate a descent. 3. Metaphorically, a golden parachute = a generous severance package.
Parents	1. Associated with a higher authority or power (e.g. God, one's boss, one's father, one's spouse, etc.). 2. May represent the individuals or whatever trait or character we most associate with them. 3. May be symbolic of our relationship with that person. See also **People**.
Paris	1. Corresponds to whatever one most associates with Paris (e.g. romance, good food or a vacation). 2. See also **Places**.
Park	1. Generally symbolic of whatever one most associated with parks (e.g. relaxation, nature, exercise, walking the dog, etc.). 2. See also **Places**.
Party	1. May represent whatever one most associates with parties (e.g. a celebration, a gathering, etc.). 2. A message of congratulations or recognition.
Password	1. Associated with personal knowledge, secrets or information. 2. Might correspond to a rite of passage.
Pediatrician	1. Generally associated with the health and wellbeing of one's children. 2. Might be connected with the wellbeing of one's own inner child. 3. Depending upon imagery, see also **Doctor** and **Children**.

Pen/Pencil	1. Associated with ideas, words, or experiences. 2. Indicative of communication.
Penis	1. Associated with male energy. See also **Phallus**. 2. Can be associated with sexuality. See also **Sex**. 3. Depending on the imagery could indicate one who is oversexed or repressing sexuality. 4. Might correspond to male vulnerability.
People	1. Generally represents various aspects of oneself, or aspects of self in relationship to that individual. 2. People are often symbolic of faults, virtues, or activities that we associate with that individual. 3. Famous people are generally symbolic of their outstanding characteristics or talent. 4. Female people can represent female traits and abilities. See also **Womb**. 5. Male people can represent male traits and abilities. See also **Phallus**.
Pets	1. Most often symbolic of whatever one most associates with her or his pets (e.g. companionship, family, love). 2. See also **Animals**.
Phallus	1. May symbolize male sexuality or masculine energy. See also **Man**. 2. The positive masculine traits of one's self or another (e.g. logical, determined or persevering). 3. The negative masculine traits of one's self or another (e.g. selfish, tactless or aggressive).

Phone	1. Generally associated with personal communication. 2. Might correspond to a message of some kind. See also **Message**. 3. A phone can be an extension of one's self. See also **Self**.
Piano	1. Associated with personal creativity. See also **Music**. 2. May correspond with whatever one most associates with the piano.
Picture	1. Often associated with an experience or personal memory. 2. Could be symbolic of the Akashic Records and/or a personal past life. See also **Akashic Records**.
Pig	1. Can correspond with greed, filth, selfishness, or gluttony. 2. Often symbolic of whatever one most associates with pigs. See also **Animals**.
Pink	1. Symbolic of higher or divine love. See also **Colors**. 2. Metaphorically, in the pink = having good health.
Places	1. Corresponds to whatever we most associate with that place 2. Can also be symbolic of activities occurring in that locale: old workplace = work; old home = homelife; school = learning experience; library = knowledge; cleaners = that which needs cleansing, etc. 3. Some historical settings can correspond to a literal past-life memory. See also **Historical Clothing/Settings**. See also **Building**.

Plates	1. That which is being presented (e.g. ideas or experiences). 2. The personal situation within one's own hands. 3. Washing dishes could symbolize cleansing a situation.
Play	1. (Noun) Often symbolic of the experience and/or journey with which one is presently involved. See also **Actor/Actress**. 2. (Verb) Could indicate the need to have more relaxation and/or balance in life.
Pledge of Allegiance	1. Associated with common beliefs, hopes, desires and dreams. 2. That to which one personally subscribes. 3. Could represent the United States. See also **United States**. 4. Might be related to personal dedication.
Pocket	1. Associated with one's personal belongings, talents, or that which one controls or can draw upon. 2. Might correspond to receptivity or female energy. See also **Womb**.
Poison	1. Represents that which is deadly, dangerous or making one sick. 2. Can symbolize a harmful experience that is occurring.
Police	1. Associated with one's higher consciousness, the law, or one's higher self. See also **Higher Self**. 2. That which provides legal and moral guidelines. See also **People**. 3. Might indicate personal protection.
Porch	1. Can correspond to whatever one most asso-

	ciates with porches (e.g. relaxation, watching the world pass by, etc.) 2. May be symbolic of one's present experience.
Post Office	1. Represents a message or a communication. 2. Information from another source (e.g. one's intuition; another person). 3. See also **Building**.
Prayer	1. Associated with spirituality, attunement and the divine. See also **God**. 2. Could be related to divine communication.
Pregnant	1. Symbolic of a new beginning, a new project, a new relationship or a new situation. 2. Might represent a literal pregnancy.
President	1. Associated with a higher authority or power (e.g. God, one's boss, one's father, one's spouse, etc.). 2. See also **People**.
Priest	1. Can be symbolic of a spiritual presence, messenger or authority. 2. Might indicate one's own higher self. 3. See also **People**.
Prison	1. That which has one caged or captive (e.g. work, a situation or a relationship, etc.). 2. Represents a confining experience. See also **Building**.
Promotion	1. Might be indicative of personal success, achievement, or personal kudos. 2. Could correspond to a literal promotion. 3. Metaphorically, that which is promoted = that which becomes the standard approach or "party-line."

Property	1. Often associated with one's current situation or experience. 2. The issue which has been presented to you. See also **Work** or **Home**.
Psychic	1. Can be associated with intuition or one's higher self. See also **Higher Self**. 2. Could be symbolic of insight or a message. 3. See also **People**.
Purple	1. Can be related to spiritual development or a regal nature. 2. See also **Colors**.
Purse	1. Symbolic or money, finance or success. 2. Associated with one's identity, energy or personal power. 3. Could correspond to female sexuality. See also **Womb**.
Pyramid	1. Symbolic of initiation, transformation or esoteric information. 2. Can correspond with whatever one may think of places with pyramids (e.g. Egypt or Mexico). 3. Might be associated with literal travel.
Queen	1. Associated with a higher authority or power (e.g. God, one's boss, one's father, one's spouse, etc.). 2. See also **People**.
Quito, Ecuador	1. Corresponds to whatever one associates with Quito or Ecuador (e.g. the equator, the Galapagos, etc.). 2. See also **Places**.

Rabbit	1. Can correspond to sexuality or pregnancy. 2. Because of the ears, could be associated with listening. 3. See also **Animals**.
Radio	1. May be symbolic of transmitting or receiving a message or information. 2. Associated with tuning to higher levels of awareness or intuition.
Rain	1. Often corresponds to an emotional experience or outburst. See also **Water**. 2. Might be associated with a physical, mental or spiritual cleansing. 3. Metaphorically, raining on a parade = dampening the enthusiasm.
Rainbow	1. Often associated with good luck or good fortune. 2. Might indicate a promise or a covenant. 3. May be symbolic of the end of a stormy experience.
Rake	1. Might correspond with gathering something together. 2. Symbolic of that upon which one is working. 3. Metaphorically, he is such a rake = he is immoral.
Rape	1. Can represent a situation or experience in which one is being violated or abused. 2. Corresponds to brutality, anger and aggression. See also **Fight**. 3. May be a warning of being violated, abused or taken advantage of.

Rat	1. Associated with one who is evil, cruel, sneaky or intimidating. 2. See also **Animals**.
Raven	1. Can be associated with a messenger of ending, bad luck or death. See also **Death**. 2. See also **Animals**.
Receptionist	1. Can be associated with communication, office politics, public outreach, etc. 2. See also **Work**.
Red	1. Symbolic of sexuality, anger or rage; can also be associated with base creativity. 2. See also **Colors**.
Refrigerator	1. Can correspond to one's personal diet (e.g. what one takes into self). 2. Might be indicative of that which is cold or emotionally "chilly."
Reoccurring	1. Generally associated with some pattern of experience that is occurring again in the dreamer's waking life. 2. May also be indicative of a warning that the subconscious is trying to bring to mind.
Restaurant	1. Where one is being fed or nurtured. See also **Places** or **Food**. 2. Could represent one's present situation or experience. 3. Might be symbolic of one's dietary habits or thoughts.
Restroom	1. Corresponds to eliminations or the need to eliminate something. 2. See also **House**.

Right	1. Associated with the future, that which is fixed, being conservative, and the east. See also **Direction**. 2. Might correspond to the right brain or intuition and emotion.
Ring	1. Can be symbolic of a relationship, that with which one is engaged, or a personal or soul commitment. 2. Might correspond to one's life journey. See also **Journey**.
River	1. Associated with the flow of emotion, spirit or intuition. See also **Water**. 2. Can correspond to one's life journey or the passage of time.
Road	1. Often represents one's present journey or experience. 2. Metaphorically, being at the crossroads = being faced with a choice of directions.
Robbed	1. That which is taken, coerced or forced from self or another. 2. Associated with personal loss.
Rocks	1. Symbolic of difficulties, obstacles, problems or life's stumbling blocks. 2. Can represent hardened emotions or stubborn immobility. 3. Worn and smooth rocks could correspond to being worn down by life's experiences. 4. Metaphorically, on the rocks = having great difficulty or being served with ice.
Rome	1. Corresponds to whatever one most associates with Rome (e.g. history, vacation, the Vatican, etc.).

	2. See also **Places**.
Roof	1. Can correspond with one's thoughts or ideas. See also **House**. 2. Might be associated with spirituality, intuition or personal protection and security. 3. That which covers one's present situation or experience.
Room	1. Can correspond with whatever is associated with that room (e.g. master bedroom = relationships; basement = unconsciousness, etc.). See also **House**. 2. Symbolic of aspects of one's self.
Rooster	1. Associated with a self-certain or a cocky male. See also **Phallus**. 2. Can be symbolic of a message or messenger of timing. See also **Animals**.
Rose	1. Symbolic of love or relationship. 2. Can correspond with one's talents or abilities. See also **Flowers**.
Rug	1. Symbolic of one's foundation. See also **House**. 2. Metaphorically, being called on the carpet = getting into trouble.
Run	1. Often associated with what one is running from (e.g. self, a present situation, one's own fears, etc.). 2. Might correspond to the race of life.
Sailboat	1. Most often associated with a spiritual or an emotional journey. See also **Water**. 2. May indicate one's present situation or experience.

Salt	1. Could correspond to a literal dietary suggestion. 2. Metaphorically, the salt of the earth = that which is the best or the finest.
Sand	1. May be related to time, the desert, and/or that which is infinite (e.g. the particles of sand). 2. See also **Places**.
Scar	1. A problem, worry or situation with which one is currently facing. 2. A past wound or memory that is affecting the present. 3. Whatever part of the body being scarred may have significance (e.g. face = self; legs = direction; head = thoughts, etc.). 4. Might be related to a past-life issue.
School	1. Generally corresponds to a present learning situation or experience. See also **Building**. 2. Can be symbolic of that with which one is presently experiencing. 3. Whatever one most associates with that locale. See also **Places**.
Scissors	1. Might represent the ending of or a separating from an experience. See also **Death**. 2. Can be associated with cutting or injurious words or actions.
Security	1. Associated with one's higher consciousness, the law, or one's higher self. See also **Higher Self**. 2. That which provides legal and moral guidelines. See also **People**. 3. Might indicate personal protection.
Self	1. Associated with one's individuality, traits,

	abilities or shortcomings. See also **Phallus** and **Womb**. 2. Can be symbolic of what one needs to work on or that with which one has to work. 3. You may also wish to see **People**, **Man** or **Woman**.
Seven	1. Might be associated with spirituality, sacredness, perfection, or the seven spiritual centers/chakras. 2. See also **Numbers**.
Sew	1. Can be indicative of personal creativity. 2. That with which one is presently involved. 3. Might be a metaphor for the passage of time—e.g. a stitch in time.
Sex	1. Corresponds to sexuality, reproduction, relationships, or self-gratification. 2. Can be associated with being oversexed or repressing one's sexual desires. 3. Symbolic of what one has been ignoring or overlooking (i.e. a sex dream can cause one to remember the experience). 4. Might represent creativity or energy. 5. Could indicate a partnership or a cooperative venture. 6. See also **Phallus** or **Womb**.
Shadow	1. Can correspond to one's shadow side. See also **Self**. 2. That which is only partially revealed or understood. 3. The projection of one's problems unto others. See also **People**. 4. Might be symbolic of memory, the unknown, that which is feared, etc.

Shampoo	1. Associated with changing or cleansing one's thoughts. 2. Can be symbolic of getting something or someone out of one's head. 3. Might represent dwelling upon a thought or an activity.
Shawl	1. May be associated with that which insulates self from the world (e.g. emotions). 2. Could indicate present situation or experience. See also **Clothing**.
Shed	1. Can correspond to that which is in storage, that which is no longer useful, that which has been neglected, or that which has been forgotten. 2. You may also wish to see **House**.
Sheets	1. Can be associated with sexuality or a relationship. See also **Bed/Bedroom**. 2. Depending on the imagery, might indicate vulnerability or protecting one's self emotionally.
Shirt	1. Associated with one's outer self, physical body or identity. See also **Clothing**. 2. Metaphorically, wearing one's shirt on his/her sleeve = being overly emotional. 3. Can be symbolic of one's outer appearance, thoughts, personal experience or occupation.
Shoes	1. Often associated with one's present direction or foundational understanding. See also **Feet**. 2. Metaphorically, being in someone else's shoes = attempting to understand another's experience; filling someone else's shoes = taking another's place.

	3. You may also wish to see **Journey**.
Shopping	1. Can correspond to free will, choices, or decisions. 2. See also **Places**.
Shoulders	1. May indicate that which weighs heavily on self or another. See also **Body**. 2. Metaphorically, he has the weight of the world on his shoulders = he has an enormous amount of responsibility.
Sidewalk	1. Generally associated with one's current direction in life. See also **Journey**. 2. The appearance of the sidewalk could be suggestive of the ease or difficulty of the path one is currently traveling.
Sing	1. May correspond with harmonious communication or the need for harmonious communication. 2. Might be suggestive of one's personal talents or abilities.
Sister	1. Most often represents the individual or whatever trait or character we most associate with that person. 2. May be associated with an aspect of our relationship with that person. See also **People**.
Six	1. Can indicate symmetry, beauty, and harmony; human dominance or Christ-mindedness. 2. See also **Numbers**.
Sky	1. Associated with spirituality, thoughts, ideas or insight. 2. The condition of the sky will have a great deal to do with the possible meaning (e.g. a

	sunny sky can indicate a bright or positive experience; a cloudy sky could be associated with a variety or worries or problems, etc.). 3. Metaphorically, the sky is the limit = all kinds of things are possible.
Skyscraper	1. Often symbolic of one's work. See also **Building**. 2. As a phallic symbol, may correspond to a male energy. See also **Phallus**.
Smile	1. Associated with joy and laughter. 2. See also **Mouth**.
Smoke	1. Can correspond with a message or a signal. 2. Could be associated with a lack of clarity. 3. Metaphorically, something is up in smoke = something is ruined.
Snake	1. Often associated with male energy or sexuality. See also **Phallus**. 2. Can represent temptation or evil. See also **Animals**. 3. Might be indicative of the creative energy of the kundalini. 4. Could be associated with healing (e.g. the caduceus).
Snow	1. Can correspond to repressed or frozen emotions. See also **Ice**. 2. Associated with an experience or situation left out in the cold. 3. Might correspond to whatever one most associates with snow (e.g. fun, winter, skiing, etc.). 4. You may also wish to see **Water**.

Son	1. Most often represents the individual or whatever trait or character we most associate with that person. 2. May be associated with an aspect of our relationship with that person. See also **People**.
South	1. Generally associated with whatever one thinks of the north (e.g. conservatism, retirement communities, etc.) 2. Could be indicative of sexuality or the lower self. See also **Direction**.
Speaking	1. Can correspond to personal communication. 2. Associated with the expression of one's talents, desires, or inner self.
Spider	1. Can represent that which is biting or bothering. See also **Bugs**. 2. May be symbolic or one who is attempting to entrap or ensnare. 3. Might indicate one who is spinning a web of deception. 4. Might be symbolic of one who is a widow.
Spirit	1. Associated with the Creator, the ultimate spiritual source, the impetus behind all that exists, and that which is Divine. 2. Might correspond to personal spirituality or one's higher self. See also **Higher Self**.
Sports	1. Corresponds to a team event or a competition. See also **Work**. 2. That which is occurring in one's present experience. 3. Any type of game or sports event can also correspond with what one literally associates with that game or event (e.g., relaxation, spe-

	cific seasons, family activities, etc.).
Stage	1. Corresponds to one's present situation or experience. 2. That which one is currently perceiving.
Statue	1. That which is solid or unmoving. See also **People**. 2. Could indicate one who is emotionally detached or one who is upon a pedestal. 3. Might represent a prize or an honor.
Statue of Liberty	1. Associated with freedom, independence or liberty. 2. Might correspond to new beginnings. See also **Statue**.
Steps	1. Can correspond to life's direction, challenges, or moving though levels of consciousness. 2. Going down steps can be associated with the subconscious or memories; going up steps can correspond to personal accomplishment or one's higher self. 3. See also **House**.
Store	1. Often symbolic of whatever one most associates with that store (e.g. a grocery store might correspond to diet and health; a mechanic could be symbolic of one's car and therefore personal journey or physical body, etc.) 2. Buying things at a store is generally indicative of free will and personal choice.
Storm	1. Can be symbolic of a challenging or an emotional situation or experience. 2. See also **Weather**.

Street	1. Can be associated with one's present experience or direction. 2. Might correspond to one's present journey. See also **Journey**.
Stuck	1. That which is controlling self or another. 2. Could be indicative of confusion, isolation, stubbornness, or even addiction.
Student	1. Generally corresponds to a learning situation or experience. 2. What one is presently learning or teaching. 3. See also **People**.
Sun	1. That which lights one's experience or warms one's way (e.g. God, spirituality, an experience, an idea, another person, etc.). 2. Associated with a pleasant experience or idea. 3. Can correspond to the masculine aspects of one's self. See also **Phallus**. 4. Could be symbolic of the higher self. See also **Higher Self**.
Sunrise	1. Associated with a new beginning or a rebirth. 2. See also **Sun**.
Sunset	1. Could correspond to personal closure or the end of something. 2. See also **Death**.
Superheroes	1. May represent one's inner talents or higher self. See also **Higher Self**. 2. The most positive qualities associated with being human. See also **Phallus** and **Womb**. 3. May be symbolic of whatever outstanding characteristic we associate with that superhero. See also **People**.

Surgeon	1. May be associated with that which needs to be extracted or removed. 2. Might indicate the current "operation" (e.g. experience or situation). 3. See also **Doctor**.
Swim	1. A spiritual or emotional journey or experience. See also **Water**. 2. That into which one is presently submerged.
Sword	1. Associated with aggression or dominance. See also **Phallus**. 2. Can correspond to that which cuts, injures or divides.
Teacher	1. Symbolic of an authority figure or one's higher self. See also **People**. 2. Associated with what is attempting to be learned from or taught to others. 3. Can correspond to a present learning situation or experience.
Teenager	1. A youthful project, experience or idea of about the same age. 2. Could be associated with one's youthful self. 3. May correspond to whatever one most associates with his or her teenagers. See also **People**.
Teeth	1. Teeth can be symbolic of words (e.g. that which is in one's mouth) or personal identity. 2. When teeth fall out is often related to things coming out of one's mouth that shouldn't (e.g. gossip). 3. Different types of teeth suggest meaning as well (false teeth = false words; baby teeth = immaturity, etc.).

	4. You may also wish to see **Mouth**.
Telephone	1. Associated with a message or communication. 2. Might indicate receiving information, insight or intuition from another source.
Telescope	1. Can correspond to clarity of vision. 2. Represents the ability to see that which is far off (e.g. the future). 3. Associated with the close inspection of an experience or activity. 4. Might indicate giving things more scrutiny that is necessary.
Television	1. Can correspond to one's present situation or experience. 2. Associated with a message or communication. 3. Might indicate the receipt of information, insight or intuition.
Temple	1. Often represents spirituality or faith. 2. Can correspond to whatever one associates with temples. See also **Building**. 3. May be indicative of a past-life memory pattern that is similar to a present-day experience. See also **Historical Clothing/Settings**.
Ten	1. Can suggest completeness and strength; or, the same as one. 2. See also **Numbers**.
Tent	1. Suggestive of a temporary experience or situation. See also **House**. 2. Might correspond to nature, the earth, or whatever one associates with Indians. See also **People**.

Terrorist	1. That which is threatening, angry, reactive, or hidden. See also **People**. 2. Might correspond to a rebellious or threatening nature in self or another.
Thanksgiving	1. Generally corresponds to whatever one most associates with the holiday. 2. Suggestive of thankfulness or the need to be thankful.
Three	1. Represents body, mind, spirit; the trinity; great strength or personal power. 2. See also **Numbers**.
Throat	1. Often associated with one's free will. 2. Can correspond to the voice or one's ability to communicate. 3. Metaphorically, to cut one's throat = to destroy someone; shoved down his throat = to force him.
Tiger	1. May be symbolic of whatever one most associates with tigers (e.g. anger, aggression, the act of hunting or being hunted, etc.). See also **Animals**. 2. Metaphorically, she is such as tiger = she is fierce or brave.
Toilet	1. Corresponds with eliminations or the need to eliminate something. 2. See also **House**.
Tomb	1. Can correspond to whatever one associates with tombs (e.g. death, resurrection, Jesus, etc.). 2. See also **Historical Clothing/Settings**.
Tornado	1. Often symbolic of emotional turmoil.

	2. Can correspond to verbal arguments and aggression. 3. Can be associated with a challenging experience or situation over which one has no control.
Tower	1. Can represent a male figure or energy. See also **Phallus**. 2. May be associated with a lofty idea or experience. See also **Building**. 3. Might be indicative of one who is emotionally isolated and withdrawn.
Tower of Babel	1. Associated with a major communication problem. See also **Tower**. 2. See also **Places**.
Train	1. Associated with a life journey. See also **Journey**. 2. Can correspond to one's present situation or experience. 3. Metaphorically, that was a real train wreck = that was a disaster. 4. Might represent a new destination or travel.
Trash	1. That which is unnecessary, needs to be eliminated, or is no longer needed. 2. Could correspond to bad language or personal eliminations.
Trees	1. Associated with growth and vitality. See also **Forest**. 2. Different types of trees have different meaning (e.g. an apple tree could represent the need to see a doctor, or personal temptation; a willow tree could indicate the need to bend in the face of a challenging experience, etc.). 3. Metaphorically, can't see the forest for the trees = one who gets caught up in details and is

	unable to see the entire experience.
Trolls	1. Corresponds to something that diverts one from a path or direction. 2. That which can steal innocence. 3. May correspond to whatever one most associates with trolls. See also **People**.
Truck	1. May be associated with one's personal direction or physical body. See also **Car**. 2. Can correspond to whatever one associates with trucks (e.g. that which is rugged, manly, independent, etc.)
Tunnel	1. Associated with one's personal journey or with other levels of consciousness. 2. Might be associated with a female figure or energy. See also **Womb**. 3. Could be indicative of the unconsciousness or memory. 4. Metaphorically, light at the end of the tunnel = positive things are on their way. 5. Might be associated with death or transition. See also **Death**.
Turning Around	1. Might indicate a change in decision or directions. 2. Corresponds to one's personal path and/or life direction. See also **Journey**. 3. May be associated with reflections on the past.
Turtle	1. Can be associated with a long life, or that which is slow and methodical. 2. May be symbolic of that which withdraws into its shell. See also **Animals**.
Twelve	1. Can correspond to cosmic order, the circle of

	life; or same as three. 2. See also **Numbers**.
Twin Towers	1. Can symbolize whatever one most associates with the Twin Towers (e.g. a major disaster, a place of work or business, the number two, etc.). 2. See also **Building** and **Places**.
Two	1. Can symbolize duality, opposites, relationships; sexuality. 2. See also **Numbers**.
Under	1. Suggestive of being contained by, controlled by, subordinate to, or involved in that which one is under. 2. Metaphorically, under the gun = under a great deal of pressure.
Uniform	1. Can correspond to occupation, present situation or state of mind. 2. Suggestive of one who falls in line or follows orders. 3. See also **Clothing**.
United States	1. May be symbolic of liberty, independence, freedom, military might, etc. 2. Most often corresponds to whatever one associates with the United States. See also **Places**.
Vacation	1. Associated with relaxation, personal escape, or taking it easy. 2. Might be symbolic of whatever one associates with the locale shown as the vacation destination. See also **Places**.
Vagina	1. Associated with female energy. See also **Womb**.

	2. Might be associated with sexuality. See also **Sex**. 3. Depending on the imagery could indicate one who is oversexed or repressing sexuality.
Vampire	1. That which feeds off of or sucks the life from another. 2. Could be associated with one who is taking advantage of another. 3. Depending upon one's personal association (e.g. *The Twilight series*) might represent romance and sexuality. See also **People**.
Vatican	1. Can correspond to a higher spiritual authority or power. See also **Higher Self**. 2. Whatever we most associate with that locale. See also **Places**.
Vegetables	1. Depending upon imagery, might be indicative of personal dietary advice. See also **Eating**. 2. Suggestive of whatever one most associates with vegetables (e.g. fiber).
Veterinarian	1. Often symbolic of one's pets or animals or whatever one associates with one's pets. See also **Pets** or **Animals**. 2. Can be associated with a health concern. See also **Doctor**.
Victorian	1. Often corresponds to whatever an individual associates with that the period. 2. May be indicative of a past-life memory pattern that is similar to a present-day experience. 3. See also **Historical Clothing/Settings**.
Violet	1. Corresponds to great spirituality or spiritual dedication.

	2. See also **Colors**.
Vomit	1. That which is making one sick or ill. 2. Could be associated with a literal health concern or something hard to deal with in one's present experience.
Vulture	1. Associated with death and decay. See also **Death**. 2. Metaphorically, a vulture = one who preys upon another. 3. See also **Animals**.
Waiter/Waitress	1. Often symbolic of whatever one thinks of the occupation (e.g. work, service, etc.) 2. Can correspond to the act of "waiting." 3. Might be associated with one who attends to or serves another. See also **People**.
Walk	1. Can correspond to one's present direction or experience. 2. May be symbolic of the journey of life. See also **Journey**.
Wall	1. That which prevents someone or something from going in or out. 2. May be representative of a barrier or limitation. 3. Metaphorically, he's like a wall = he's emotionally closed off.
Wallet	1. Symbolic or money, finance or success. 2. Associated with one's identity, energy or personal power. 3. Depending on imagery, could correspond to either male or female sexuality. See also **Phallus** and **Womb**.
Walt Disney	1. Can be associated with creativity, imagina-

	tion, Disneyland, etc. 2. Generally corresponds to whatever we most associate with that individual. See also **People**.
War	1. Can correspond to a physical or emotional conflict or confrontation. 2. Symbolic of anger, aggression or a personal struggle with self or others. 3. Often associated with a current situation or experience. 4. Metaphorically, may suggest something is at war.
Wash	1. That which needs to be cleansed, purified or released. 2. Metaphorically, to wash one's hands = to relinquish responsibility; all washed up = completely ruined. 3. You may also wish to see **Water**.
Washington Monument	1. Generally symbolic of the United States and whatever one associates with the United States. See also **Places**. 2. Because of its shape, might be representative of male energy. See also **Phallus**.
Watch	1. Associated with time and the sequencing of events. See also **Clock**. 2. Might be indicative of what one is doing with his/her time.
Water	1. Associated with spirituality and the emotions. 2. Depending on the imagery might represent a spiritual or emotional journey or experience. See also **Journey**. 3. Can be indicative of insight, intuition or the unconscious.

	4. Might be symbolic of metaphorical associations (e.g. making one's mouth water = a strong desire for; being in hot water = being in trouble). 5. May represent a physical or emotional release.
Waterbed	1. Associated with a relationship or sexuality. See also **Bed/Bedroom**. 2. Might correspond to an emotional situation or experience. See also **Water**.
Weather	1. Positive or beautiful weather can correspond to positive or upbeat experiences upon the journey of life. 2. Negative or challenging weather can indicate turmoil or upheaval (e.g., a hurricane or tornado = emotional turmoil). See also **Emotions**.
Wedding	1. Represents a partnership, a new venture, or a relationship. 2. Could indicate a cooperative situation or experience. 3. Might be literal or symbolic. 4. Associated with coming to terms with another.
Weeds	1. Can correspond to problems or a situation that needs to be dealt with. 2. Associated with that which is unwanted. 3. May be symbolic of obstacles that need to be removed.
West	1. Generally associated with whatever one thinks of the west (e.g. a pioneering spirit, the setting sun, etc.) 2. Could be indicative of the right and be suggestive of the future. See also **Direction**.

Whale	1. Can represent a large situation or experience. See also **Animals**. 2. Might be associated with repressed emotions.
White	1. Associated with purity, innocence, and holiness. See also **Colors**. 2. Metaphorically, one who sees things as black and white = one who is extremely focused in perspective seeing only yes or no, right or wrong, etc.
Wife	1. Might correspond to a partnership or a co-operative venture. See also **Marriage** or **Wedding**. 2. May represent the individual or whatever trait or character we most associate with that person. 3. Can be symbolic of our relationship with that person. See also **People**.
Wind	1. May be associated with an emotional situation or experience. 2. Depending upon imagery, see also **Hurricane** or **Tornado**.
Window	1. Can correspond to the perception of new possibilities or opportunities. See also **House**. 2. Associated with clarity and insight, or personal reflection. 3. Looking out the front window might correspond to seeing glimpses of the future; looking out the back window might be associated with one's personal past.
Windshield	1. Can be symbolic of insight related to one's direction or journey. 2. See also **Car** and **Journey**.

Witch	1. Associated with a female energy or influence. See also **People**. 2. Can represent magic, the enchanted or the mysterious. 3. Could indicate one who is bewitching or charming. 4. You may also wish to see **Woman**.
Woman	1. Can indicate the feminine side of one's self or another. See also **Womb**. 2. Could be associated with feminine traits (e.g. emotional receptivity, intuition, cooperation, etc.). 3. See also **People**.
Womb	1. May symbolize female sexuality or feminine energy. See also **Woman**. 2. The positive feminine traits of one's self or another (e.g. empathetic, patient or intuitive). 3. The negative feminine traits of one's self or another (e.g. moody, critical or possessive).
Woods	1. One's present situation or experience. 2. Can indicate growth and stability or overgrowth and confusion. 3. Metaphorically, not out of the woods = there are still problems. 4. You may also wish to see **Trees** or **Forest**.
Work	1. Generally associated with work and/or any group activity or experience with which one is presently involved. 2. The imagery of one's old workplace is usually symbolic of one's current occupation. 3. Might be symbolic of whatever you associate with the company/workplace (e.g., an obligation, an enjoyable endeavor, the channel

	of one's creativity, a horrible situation, etc.).
World Trade Center	1. Can symbolize whatever one most associates with the Twin Towers (e.g. a major disaster, a place of work or business, the number two, etc.). 2. See also **Building** and **Places**.
Wound	1. Associated with a personal hurt or injury inflicted by self or another. 2. That which is bothering self. 3. See also **Doctor**.
Wrist	1. Can be associated with the self or one's free will. 2. An extension of the self. See also **Body**.
X-ray	1. Can correspond with the ability to see through an obstacle, a situation, a person or an experience. 2. Associated with clarity of vision. See also **Eyes**. 3. Might indicate the need to take a closer look at something.
Yard	1. Associated with one's current situation or experience. 2. That which needs to be addressed, dealt with or taken care of. 3. A front yard can indicate the future or that which is in public view; a backyard can indicate the past or that which is hidden from public view. 4. You may also wish to see **House**.
Yellow	1. Represents intelligence or personal power. 2. See also **Colors**.

Zebra	1. Can represent the act of seeing things black and white. See also **Animals**. 2. Associated with a messenger. See also **Horse**.
Zero	1. Symbolic of nothing, that which is absent or the all-encompassing. 2. See also **Numbers**.
Zoo	1. Associated with untamed aspects of one's self, one's environment or an experience. 2. Metaphorically, this place is a zoo = this place is filled with confusion and chaos. 3. You may also wish to see **Animals**.

References and Recommended Reading

Cayce, Edgar (readings). *Dreams and Dreaming. Volumes I and II.* Association for Research and Enlightenment, Inc.: Virginia Beach, Virginia. 1974, 1976.

Crisp, Tony. *Dream Dictionary: An A to Z Guide to Understanding Your Unconscious Mind.* Dell: New York. 2002.

Gottlieb, Annie and Slobodan D, Pesic. *The Cube . . . Keep the Secret.* HarperSanFranciso: San Francisco. 1995.

Pehrson, John B. and Susan E. Mehrtens. *Intuitive Imagery: A Resource at Work.* Butterworth-Heinemann: Boston. 1997.

Pimm, Bobbie Ann. *Notes from a Dreamer on Dreaming.* notesfromadreamer.com. 2010.

Reed, Henry, Ph.D., editor. *Sundance Community Dream Journal (1976-1979).* Atlantic University: Virginia Beach, Virginia. 1977-1979.

Rodriguez, Magaly del Carmen. *Creative Imaging Work.* Privately Published. 1988/89.

Sechrist, Elsie. *Dreams: Your Magic Mirror.* A.R.E. Press: Virginia Beach: Virginia. 1995.

Tanner, Wilda B. *The Mystical, Magical, Marvelous World of Dreams.* Sparrow Hawk Press: Tahlequah, Oklahoma. 1988.

The Jewish Encyclopedia. Funk and Wagnalls: London. 1901.

Todeschi, Kevin J. *Dream Images and Symbols.* A.R.E. Press: Virginia Beach: Virginia. 2003.

Todeschi, Kevin J. *Soul Signs.* A.R.E. Press: Virginia Beach: Virginia. 2003.

Todeschi, Kevin J. and Liaros, Carol Ann. *Edgar Cayce on Auras & Colors*. A.R.E. Press: Virginia Beach: Virginia. 2011.

Van de Castle, Robert L., Ph.D., *Our Dreaming Mind*. Ballantine Books: New York. 1994.

Webster's New Universal Unabridged Dictionary. Simon & Schuster: New York. 1979.

Made in the USA
San Bernardino, CA
25 February 2015